MANCHESTER MEDIEVAL LITERATURE AND CULTURE

BORROWED OBJECTS AND
THE ART OF POETRY

Manchester University Press

Series editors: Anke Bernau, David Matthews and James Paz

Series founded by: J. J. Anderson and Gail Ashton

Advisory board: Ruth Evans, Patricia C. Ingham, Andrew James Johnston, Chris Jones, Catherine Karkov, Nicola McDonald, Sarah Salih, Larry Scanlon and Stephanie Trigg

Manchester Medieval Literature and Culture publishes monographs and essay collections comprising new research informed by current critical methodologies on the literary cultures of the Middle Ages. We are interested in all periods, from the early Middle Ages through to the late, and we include post-medieval engagements with and representations of the medieval period (or 'medievalism'). 'Literature' is taken in a broad sense, to include the many different medieval genres: imaginative, historical, political, scientific, religious. While we welcome contributions on the diverse cultures of medieval Britain and are happy to receive submissions on Anglo-Norman, Anglo-Latin and Celtic writings, we are also open to work on the Middle Ages in Europe more widely, and beyond.

Titles available in the series

11. *Reading Robin Hood: Content, form and reception in the outlaw myth*
    Stephen Knight
12. *Annotated Chaucer bibliography: 1997–2010*
    Mark Allen and Stephanie Amsel
13. *Roadworks: Medieval Britain, medieval roads*
    Valerie Allen and Ruth Evans (eds)
14. *Love, history and emotion in Chaucer and Shakespeare:* Troilus and Criseyde *and* Troilus and Cressida
    Andrew James Johnston, Russell West-Pavlov and Elisabeth Kempf (eds)
15. *The Scottish Legendary: Towards a poetics of hagiographic narration*
    Eva von Contzen
16. *Nonhuman voices in Anglo-Saxon literature and material culture*
    James Paz
17. *The church as sacred space in Middle English literature and culture*
    Laura Varnam
18. *Aspects of knowledge: Preserving and reinventing traditions of learning in the Middle Ages*
    Marilina Cesario and Hugh Magennis (eds)
19. *Visions and ruins: Cultural memory and the untimely Middle Ages*
    Joshua Davies
20. *Participatory reading in late-medieval England*
    Heather Blatt
21. *Affective medievalism: Love, abjection and discontent*
    Thomas A. Prendergast and Stephanie Trigg
22. *Performing women: Gender, self, and representation in late-medieval Metz*
    Susannah Crowder
23. *The politics of Middle English parables: Fiction, theology, and social practice*
    Mary Raschko
24. *Contemporary Chaucer across the centuries*
    Helen M. Hickey, Anne McKendry and Melissa Raine (eds)
25. *Borrowed objects and the art of poetry:* Spolia *in Old English verse*
    Denis Ferhatović

Borrowed objects and the art of poetry

Spolia in Old English verse

DENIS FERHATOVIĆ

Manchester University Press

Copyright © Denis Ferhatović 2019

The right of Denis Ferhatović to be identified as the author of this work has been asserted by him in accordance with the Copyright, Designs and Patents Act 1988.

Published by Manchester University Press
Oxford Road, Manchester M13 9PL

www.manchesteruniversitypress.co.uk

British Library Cataloguing-in-Publication Data
A catalogue record for this book is available from the British Library

ISBN 978 1 5261 3165 2 hardback
ISBN 978 1 5261 7914 2 paperback

First published 2019

The publisher has no responsibility for the persistence or accuracy of URLs for any external or third-party internet websites referred to in this book, and does not guarantee that any content on such websites is, or will remain, accurate or appropriate.

Typeset
by Toppan Best-set Premedia Limited

Contents

Acknowledgements	vii
Introduction Powerful fragments: Ruin, relics, *spolia*	1
1 Encyclopedic miniatures: Combinatory powers of loot in the Exeter Riddles	33
2 Architecture of the past and the future: Transformative potential of plunder in *Exodus*	61
3 Animated, animating: Bringing stone, flesh, and text to life in *Andreas*	86
4 Zooming out, cutting through: Resistance to incorporation in *Judith*	115
5 A hoard full of plunder: Paradoxical materiality of loss in *Beowulf*	143
Afterword Resistant material remnants in Old English and beyond	164
Bibliography	169
Index	183

Acknowledgements

I wish to thank:

My parents, Emir and Dubravka, and sister Sabina Ferhatović Bharwani, nije moguće zahvaliti im se na svemu što su učinili i što čine za mene.

My two anonymous readers for MUP, the series editors Anke Bernau and David Matthews, the acquisitions editor Meredith Carroll, and the assistant editor Alun Richards for their help and feedback, incredible patience, and promptness.

Roberta Frank, Jessica Brantley, Alastair Minnis, and Nicole Rice for their aid in the earliest days of this project.

My *weorod*, Irina Dumitrescu, Mary Kate Hurley, and Jordan Zweck for reading and commenting on countless proposals and drafts, inviting me to give talks and participate in workshops, publishing inspiring scholarship with which I could engage, sending daily encouragement ('you are almost there!', 'you are doing the work!'), and at times putting some sense into me.

Eric Weiskott for being a very generous *Doktorbruder* and a model of unflappability.

My department at Connecticut College, especially Ken Bleeth, Janet Gezari, Julie Rivkin, Jeff Strabone, and Lina Wilder, for continuous support (I also acknowledge the financial support of Hodgkins, R. F. Johnson, William Meredith, and Judith Opatrny funds).

Our administrative assistant, Katie Trautlein, for saving me many a time.

My friends from other departments – Suzuko Knott, Ari Rotramel, and Ben C. Williams – for conversations, feedback on drafts, dinners, cocktails, Reyhan Şahin, nineteenth-century French poetry, birdlore, and queer aliens.

Josh Davies and James Paz, my colleagues in the UK; I am happy to appear in the same book series with them.

The library staff of Yale University and Connecticut College.

Rachel DeGregorio, Amra Đumišić, Daanish Masood, Ali Aghazadeh Naini, Dilek Uygül and Daniel Barry for hosting, entertaining, and nourishing me in the City.

Elise Dunphe and Bernard Mishmish for Connecticut and Maine adventures.

Chienchuan Chen for being a constant, calming presence in my life, whether from New York, Boston, or Shanghai.

Bilal Qureshi for a Mughal palace on Dupont Circle, delicious cooking, and literary gossip.

Iskandar Ding for his myriad languages, sense of fun, and sheer persistence.

Vanja Stegić for his friendship of many years.

Mustafa Nakeeb, Ayşe Çelikkol and William Coker, Colleen Kennedy-Karpat, Begüm Kalyoncu, Serbaykuş, and Nazlı Nuran Yanıköz for making my time in Turkey always so pleasant and rewarding, hepiniz sağolun.

John Angliss for various types of nerdiness.

Maja Muhić for sharing many brilliant and hilarious moments across the Balkans, but especially in Macedonia.

Starr St crew: M. J. Brioness, Carolyn Johnson, and their cats for everyday acts of neighbourly kindness.

Fuat, sana herşey için teşekkür ederim, seni çok seviyorum.

Introduction
Powerful fragments: Ruin, relics, *spolia*[1]

The Ruin

An influx of sensuality can come at the least expected places in Old English literature. For instance, at the end of a short Exeter Book lyric now titled *The Ruin*, the speaker who has just brought to life an entire dilapidated city with walls, roofs, gates, and buildings, imagines a bathhouse:

> Stanhofu stodan, stream hate wearp
> widan wylme; weal eall befeng
> beorhtan bosme, þær þa baþu wæron,
> hat on hreþre. Þæt wæs hyðelic.
> Leton þonne geotan [........]
> ofer harne stan hate streamas
> un[........
> .] þþæt hringmere hate [........
> ....] þær þa baþu wæron.
> Þonne is [........
> ....]re; þæt is cynelic þing,
> huse [........] burg [........] (38–49)[2]

[Stone houses stood; water gave off heat in a great wave. The wall enclosed everything in its bright breast, hot in its embrace (the place) where the baths were. That was as it should be. Then they let flow ... the hot streams over the grey stone ... un-... into the ring-shaped pool. Hot ... (the place) where the baths were. Then is ... that is a proper/noble thing, the house ... the city.]

Two elements commonly emerge in critical discussions of this text: the strong illusion of specificity, and the bringing together of the past and present of the poem with a suggestion of its future. The author's attention to detail, down to the original binding agent for the wall, the loops of wire that with time gave way to congealed clay (19), has sent scholars in search of the actual place that supposedly inspired the lyric. Many have suggested the Roman ruins at Bath; some prefer Hadrian's Wall; still others argue for Chester.[3] But no single *locus* needs to be discovered as the setting for *The Ruin*; the poem reaches, through all its carefully observed ephemera, towards something larger. Bruce Mitchell and Fred Robinson call the work 'a composite of various Roman ruins that the poet had seen'.[4] Alan Renoir sees the alternating scenes as 'a series of tableaux rather than a narrative or philosophical monologue'.[5]

In addition to the quick succession of particulars in this passage, from the wall to the inside of the building to the circular pool, there is temporal switching. The past tense predominates. But, near the end, two instances of the present tense appear; the exclamation 'þæt is cynelic þing' [that is a proper/noble (lit., kingly) thing] seems to echo the preceding appreciation of the baths, 'Þæt wæs hyðelic' [that was as it should be (lit., that was convenient)]. In an earlier tableau, the speaker familiarises the ruin by peopling it in his imagination with a multitude of men in war-gear who gaze at their material belongings. Those treasures, lovingly enumerated, accord better with the world of the vernacular epic such as *Beowulf* than with the urban pleasures of an outlying Roman province: the men look 'on sinc, on sylfor, on searogimmas, / on ead, on æht, on eorcanstan, / on þas beorhtan burg bradan rices' [at (their) treasure, at silver, at expertly wrought gems, at riches, at possessions, at precious stones, at this bright citadel of the broad realm] (34–7). Imagining the individuals who came before him, the poet transforms them into figures from a literary convention closer to him in time. Yet in positioning himself as one who comes after them, he becomes 'not only a witness to a heroic past, but ... also its survivor'.[6] The ruin is, simultaneously, his and our own past, present, and future.[7]

Different temporal and spatial layers come into being through a particular imaginative intersection of the human, artefactual, elemental, and cosmic that, I will argue, characterises the artistic endeavour in Anglo-Saxon poetry and often signals meta-poetic reflection within that corpus. Artefacts appearing at that intersection are often *spolia*, reused fragments of past material culture, which I discuss in some detail later in this introduction, or akin to it. The inanimate acquires not only life but also invigorating mobility from being touched by the animate; it then energises the text which it inhabits before leaving it behind, and enables the text to move its focus from a bounded, concrete object (itself) to a region far outwards, to jump from the micro- to the macro-level. At the conclusion of *The Ruin*, at least in the state in which it survives, we catch glimpses of such a dynamic. The observer depicts the baths in admiring, or at least non-negative terms.[8] From his contemplation of the materials, stones that retain their colours, he imagines gushing, streaming hot water. These images, rather than seeming strange and perverse for an Anglo-Saxon (whose people did not share the communal bathing culture of the Romans[9]), bring about sensations of warmth, bodily comfort that can connect, however briefly and intermittently, embodied human beings across time. The walls protect all in their bright embrace, while the baths, hot to their very core, fulfil their pleasant purpose. Architectural features unite with bodies and elements. Everything is proper, fitting, even royal (*hyðelic* has the first two meanings, *cynelic* all of them). Here the author imprints the image of the circle onto the text both with the wonderfully specific *hringmere* [ring-pool], and the repeated plainest of statements '(the place) where the baths were'. Gaston Bachelard's insight comes to mind that 'images of *full roundness* help us to collect ourselves, permit us to confer an initial constitution on ourselves, and to confirm our being intimately, inside'.[10] After a quick series of heated images internalised and shored against ruin, we encounter two simple words (admittedly only after the ravages of time on the manuscript), *hus*, *burh*, waiting to be filled with future imaginings.

Despite the distance that separates them from later observers, evocative objects, remnants from other times and places, bring with themselves an indication of their use. They allow for historicisation and, at the same time, a more anachronistic use: in the case of *The Ruin*, for a reconstruction of a Roman bath, and for a projection of an Anglo-Saxon literary staple, the treasure hall. That the early medieval English could identify and employ certain aspects of hermeneutically charged material culture in their verse-making testifies to a high level of consciousness about the artful interweaving of people and things in general, and the place of the Other in that interweaving in particular. It also shows some measure of awareness that in time their own work will become fragmented and in need of creative refurbishing, like a ruin.

In this monograph I investigate artefacts handled and animated by the human and/or the divine in seven Old English riddles (numbered 14, 20, 29, 40, 49, 60, and 95)[11] and four longer poems (three biblical: *Exodus*, *Andreas*, and *Judith*, and one not: *Beowulf*). These artefacts create a particular force in the texts, but do not remain in sight for long, thus preserving the mystery enveloping them. These objects, usually shaped like and named after a recognisable, contained, metonymic item, such as a horn, a pillar, a head, a bed, or a sword, break out of the narrative in order to connect it to other worlds. They occur in image clusters with individuals or enclosures, at crucial junctures in the story, at a turning point or near the end. When there exist sources or analogues in three out of four of the longer poems and at least one enigma that I discuss, comparison reveals that the artefacts in the Anglo-Saxon versions receive much more attention. Investigating the role and place of evocative objects might, therefore, provide clues towards recovery of one important aspect of Old English poetics. This book, moreover, intends to reveal some ways in which the sense of affinity and competition could develop between literary artists and their visual-arts colleagues. On an even larger level, it will become clear that art for the Anglo-Saxons, whether textual or plastic, represents an encounter of a person, or a group of people, not with an abstraction but with a thing.

I begin this book with a consideration of several Exeter Riddles that take on *spolia* and accumulation in different ways. My goal there is to prepare the reader for later invocations of the enigmatic, in the longer poems. The riddles could provide a guide for reading other verse while remaining quite distinct from the epics, in terms of their form, tone, and sheer diversity and rarity of their subject matter. I examine *Exodus*, *Andreas*, and *Judith* because they are all versions of biblical or apocryphal narratives, and they are stylistically distinct from each other and other poems. All three of them foreground the issue of translation, in its literal sense of carrying across and also more broadly. They thus show a range of possibilities for an Old English poetics rooted in its own time and language, but extending to the wider world, spatially and temporarily. These texts all deal with the past, acts of war, and cataclysmic changes. They include fragments in motion, objects come to life, and bodies turned to objects. While other poems sometimes have similar motifs, the ones I have chosen stand apart from the extant corpus more explicitly. For instance, these poems present such images in clusters (*burh*-woman-pillar; sculpture-pillar; bed-head-*burh*). *Exodus*, *Andreas*, and *Judith* all weave back and forth between references to heroic individuals and masses of people (the Israelites, the pre- and post-Conversion Mermedonians) that attempt to incorporate them, the way an artist would try to make a *spolium* fit into its surroundings. *Beowulf* always stands apart among the surviving Old English poetry, even though the scholarship often treats it as paradigmatic. It accumulates, even hoards, references to war plunder. *Beowulf*

Introduction: Powerful fragments

comes at the end because it follows the thematic and structural patterns described above, but, unlike the religious verse in *Borrowed Objects*, has a cloud of uncertainty hanging over it: the narrator cannot say what happens to his heroic pagan characters after death. The order of *Exodus* and *Andreas* in the book is mostly chronological according to the events depicted therein, while *Judith* comes before *Beowulf* to underline their proximity in the manuscript and their protagonists' more problematic status than Moses or Andrew. I argue that the riddles, *Exodus*, *Andreas*, *Judith*, and *Beowulf* show that the Anglo-Saxon vernacular verse, often considered conventional and doctrinally unswerving, not only allows for great variation and divergence, but also foregrounds and thinks deeply about them.

Concepts of 'art' in Old English

The question of what the Anglo-Saxons thought about art is still open. No extensive treatise on visual arts survives from early medieval Britain. Paul Szarmach considers a few passages from St Augustine, Gregory, and Bede, but none of them offers specific information. The most they do is to allow for some use of images in churches, to help the congregation recall biblical stories from memory or to encourage a simple typological exercise with juxtaposed pictures from the Old and New Testament.[12] In the first chapter of his book on pre-Conquest English art, C. R. Dodwell states with some frustration that '[n]o written material which relates to the Anglo-Saxon period has primary or even significant interest in art'. A search through a variety of materials, including chronicles, hagiographies, verse, legal and theological writings, and correspondence yields only a 'few references … usually made *en passant*'.[13] These references often give much less than a scholar might desire, and tend to express the object's splendour, value, or association with a particular, usually sacred personage.[14] The artworks that survive from early medieval England indicate that people made, commissioned, appreciated, and used artefacts; they just did not write about them in ways recognisable to us. Catherine Karkov emphasises that our involvement with Anglo-Saxon art would not have appeared so alien to its creators. She writes that 'Anglo-Saxons themselves viewed works of art as existing within a continuing process of creation, recreation and changing meanings.'[15] Elsewhere, Karkov notes that text and image flow into each other more in this period than any other time in the Middle Ages, moving beyond the illuminated manuscript to other kinds of material culture, including even buildings.[16] If what we consider distinct artistic expressions are so thoroughly integrated, perhaps we can look to poetry for oblique insight on other branches of art. Benjamin C. Tilghman turns to the Exeter Riddles with their persistent suggestion of ultimate obscurity of all matter to conclude that modern art historians studying Anglo-Saxon England are not at fault for being baffled: 'the continuing elusiveness of our objects of study comes not from our inability to master them, but from their innate resistance to disclosure'.[17] A lack of a larger, unified, explicit meta-discourse on art enables rather than prevents poets from engaging with the topic in creative, complex, and multifold ways.

Many possibilities that the Anglo-Saxons imagined art to afford come through lexicographic evidence, another extant source for a recovery of their attitudes. Searching through *A Thesaurus of Old English* for 'art' words, one encounters the term *cræft* in its several incarnations: *acræftan*, 'to think out/up, devise, design'; *leopcræft, scopcræft, wordcræft*, 'art of poetry'; *cræft(e)lic*, 'skilful, skilled'; *cræftig*, 'crafty, cunning, skilful, artful'; *(ge)cræftan*, 'to construct, form, fashion'.[18] The *Dictionary of Old English* remarks, before giving their definitions:

> The most frequent Latin equivalent of *cræft* is *ars*, yet neither 'craft' nor 'art' adequately conveys the wide range of meanings of *cræft*. 'Skill' may be the single most useful translation for *cræft*, but the senses of the word reach out to 'strength,' 'resources,' 'virtue' and other meanings in such a way that it is often not possible to assign an occurrence in one sense in [Modern English] without arbitrariness and the attendant loss of semantic richness.[19]

Some idea of the complex attitude towards art and the artificial can be gleaned from this 'semantic richness'. The word can have neutral ('strength, power, might'), negative ('vice'; 'a trick; stratagem, wile'), or positive implications ('skill, ability, dexterity, facility [physical]'). In compounds it joins with *woruld*, to form *woruldcræftig*, 'Skilled in secular arts', and *sundor* and *wundor* to make *sundor-* and *wundorcræftlice*, 'with special/wondrous skill'.[20] The semantic range of *cræft* suggests that the Anglo-Saxons thought of skill, ability for good or evil, potency, craft, and art as being so related that they could be expressed by the same word. They used the term for divine ('God's skill in creating and maintaining the world'), human ('trade, work, livelihood'), and demonic (*deofles/feondes cræft*, 'devil's cunning') endeavours. Danger, excitement, and potential – these

Introduction: Powerful fragments

are some responses to artful speech or creation in general, and to the enchanted artefact in particular.[21]

Another word, the adjective *wrætlic*, 'wondrous, awe-inspiring' helps us uncover a certain characteristic Anglo-Saxon aesthetic sensibility. Peter Ramey dedicates an entire essay to the term.[22] He concludes by listing and discussing the four elements that he discovers the word implies: materiality, intricacy, singularity, and mystery. All four elements work well with the objects considered in *Borrowed Objects*, and the first and last components illustrate the paradox which I trace throughout, of something concrete but elusive, clear yet perplexing. With reference to Hans Robert Jauss's theory of reception, Ramey discusses how *wrætlic* functions as a force in the Exeter Riddles, a collection of poems conscious of their craft. A textual artefact contains within itself not only that which the maker places in it, but also that which the viewer or reader derives from it; in other words, *wrætlic* as a quality results from authorial intention and audience reception.[23] This mutually constitutive process closely resembles the effect that people and things have on each other, as discussed in recent theory. Such an effect requires strenuous cogitation on the part of humans, which brings about pleasure as well as a sense of danger, according to Irina Dumitrescu. Dumitrescu's preferred translations of *wrætlic* include 'astonishing', 'striking', 'staggering', 'stupefying', and simply 'awful'. '[A] mixture of horror and admiration that provokes reflection', *wrætlic* implies an ongoing challenge, an intense force that can turn either way.[24]

Theories of things

By exploring the forms of interaction between people and objects in Old English verse, I hope not only to illuminate one overlooked aspect of an old, incompletely theorised poetics, but also to make a contribution to the emergent body of criticism focusing on materiality. In the first decade of the new millennium, as various theories beginning with thing theory were gaining ground, scholars turned mostly to later artistic expression. More recently, Anglo-Saxon literature (especially *Beowulf*) and visual art have had their turn, and I will briefly discuss two instances of this response later in this section.

Several general conclusions by various critics interested in objects apply well to the depiction of artefacts within Old English verse. In her essay 'What Makes an Object Evocative?' Sherry Turkle discusses how objects help people 'by bringing the world within'.

From a very early age, humans enrich and give expression to both their emotional and intellectual lives by focusing on toys. 'Far from being silent companions', Turkle writes, 'objects infuse learning with libido'.[25] One can recall the sensuous ending of *The Ruin*, where fragments of a Roman bathhouse inspire visions of corporeal pleasure in the Anglo-Saxon poet, leading him to a fairly faithful recovery of a building alien to his own culture. But we need not take 'libido' in strictly limited, psychoanalytic terms. Mihaly Csikszentmihalyi and Eugene Rochberg-Halton prefer to see a Nuer warrior's close attachment to his spear and a twentieth-century Westerner's to his car not as 'a libidinal, phallic fixation', but rather as 'an expression of Eros in the broadest sense, a need to demonstrate that one is alive, that one matters, that one makes a difference in the world'.[26] The manipulation of artefacts by Anglo-Saxon heroes and their poets has a very similar effect. Consolation to the Israelites in *Exodus* and *Judith*, and to Andrew and the Mermedonians in *Andreas*, arrives from the things that burst in from the past or a different place, or both. In *Beowulf*, that consolation is mixed with intimations of destruction, and loss and survival come together in the final image of the hoard-turned-barrow. By means of an instrument, an agent leaves a trace on the world, but also, through this process, the instrument becomes a part of the agent. The horn in Riddle 14 helps bring together the aristocratic world of art-making, feasting, and warfare that had removed it from a bovine's head. '[A]ll sentient beings', Ian Hodder reminds us, 'depend on things to bring their sentience into being', and are 'entangled' with each other.[27]

The intimate association of individuals with objects has great implications for human imagination. While for ethical and philosophical reasons the separation of thing and people within a society is tantamount, in art rigid lines need not be drawn; here, invocation of one often brings the other to the fore. Moreover, artefacts often ensure survival of the trace of the human because they have much longer temporalities. Bruno Latour claims that we read persons in terms of objects, and vice versa: 'Consider humans, and you are by that very act interested in things. Bring your attention to bear on hard things, and see them become gentle, soft or human. Turn your attention to humans, and see them become electric circuits, automatic gears or softwares.'[28] Latour's examples come from more recent technological discoveries (electricity, machines, computers), but they might also include robots, or animated sculptures, like the one in *Andreas*. Latour goes so far as to state that the modern period created the distinction between 'inanimate object and human

Introduction: Powerful fragments

subjects', falsifying the world in which 'quasi-objects' and 'quasi-subjects' proliferate.[29] Early medieval literature might provide an abundant hunting ground for such hybrids, or at least set us to talking around and about them. Lorraine Daston finds 'things' so central to human linguistic production that she declares that '[w]ithout things, we would stop talking'.[30] Approximately one half of the Exeter Riddles, about forty-six in number, feature non-human speakers, out of which fifteen challenge the listener or reader to say what they are called ('saga hwæt ic hatte'), thus asking for more speech.[31]

The anthropologist Carl Knappett discusses twentieth-century French stoneware that moves from an obsolete mundane commodity to a sought-after antique item to articulate the existence of 'different registers of objecthood' into and out of which artefacts move. The discussion takes him to three important conclusions:

> to see the status of objects as transitory rather than fixed; to imagine that the status of objects relies not only on the objects themselves but on the manner of their articulation within human-nonhuman networks; and to conceive of objects as leading lives that may be eventful and multiphased.[32]

The pillar in *Andreas* does not move from its place, but its status definitely changes. Even though it is, at the moment when the apostle meets it, one of the many architectural supports in a Mermedonian prison, St Andrew recognises its past incarnation as the tablet on which God wrote the Ten Commandments. Its role as a vessel for the cleansing flood brings up questions of its future use. It continues to live, as does the angel-shaped sculpture from earlier in the narrative. Knappett argues that objects move easily on a continuum between the mundane and the magical, and that human engagement with either kind demonstrates that mind and cognition do not remain limited to the brain, but 'seep out into the body and the world'.[33] In his own work on twentieth-century French stoneware and ancient Minoan drinking vessels, Knappett draws on the contiguity of the objects he studies, in order to discover their resonance; he investigates with what other objects they were found, and near what spaces. A carinated cup, for instance, may 'nest' in a particular room, which is in a particular building, which is in a particular region.[34] Thinking-with-objects necessarily involves the surrounding environment, architectural, geographical, and cosmic. The artefacts I am interested in draw their power and associations from their backgrounds, even while they break out of them. The narrators of the Exeter Riddles insist on the subjects' connection to the larger material context, whether of forging and recycling of swords, manuscript production, or the entire cosmos, while distracting us sufficiently to prevent an easy answer. Though the biblical poems do not envision the exact past or future of these objects, they acknowledge that they were activated before and will be again, somewhere outside the text, as the text itself would be. *Beowulf* works somewhat differently, since it reveals the past and future of a number of its important treasures, but it often suggests further depth or further continuation, which it cannot address because they are veiled in mystery.

Scholars have recently turned to the body of twenty-first-century theory dealing with materiality to illuminate how certain enigmatic things operate in *Beowulf*. James Paz draws our attention to 'riddle-like things' (both objects like the famed swords and creatures treated as such like Grendel's mother) to demonstrate that artefacts commonly thwart the attempts of people to place them within an interpretative frame;[35] in this dynamic lies their frustrating usefulness. Aaron Hostetter acknowledges Paz's 'sense of material recalcitrance', but prefers to look at moments of productive interaction between human characters and material culture.[36] He employs Jane Bennett's notion of 'thing-power' to explain the draw enigmatic objects have on characters of *Beowulf*. Though he emphasises the interdependence of the two – people create things, which influence people who then have to maintain them – Hostetter still notes that a certain excess or surplus resides in artefacts 'that exceeds the human social activity that constitutes the commodity'.[37] In *Borrowed Objects* I am interested precisely in this central paradox, whereby physical objects that both depend on and constitute their creators and users refuse full incorporation, whether textual or architectural. This phenomenon further ensures their survival and relevance: mysteries keep their currency until they are satisfactorily solved. Due to their resistance and flexibility alike, the evocative artefacts play a crucial role not only for Anglo-Saxon poetry but also for its implicit poetics.

Relics

If these theoretical discussions still seem removed from the Middle Ages, one well-known medieval category exists that blends the animate and the inanimate; appeals to the elemental and the cosmic;

Introduction: Powerful fragments

brings together the near and the far; and incites discussions of origins and purpose of especially marked material culture. Relics are small, compact fragments, either body parts belonging to Christ or a saint, or objects owned or touched by them, 'around which boundless associations clustered'. They serve as visual proofs of spiritual triumph over time and place, and thus over human mortality.[38] Patrick Geary, having remarked that relics belong to 'that category ... of objects that are both persons and things', invents the word 'person-objects' to refer to them.[39] The spiritual certainty surrounding a martyr's nail, his sandals, or cup does not extend to an animated sculpture of an angel or a tyrant's decapitated head; one type of fragment inhabits a stable sacred context for eternity, while the other seems only momentarily tamed. However, the transfer of immense power occurs in both types along spatial lines. 'Previously peripheral region[s]', including Central Europe and Anglo-Saxon England, show their increased political significance by bringing into their midst relics from the Mediterranean lands, like Italy.[40] But, by virtue of already being Christian, such relics need not be subjugated or wrestled with in the same way that other numinous artefacts do. Peter Brown writes that '[b]ehind every relic that was newly installed in its shrine throughout the Mediterranean, there had to lie some precise gesture of good will and solidarity'. 'Good will and solidarity' are often missing, or complicated, in the things discussed in *Borrowed Objects*, as is the precision. Unlike the bits or effects of holy persons, evocative objects in the riddles of the plunder cluster, *Exodus*, *Andreas*, *Judith*, and *Beowulf* do not inspire extended accounts of their 'discovery, translation, and installation':[41] like the Old English texts that house them, they incorporate clarity and obscurity. Finally, if relics serve as 'instruments of approach in communicating with the godhead',[42] our artefacts both inspire and question communication, without always involving the divine.

When a relic emerges in an Anglo-Saxon poem, the author positions it explicitly with regard to its past, present, and future, similarly to the way that *The Ruin* poet does the ruin, as we have seen earlier in this introduction. *The Dream of the Rood*, a work that survives, like *Andreas*, only in the late tenth-century Vercelli Book, is known for being the first extended dream-vision in the Anglophone tradition. It is also famous for repeating – or providing – parts of the early eighth-century Northumbrian Ruthwell Cross. The text features the voice of the narrator-visionary alongside that

of his envisioned object, the True Cross in its many manifestations.
The latter speaks of its origins thus:

> Ongan þa word sprecan   wudu selesta:
> 'þæt wæs geara iu,   (ic þæt gyta geman),
> þæt ic wæs aheawen   holtes on ende,
> astyred of stefne minum.   Genaman me ðær strange feondas,
> geworhton him þær to wæfersyne,   heton me heora wergas hebban.
> Bæron me ðær beornas on eaxlum,   oððæt hie me on beorg asetton,
> gefæstnodon me þær feondas genoge.' (27–33)[43]
> [Then the most chosen of wood began to speak these words: 'It was long ago (I still remember it) when I was cut down at the edge of the forest, pulled from my root. Strong enemies took me from there, put me on display for themselves, ordered me to lift up their outlaws (or: they ordered their outlaws to lift me up).[44] Men carried me on their shoulders until they set me down on a hill. So many foes fastened me there.']

The Rood gives an account of the Crucifixion, Christ's removal from the Cross, and his entombment. Then it relates how men cut it down, buried it and its colleagues (the two crosses of the thieves crucified with Jesus) in a deep pit, and how, later, 'Dryhtnes þegnas, / freondas gefrunon, [a missing line] / gyredon me golde ond seolfre' [the Lord's thanes, his friends found out (where I was), they adorned me with gold and silver] (75–7). Not only do we learn the entire story – the one that we presumably already know, since the Cross expects the audience to understand a hint like 'God's friends'[45] – but we also hear it from the artefact itself. The artwork provides its own caption, or, to use an apt medieval term, its own *titulus*.[46] Szarmach singles out *The Dream of the Rood* as an unusual case of Anglo-Saxon ekphrasis because it describes more than Bede and Gregory could theorise about uses of art: the typically un-described, aesthetically appealing details of the artefact's physical appearance and the emotional reaction of the viewer. Furthermore, *The Dream of the Rood* in Szarmach's estimation moves beyond what the poets of *Andreas* and *Beowulf* could offer with their meditations on the animated sculpture and the inscribed giant-made hilt, respectively. His conclusion is suggestive: 'Ultimately, this paper suggests the triumph of art over criticism or, more sharply, ekphrasis and the experience of the verbal description of the visual over the discursive formulation of any particular ekphrastic moment.'[47]

The wholeness and groundedness of the vision presented in and by the Rood cannot be paralleled in textual moments of exhibited

Introduction: Powerful fragments

artworks in the Exeter Riddles, *Exodus*, *Andreas*, *Judith*, and *Beowulf*, and not merely because the coherent, well-known narrative does not exist for each case of artefactual manipulation in Old English verse. *The Ruin* teasingly invites comparisons with existing Roman ruins in Britain, and *The Dream of the Rood* interacts in some inter-media way with the objects we have at hand, the Ruthwell Cross and the eleventh-century silver reliquary called the Brussels Cross.[48] On the contrary, no real fragment could be retrieved, at this or probably any future point, that corresponds to the bookcase/oven of Riddle 49, the shape-shifting pillar in *Exodus*, the angel-sculpture in *Andreas*, or the golden net in *Judith*. The things that speak and are spoken about in the short vernacular enigmas typically do not allude to a specific item of material culture but to concepts more generally, sometimes even words covering more than one particular referent.[49] The sheer number of artefacts mentioned in *Beowulf* has led many scholars to find equivalents in the early Germanic archaeological record, which is an understandable but problematic endeavour; more careful analyses of material culture in the poem by Roberta Frank and Emily Thornbury demonstrate a greater adherence to imagination and blending of various material contexts.[50] In working with evocative objects, three different Anglo-Saxon biblical poems seek to distance the specific-visual from the textual while, at the same time, taking advantage of the specific charge of physical artefacts that combine the elemental and the cosmic, the concrete and the abstract. *Beowulf* reproduces the same dynamic, but with a larger number of things that it displays, hoards, and buries out of sight. The riddles in their sheer diversity combine these two approaches.

The fleeting nature of the image, coupled with its materiality, comes up both in the depiction of the Rood and the less contextualised objects from the poems I discuss in subsequent chapters. We need only recall the resplendent scene of the Cross changing 'wædum ond bleom' [garments and colours], being, one moment, 'mid wætan bestemed, / beswyled mid swates gange' [wet with moisture, drenched with blood-flow], and the next, 'mid since / gegyrwed' [adorned with treasure] (22–3). But a crucial difference emerges, as well. Chaganti argues that the object in the poem moves between the two poles represented, respectively, by the Brussels Cross and the Ruthwell Cross: a small, portable keepsake versus a large, fixed monument; private reading versus a more communal engagement. *The Dream of the Rood* synthesises 'the inscriptional and performative modes elucidated in its metal and stone manifestations'.⁵¹ The artefacts that I shall discuss do not compare to the Brussels Cross, the Ruthwell Cross, or the Rood in the effect they have on the viewers. They urge contemplation of more intimate, mysterious, and fleeting uses of art rather than public, illuminated, and fixed. They may manifest themselves in front of groups of people, but they are manipulated by a special individual (a craftsperson, Moses, God, St Andrew, Beowulf, Judith); they are exhibited (at a feast; on the city streets; on the road to Canaan; in an uncovered hoard and as they burn in a funeral pyre; on the edge between the sea, sky, and earth), but they easily vanish from our view.

One similarity between the Cross in *The Dream of the Rood* and various instances of evocative objects in Old English verse is that they do what ekphrasis, 'the verbal representation of the visual',[52] usually does: show the desire of the verbal to incorporate and extend the visual. Putting aside the question of whether Anglo-Saxon texts even provide examples of the phenomenon considered in pre- and post-medieval rhetoric as ekphrasis, we can turn to theories developed to explain more conventional cases of the figure to illuminate Old English poetics, even if only to provide contrast. In her book on *The Stone Sleeper* by Mak Dizdar, a twentieth-century Bosnian poet, Adijata Ibrišimović-Šabić gives the definition of the third type of ekphrasis following Maria Rubins, a Russian literary scholar of nineteenth- and twentieth-century poetry. According to Ibrišimović-Šabić, in the psychological or expressive ekphrasis, 'the artefact itself does not receive the focus of attention as much as the poet's experience of the given object … Ekphrases of this type are actually a modified text, not a text that imitates but one that reworks creatively …'[53] The critic then discusses a particular poem as an example of the expressive ekphrasis, in order to conclude that 'it is only with words, with speech that one can completely reveal, supplement, or adequately communicate the meaning and sense of an artwork'. 'Without mediation of the words', Ibrišimović-Šabić continues, 'the medieval tombstone [as depicted by Dizdar's text] would become mute and unnecessary, alien and incomprehensible to a modern person', and potentially cause the past to be forgotten.[54] We cannot claim the same for the Cross, which does not lose its currency with time, and it would be challenging to argue for individualised poetic experience of a non-existent artefact in entirely anonymous Old English works. Still, the ideas of reworking the visual to enrich a text and of preserving the past by speaking around a fraught and incomplete object from it are extremely helpful in reading poetry from pre-Conquest England.

Spolia

Relics are not the only examples of early medieval intellectual and artistic fascination with significant artefacts that complicate the boundary between temporal layers, elements, global and local, textual and visual, and animate and inanimate forces. An entire discourse, permeating religious, political, and artistic culture, arises around the idea of *spolia* in the Middle Ages. The earliest meaning of *spolium*, 'the skin or hide stripped off an animal', already shows the melding of bodies and things. From there, the word becomes generalised as 'the spoils of war', possessions taken from an enemy for reuse by the vanquishing force.[55] In the language of art history, *spolia* refer to artefacts in a new, physical context, especially in a manner that highlights their Otherness, their difference. For instance, one could take a capital from an antique pillar and put it to the same structural use in a post-antique building, or turn it into a receptacle for holy water; in either case, the capital stands out as an object from the past which carries a particular charge despite and because of its new position.[56] Foregrounding questions of continuity and discontinuity, this practice has a long history. The earliest examples of architectural *spolia* in Greece occur in the foundations of the Acropolis, while some of the latest, in St Photeine in the Peloponnesus, appear in a church dating from 1970.[57] The Roman theatre in the centre of Apt (the south of France) decreased in size over the ages, as it provided materials for the building of the Apt Cathedral in the twelfth century in addition to its expansion between the fourteenth and seventeenth centuries, until not a trace of the theatre remained in 1870.[58]

While pre-sixteenth century texts never employ the term *spolia*, but rather speak of specific artefacts,[59] the art-historical practice of spoliation was widespread throughout the Middle Ages, from after the fall of Rome (that is, the conventional end of the classical period), to the time of the Anglo-Saxons in England, and beyond. One can follow the power shifts from the south to the north of Europe by looking at paradigmatic instances of this practice. The first Christian Roman emperor, Constantine, took the ideological manipulation of material fragments belonging to his predecessors to a new level in the process of building his triumphal arch and the Lateran Basilica.[60] As the seat of power moved from Rome northwards, grand imperial statements of this type followed. One ruler attempted to upstage another. Charles the Great had pillars and marble removed from Rome and Ravenna to uphold and adorn his chapter at Aachen; he also took along the equestrian statue of Theodoric. The long-distance transportation of construction materials from Theodoric's Italian palace to Charlemagne's residence at Ingelheim struck the latter emperor's contemporaries as such an unprecedented move that it immediately became 'stylized into a literary topos'.[61] Artefacts wrenched from their past contexts contributed to the larger project of *renovatio*, later dubbed the Carolingian Renaissance, which had as its goal nothing less than the creation of 'a new Athens ... in France' in the words of Charlemagne's *magister* the Englishman Alcuin.[62] Transferring Rome to Aachen or turning France into a second Athens does more than appropriate the power of one's predecessors: it contests the status of a major contemporary rival, Byzantium, as the new Rome.[63] Ottonians, another people proximate to Anglo-Saxons, went a step further when they incorporated *spolia* from backgrounds other than Roman. In the so-called Egbert shrine, a jewelled reliquary from the late tenth century (also known as the portable altar of St Andrew), scholars have identified earlier 'Fatimid (?), Anglo-Saxon, Merovingian, and Byzantine' fragments. Such a conglomeration reveals a larger appetite for power, a *culminatio* rather than a *renovatio*.[64]

The Anglo-Saxons who headed on pilgrimage to Rome certainly observed the results of spoliation on the Continent as they crossed the realms of the Carolingians and Ottonians; Nicholas Howe notes that, just as Paris was the capital of Europe before the Second World War, so Rome can be considered the capital of early medieval England.[65] But *spolia* are amply attested in the British Isles, as well. Tim Eaton's detailed study *Plundering the Past: Roman Stonework in Medieval Britain* reveals such items as a Roman altar from St Oswald-in-Lee (Northumberland) re-contextualised as a cross base at the marketplace in Corbridge, and a relief of a spear-wielding warrior (or god) from a Roman monument reused in Hexham Abbey.[66] One mid-seventh-century work, the church of St Peter from Bradwell-on-Sea (Essex) was compiled almost entirely of *spolia*.[67] Pagan figures did not necessarily suffer demotion in their new backgrounds. Richard Morris reports that a sculpture of a Roman *genius* graces the outside of the south wall of St John's church at Tockenham (Wiltshire); he speculates that this figure gained such prominence because of its resemblance to a saint or even Christ.[68] Ordinary Anglo-Saxons would not only encounter

Introduction: Powerful fragments

re-contextualised fragments from late antiquity or the classical past in and outside churches and in other public places, such as the St Oswald-in-Lee marketplace with its Roman altar, but would also sometimes directly interact with them in the rural landscape. Human engagement with plundered artefacts did not always need to be grand, politically or aesthetically. Pre-Roman monoliths appeared as boundary-markers, way-markers, and gate-posts, and as such seem difficult to distinguish from more recent objects serving the same function.[69] Recycled Roman inscriptions, *spolia* that powerfully combine the textual with the visual, seem more upfront about their former identity. One inscription, on a Roman altar repurposed as a stoup at St Michael's church at Michaelchurch (Herefordshire) reads, 'DEO TRIDAM ... | BELLICUS DON | AURIT ARA[M]', 'To the god Tridam ... Bellicus presented this'. Another stoup from St Andrew's at Corbridge, features a Greek text, 'To Heracles of Tyre Diadora the priestess (set this up)'.[70] Educated Anglo-Saxons could read the Latin inscriptions at least.

Physical spoliation might have become a literary trope among some Anglo-Saxons. St Augustine[71] writes in *On Christian Teaching* (Book Two, section 44ff.) that Christians should appropriate the learning of pagans that does not clash with their faith. To speak of this process, he focuses on a key scene from the Book of Exodus:

> Like the treasures of the ancient Egyptians, who possessed not only idols and heavy burdens, which the people of Israel hated and shunned, but also vessels and ornaments of silver and gold, and clothes, which on leaving Egypt the people of Israel, in order to make better use of them, surreptitiously claimed for themselves (they did this not on their own authority but at God's command, and the Egyptians in their ignorance actually gave them the things of which they had made poor use) [Exod. 3:21–2, 12:35–6] – similarly all the branches of pagan learning contain not only false and superstitious fantasies and burdensome studies that involve unnecessary effort, which each of us must loathe and avoid as under Christ's guidance we abandon the company of pagans, but also studies for liberated minds which are more appropriate to the service of the truth, and some very useful moral instruction, as well as the various truths about monotheism to be found in their writers.[72]

Augustine then compares this pagan scholarship again to the two precious metals, and likens the Egyptian clothing to 'human institutions' ('hominum quidem instituta') grudgingly allowed because they are indispensable for earthy life. He goes on to list several names, among them Cyprian, Hilary, and '[some] people still alive, and countless Greek scholars' ('... vivis ... innumerabiles Graeci') as beneficiaries of Egyptian gold, silver, and textiles.[73] The enemies of the believers would not have willingly allowed them to take up their arts if they had known that those would be employed to overturn heathenism; therefore, Augustine claims, it is all the more important to engage in such a process to facilitate the triumph of the one true religion. Finally, Augustine summarises his argument by calling the act of spoliation in Exodus a foreshadowing of Christian appropriation of pagan knowledge. He quickly adds, 'I say this without prejudice to any other interpretation of equal or greater importance' ('Quod sine praeiudicio alterius aut paris aut melioris intellegentiae dixerim').[74] Throughout this discussion, Augustine suggests that some artefacts are not tarnished by association with previous users, yet he does not address the difficulty of separating the useful from the dangerous. He does mention the existence of other readings, although he does not explore them in any detail. The scene of spoliation in Exodus encourages a certain mystery alongside interpretive proliferation.

The transformation of pagan learning into Christian has another textual equivalent, with extremely corporeal images, in claiming classical and Old Testament figures for Christianity. When Augustine speaks of foreshadowing, he means typology, that is, taking certain events in the Hebrew scriptures as looking ahead to Christ, his deeds, and the actions of his followers. The phenomenon begins in the New Testament itself, where Moses's raising of the snake in the wilderness is interpreted as a type of Christ's 'exaltation on the cross' (John 3:14) and Jonah's three-day sojourn in the innards of the whale becomes Christ's three-day journey through death (Matthew 12:39 ff).[75] Reading the Old Testament with an eye to the New Dispensation allows for recuperation of much of the older narrative, which might otherwise appear strange or unacceptable to an orthodox Christian;[76] through typology unusual situations continue to live on in a new context.

Spoliation in the New Testament flows into the apocryphal story of the Harrowing of Hell, a theme popular in Anglo-Saxon England, 'widely adopted but never fully or consistently elaborated'. During the three days between his death and resurrection, Christ journeys into the underworld to release 'Adam, the patriarchs, and the prophets, including John the Baptist' from infernal suffering.[77] An Old English poetic account surviving in the Exeter Book mentions by name Adam, Abraham, Isaac, Jacob, Moses, David, Isaiah, Zachariah, and John the Baptist.[78] Several Anglo-Saxon homilies concern themselves with the subject. There exists a prose translation as well as references to the theme in *Christ I* and *II*, *Phoenix*, Riddle 55, *Elene*, and *The Dream of the Rood*, just to list the most famous texts.[79] Additionally, at least one manuscript from pre-Conquest England visually depicts the Harrowing. The Tiberius Psalter, or MS, BL Cotton Tiberius C vi, from the mid-eleventh century, features the drawing of Jesus's rescue of Adam and Eve and other figures from Hell's mouth and crushing of the shackled devil with his foot; this image 'not only explicitly portrays the battle between Christ and Satan', but it also provides 'the visual key to the whole group of images' in the Psalter.[80] The Old English word for 'harrowing', *hergung*, covers a variety of meanings that connect Christ's attack with spoils of war, his action with its results: 'Harrying, harrowing, plundering, devastation, waging war, an irruption, incursion, invasion, a raid, plunder'.[81] Indeed, medieval England (and elsewhere) envisioned Jesus 'both breaking down [the] gates [of hell] ... and robbing Satan of its spoils, the souls of the righteous'.[82]

The centrality of plundering in Anglo-Saxon imagination becomes apparent in another common word for the practice. *Reafian*, 'to plunder', comes from *reofan*, 'to tear apart', deriving from the same Indo-European root as *rupture*; *reaf*, 'garment', also means 'spoils'.[83] Spoils signify something snatched away and employed to cover one's body. If we wished to find an approximate translation of *spolia*, broadly conceived, in Old English, we could turn to *laf*. Phyllis Portnoy has extensively argued that this polysemic noun plays a key role in Anglo-Saxon vernacular poetry, from biblical verse to Exeter Riddles.[84] She gives the following definitions: 'what is left', 'remnant', 'survivor', 'widow', 'treasure', 'heirloom', 'sword', and 'relic'. Like *spolia*, the concept applies to both terms of the human/non-human and live/dead binaries; it could refer to either side of a conflict, the attacker or the attacked, as well as to a male or female individual; it fuses creativity with deadliness (resembling in this aspect the idea of *wrætlic*). Portnoy elegantly articulates the striking effectiveness of *laf*: 'the one word adds several layers to a simple subject'.[85] Reused artefacts, whether architectural or textual, contribute to and highlight compositeness of the larger structure that they are harnessed to uphold.

In late antique poetry, Christian and pagan, we see the metaphor of plundering the ancients alongside statements that the ancients plundered the ancients, as well. Prudentius creates his *Psychomachia* out of verses from Virgil in a technique called the *cento*, lifting verses wholesale and fitting them into a new text. Macrobius, in the sixth book of his *Saturnalia*, uses the metaphor of 'plundering a library' to refer to the work of Roman *auctores* who helped themselves to 'a deposit of texts, both Latin and Greek'.[86] Isidore of Seville, in his *Etymologies*, refers to Virgil's being called a plunderer (*compilator*).[87] The metaphor comes to Anglo-Saxon England through the *grammatica* tradition. Bede knew that the Augustinian trope of plundering the Egyptians could be used to 'defend the value of grammatical studies', something he could have learnt from the *Anonymous ad Cuimnanum*, an eighth-century commentary to Donatus's *Ars maior*.[88] Two centuries later, King Alfred speaks of writing as *compilatio* in his English translation of St Augustine's *Soliloquies*. An author, he says, cuts down some remarkable trees from the woods, and transports the materials in wagons to the site where he can 'windan manigne smicerne wah, and manig ænlic hus settan, and fegerne tun timbrian' ['weave many a beautiful wall and build many an excellent house and build a fine town'], in which one can live in comfort with one's kin throughout the year, 'swa swa ic nu ne gyt ne dyde' ['as I have not yet done'].[89] One last Anglo-Saxon example of material reuse and textual production appearing together is also associated with Alfred. The remarkable Alfred Jewel, which probably contains a repurposed Roman crystal, formed the top part of a pointer and could have 'mirror[ed]' *The Pastoral Care*, Gregory the Great's canonical text that Alfred translated into his vernacular.[90]

Drawing parallels between textual production and spoliation continues to our day. In conversation with the poet Robert Hass, Seamus Heaney discusses two types of translation: the raid, in which a poet-translator like Robert Lowell plunders various languages to 'end up with booty that you call *Imitations*', and the settlement, in which someone like Robert Fitzgerald 'stayed with Homer', or Heaney himself, who 'settled with *Beowulf* and stayed with it, formed a kind of conjugal relation for years'.[91] Another translator of *Beowulf*, Roy M. Liuzza, goes even further, comparing the structure of the poem to 'an Anglo-Saxon church made from the salvaged stones of a Roman temple'.[92] The scholar Haruko Momma speaks similarly when she likens an Old English poem to composite medieval architecture 'whose construct has been repeatedly altered by renovations, additions, and demolitions'.[93] The ultimate source for Liuzza and Momma's analogies may well be Tolkien's allegory of a man who uses ancient stones found in an inherited field to build a tower from which he can 'look out upon the sea'.[94]

Both textual and architectural *spolia* contribute to the larger medieval aesthetic called *varietas* in Latin and *poikilia* in Greek

Introduction: Powerful fragments

that delights in juxtaposed difference and richness of materials. For instance, ancient sculptures built into a wall of a Byzantine church 'endowed it with variety (*poikilia*), prerequisite of any building of high repute in Byzantium', which requires 'surfaces … [to] glitter and walls [to] gleam and an embroidery-like texture [to appear] in facades'.[95] *Varietas* pervades textuality, manifests itself in the 'jeweled style' of late antiquity, and finds its biblical justification in the multivocal modes of the psalms and the miraculous speaking of tongues in the story of the Pentecost.[96] In opposition to classical ideals of homogeneity, symmetry, and harmony in styles, this aesthetic champions heterogeneity, rupture, and mixing of styles, and, as a result, early medieval art moves away from a certain 'corporeality and coherence' to a new type of sensibility focused on the spiritual and mystical.[97] Maria Fabricius Hansen explains a significant effect of such a change: 'This new mental habit contained an awareness of rhythm, punctuation, and intervals, of pauses and space, an awareness alien to the ancient Greek and Roman cultures.'[98] *Varietas* highlights gaps and breaks, marking a rearrangement of the pagan heritage and leaving spaces for contemplation of the divine. At the same time, it celebrates unity in multiplicity, the bewildering richness of God's creation that comes from a single, all-powerful source.[99] It is a powerful, paradoxical dynamic, a result of coming together of Christianity and paganism, of Latin learning and 'barbarian' artists and authors. A certain affinity seems to exist between *varietas/poikilia* and later aesthetic developments in colonial and post-colonial contexts. Indigenous and colonial influences fuse to produce intricate, variegated new forms in literature, visual arts, music, and so on.[100] *Spolia* are useful as a conceptual framework for a number of reasons. Strategically recycled artefacts, textual and architectural, add depth and texture. They invoke, metonymically, different times and places; they break down the boundary between life and death; they carry enormous, nearly cosmic energy, often appearing at the intersection of various elements or under extreme weather conditions in poems under discussion in *Borrowed Objects*. They simultaneously suggest rupture and continuity, utter loss and palpable lingering presence.

Chapter summaries

The book opens with the first chapter dedicated to a selection of Exeter Riddles that deal with *spolia* or their effects. While their solutions are not always certain, they cover a wide swathe of the

Anglo-Saxon world that does not emerge in any other surviving poetic source. Participating in the larger Latinate textual tradition of riddles, yet distinct from them, these vernacular riddles speak of weather events, flora and fauna, everyday implements, writing utensils, and even sexual organs and activities. While they differ from the rest of the poems under consideration, they do illuminate the enigmatic force of fragmented artefacts in biblical verse and *Beowulf*. The riddles speak to each other; they often come in larger thematic clusters, sometimes in pairs and triads and oppositional groups. Like *spolia*, they gain their meaning and allure from juxtaposition, mystery, and elusiveness, and they contain multitudes in a small space. In this chapter, I identify a 'plunder cluster' within the collection, consisting of, at least, Riddles 14, 20, and 29, those with the proposed solutions of 'Horn', 'Sword', and 'Moon and Sun'. Then I proceed to four other riddles, numbered 49, 40, 60, and 95 ('Bookcase/Oven', 'Creation', 'Creation', 'Book'), that, like *Beowulf*, ponder accumulation. The selected Exeter Riddles begin to reveal traces of a sophisticated *ars poetica*, at once playful and deeply serious, that conceives of texts as remnants that paradoxically communicate while holding back.

In the second chapter, I look at the Old English *Exodus*. I begin with a sudden, enigmatic appearance that has puzzled the scholars, that of an African woman, who helps the Israelites divide the treasure stripped from the drowned Egyptian army. I frame this episode with the repeated figure of *burh* [city or enclosure] that follows Moses and his people in their journey, and the metamorphosing pillar of cloud, a biblical element largely expanded in Old English. Both iconic images exhibit *spolia*-like effects due to their specific relationship to space and time. Functioning at once as a memory of old cities and a premonition of future cities for the Israelites, the *burh* constantly changes and acquires new meanings. The pillar, on the other hand, functions as a fragment of the future, able to suggest on its own the larger protective structure of the Christian church. These three remarkable textual moments together provide the key to the work's modus operandi. *Exodus* seems to encourage both exegetical and political readings, as scholars have repeatedly shown, but it also produces an excess of meaning, indicating that something irreducibly strange always remains.

The third chapter concerns itself with *Andreas*, a poetic version of the apocryphal narrative about the Apostle Andrew's journey to Mermedonia, an island of cannibals, and his subsequent martyrdom and conversion of Mermedonians. Two clear examples of architectural *spolia* emerge in *Andreas*. They are unique to the Old English poem, diverging greatly from its Latin and Greek analogues. In the first scene, Jesus animates an angel sculpture in a Jerusalem temple to manifest his divinity to the unbelievers. In the second passage, Andrew speaks to a stone pillar in his prison cell, causing it to issue a flood that drowns – and baptises – the violent Mermedonians. I argue that both artefacts come to life thanks to powerful figures, Jesus and Andrew, who function as the author's alter egos as they animate artefacts from the past. Their status as material fragments in search of a new integration fits with the larger pattern in *Andreas*. This pattern occurs twice more: the hero's bodily fragmentation caused by the Mermedonians, and the metatextual excursus in which the narrator admits to his method of presenting the material 'lytlum sticcum' [in little bits]. Far from reading *Andreas* as an incompetent poem, I argue that attending to *spolia* and other textual and physical fragments found in the text helps us uncover sophisticated, self-conscious poetics behind the work.

The fourth chapter focuses on *Judith*. This poem describes the eponymous Hebrew heroine's successful decapitation of the evil Assyrian king Holofernes. Holofernes's head provides a literal example of plunder. Unlike her biblical inspiration, Judith accepts the Assyrian's gore-smeared armour as an offering from her people. The irony of this instance of *spolia* increases because the woman whom Holofernes wishes to claim as his plunder in the end plunders him. Two sets of opposing methods surface regarding *spolia* and similar objects. Certain passages in *Judith* feature zooming out and quickening of the narrative pace, while in others zooming in and slower rhythm predominate. The narrative allows us neither to neglect the dangerous, seductive detail (often a type of *spolium*) nor to linger too long on it. The foreshortened narrative itself invites and resists appropriation through allegorisation, whether religious (as a Christian typological exercise) or political (as a statement about the eighth-century Viking attacks). I argue that *Judith* thus complicates two common, contrasting theoretical approaches to it: the psychoanalytical criticism emphasising the heroine's subversion and the exegetical interpretations that contain the protagonist and her actions within orthodox medieval belief.

Beowulf is the subject of the fifth chapter. Although the poem features too much plunder to fully enumerate, I look at several memorable and representative examples in which objects escape human efforts to contain them. They include the torque that the Danish queen Wealhtheow gives to Beowulf, and the sword carried by a Dane but formerly belonging to a Heathobard that will bring about discord, according to Beowulf's prophecy. The chapter then turns to the hoard at the end of the poem. Acts of hoarding would seek to deactivate individual objects, but even so some of their previous change remains. The interplay between hoards and plunder, or the subsuming and the subsumed, highlights the paradox at the heart of *Beowulf*: a poignant, pervasive sense of loss seems to carry a material weight. Rather than arbitrate between positive (Germanic/ heroic) and negative (Christian/spiritual) interpretations of use of treasure in the poem, I show the poet's ambivalence towards pagan material culture, which he can neither fully embrace nor condemn.

In the afterword, I bring together my texts, suggesting that the riddle might be added to the list of Martin Irvine's macrogenres that constitute early medieval literature (such as gloss, lexicon, compilation, encyclopedia, and library).[101] I further argue that the *spolia* contribute to the larger Old English poetics of challenging and playful obliqueness, and prove the sophistication of Anglo-Saxon poets and their generosity in leaving gaps for their readers to fill. Finally, the afterword draws on the work of both medievalists and scholars working on more recent time periods to identify any transhistorical echoes.

The issue that relics and *spolia* dramatically put forward is the relationship of the specific to the general.[102] What does the movement in and out of the narrative of a material object tell us about the world at large? The physical artefact that breaks out of the temporal and spatial boundaries inside a text urges the readers to estrange their own world, or the world of the text. Additionally, it encourages them to see that the object hints at another world above, alongside, before, beyond, within the new architectural or textual structure that houses it. The need in the medieval (and post-medieval) periods to move beyond the present moment, and to do so through animated and animating objects, signifies more than a shiver of aesthetic pleasure. Writing on relics, Sobin states that 'the quest – by the intermediary of bone, splinter, or effigy – [for] a dimension *past themselves*' can help people transcend 'the often dire circumstances of their day-to-day lives'.[103] A certain hope seems implied by this belief: the hope that some fragment of us, or the work of our hands – or, better, both blended together – would survive and be sufficient in recreation of the contours of our entire world, all that was lost with our death. Still, paradoxically, the fragment by its nature

Introduction: Powerful fragments   25

would leave something out, creating a space, maybe even a ruin, to be filled pleasurably with future imaginings.

Notes

1 Parts of this chapter appeared, in different form, in Denis Ferhatović, '*Burh* & *Beam*, Burning Bright: A Study in the Poetic Imagination of the Old English *Exodus*', *Neophilologus*, 94:3 (2010), 509–22; and '*Spolia*-Inflected Poetics of the Old English *Andreas*', *Studies in Philology*, 111 (2013), 199–219.
2 I quote *The Ruin* according to George P. Krapp and Elliot V. Dobbie's edition of *The Exeter Book*, ASPR 3 (New York: Columbia University Press, 1936), pp. 227–9. Another reading of the last line is 'hu se ... burh' [how that city ...]. See *The Ruin* in Bernard J. Muir (ed.), *The Exeter Anthology of Old English Poetry* (Exeter: University of Exeter Press, 1994), pp. 360–1. All translations from Old English are mine unless otherwise noted.
3 For specific references, see note 3 in Eileen Joy, 'On the Hither Side of Time: Tony Kushner's *Homebody/Kabul* and the Old English *Ruin*', *Medieval Perspectives*, 19 (2005).
4 Bruce Mitchell and Fred Robinson, *A Guide to Old English: Fifth Edition* (Oxford: Blackwell, 1992), p. 252.
5 Alain Renoir, 'The Old English *Ruin*: Contrastive Structure and Affective Impact', in Martin Green (ed.), *The Old English Elegies: New Essays in Criticism and Research* (Rutherford, NJ: Farleigh Dickinson Press, 1983), pp. 148–73, at 149.
6 Joy, 'On the Hither Side of Time', p. 11.
7 See Joshua Davies's discussion of the poem in his 'The Literary Languages of Old English: Words, Styles, Voices', in Clare Lees (ed.), *The Cambridge History of Early Medieval English Literature* (Cambridge: Cambridge University Press, 2013), pp. 257–77, esp. pp. 273–7.
8 Joy, 'On the Hither Side of Time', p. 8.
9 Nicholas Howe, *Migration and Mythmaking in Anglo-Saxon England* (New Haven: Yale University Press, 1989), p. 48.
10 Gaston Bachelard, *The Poetics of Space*, trans. Maria Jolas (Boston: Beacon Press, 1969), p. 234. The italics are in the original.
11 While agreeing that the riddles are often not exhausted by a single solution, I accept the following solutions, respectively: 'Horn', 'Sword', 'Moon and Sun', 'Creation', 'Bookcase/Oven', 'Creation', and 'Book'. For more, see Chapter 1 below. I take the numbering from Krapp and Dobbie's edition, *The Exeter Book*, ASPR 3. Because of Craig Williamson's influential edition and commentary, from which I have benefited, I here give his numbering for the riddles under discussion, as well: 12, 18, 27, 38, 47, 64, 91. Craig Williamson (ed.), *The Old*

English Riddles of the Exeter Book (Chapel Hill: University of North Carolina Press, 1977).
12 Paul Szarmach, 'The Dream of the Rood as Ekphrasis', in Alastair Minnis and Jane Roberts (eds), *Text, Image, Interpretation: Studies in Anglo-Saxon Literature and its Insular Context in Honour of Éamonn Ó Carragáin* (Turnhout: Brepols, 2007), pp. 267–88.
13 C. R. Dodwell, *Anglo-Saxon Art: A New Perspective* (Ithaca: Cornell University Press, 1982), pp. 15–16.
14 Ibid.
15 Catherine Karkov, *The Art of Anglo-Saxon England* (Woodbridge: Boydell, 2011), p. 9.
16 Catherine Karkov, 'Art and Writing: Voice, Image, Object', in Clare A. Lees (ed.), *The Cambridge History of Early Medieval English Literature* (Cambridge: Cambridge University Press, 2013), pp. 73–98, at 73.
17 Benjamin C. Tilghman, 'On the Enigmatic Nature of Things in Anglo-Saxon Art', *Different Visions: A Journal of New Perspectives on Medieval Art*, 4 (2014), 1–43, at 9.
18 s.v. *art* in Jane Roberts et al., *A Thesaurus of Old English*, vol. 1 (New York: Rodopi, 2000).
19 *DOE*, s.v. *cræft*.
20 Ibid. for the examples of 'semantic richness'. The information about the *woruld*, *sundor*, and *wundor* constructions is taken from Roberts et al, *A Thesaurus*.
21 For a thorough treatment of usage of *cræft*, see Helen Price, 'Human and NonHuman in Anglo-Saxon and British Postwar Poetry: Reshaping Literary Ecology' (unpublished doctoral thesis, University of Leeds, September 2013), pp. 54–82.
22 Peter Ramey, 'The Riddle of Beauty: The Aesthetics of *Wrætlic* in Old English Verse', *Modern Philology*, 114 (2017), 457–81.
23 Ibid., p. 467.
24 Irina Dumitrescu, *The Experience of Education in Anglo-Saxon Literature* (Cambridge: Cambridge University Press, 2018), p. 128.
25 Sherry Turkle, 'What Makes an Object Evocative?', in Sherry Turkle (ed.), *Evocative Objects: Things We Think With* (Cambridge: Massachusetts Institute of Technology Press, 2007), pp. 307–26, at 307 (within) and 309 (libido).
26 Mihaly Csikszentmihalyi and Eugene Rochberg-Halton, *The Meaning of Things: Domestic Symbols and the Self* (Cambridge: Cambridge University Press, 1981), p. 27.
27 Ian Hodder, *Entangled: An Archaeology of the Relationships between Humans and Things* (Oxford: Blackwell, 2012), p. 9.
28 Bruno Latour, 'The Berlin Key or How to Do Words with Things', in Paul M. Graves-Brown (ed.), *Matter, Materiality, and Modern Culture* (New York: Routledge, 2000), pp. 10–21, at 20.
29 Bill Brown, 'Thing Theory', in Bill Brown (ed.), *Things* (Chicago: University of Chicago Press, 2004), pp. 1–16, at 12.

30 Lorraine Daston, 'Introduction: Speechless', in Lorraine Daston (ed.), *Things that Talk: Object Lessons from Art and Science* (New York: Zone Books, 2004), pp. 9–24, at 9.
31 I use Wim Tigges's numbers. Wim Tigges, 'Snakes and Ladders: Ambiguity and Coherence in the Exeter Book Riddles and Maxims', in Henk Aersten and Rolf H. Bremmer, Jr (eds), *Companion to Old English Poetry* (Amsterdam: Vrije Universiteit Press, 1994), pp. 95–118, at 109. Craig Williamson calls the first-person category 'projective riddles', as they result from humans giving a description of non-human subjects in human terms (*The Old English Riddles*, p. 25).
32 Carl Knappett, *Thinking Through Material Culture: An Interdisciplinary Perspective* (Philadelphia: University of Pennsylvania Press, 2005), p. 118.
33 Ibid., pp. 138–9.
34 Ibid., p. 150.
35 James Paz, *Nonhuman Voices in Anglo-Saxon Literature and Material Culture* (Manchester: Manchester University Press, 2017), p. 34.
36 Aaron Hostetter, 'Disruptive Things in *Beowulf*', *New Medieval Literatures*, 17 (2017), 34–61, at 37.
37 Ibid., p. 41.
38 Peter Brown, *The Cult of the Saints: Its Rise and Function in Latin Christianity* (Chicago: University of Chicago Press, 1981), p. 78. Brown writes about the late classical/early medieval period, but his assertion applies to later practices, too. See, for instance, Caroline Walker Bynum, who characterises the twelfth and thirteenth centuries in Western Europe as 'a period in which the overcoming of partition and putrefaction – either through reunion of parts into a whole or through assertion of part *as part* to *be* the whole – was the image of paradise' (her italics). 'In Praise of Fragments: History in the Comic Mode', in Caroline Walker Bynum, *Fragmentation and Redemption: Essays on Gender and the Human Body in Medieval Religion* (New York: Zone Books, 1991), p. 13.
39 Patrick Geary, 'Sacred Commodities: The Circulation of Medieval Relics', in Arjun Appadurai (ed.), *The Social Life of Things: Commodities in Cultural Perspective* (Cambridge: Cambridge University Press, 1986), pp. 169–91. When he defines the category on page 169, Geary says that it is 'unusual in Western society', yet, on page 188, he explains that while relics, slaves, icons, regalia, and art qualify as 'objects of commerce', they look more like persons 'under other circumstances'.
40 Brown, *The Cult of the Saints*, n. 17 on p. 163.
41 Ibid., pp. 89 ('precise gesture'), 92 ('discovery…').
42 Gustaf Sobin, *Ladder of Shadows: Reflecting on Medieval Vestige in Provence and Languedoc* (Berkeley: University of California Press, 2009), p. 37.
43 I quote the text from Michael Swanton's edition, *The Dream of the Rood*, new edn (Exeter: University of Exeter Press, 1996).

44 Swanton explains that 'either *me* or *wergas* might be understood as the object of either *heton* or *hebban*. [The first possibility,] representing normal OE word order, accords well with the dramatic sense in *wæfersyn*' (p. 116).

45 It refers to Constantine's mother Helen and Cyriacus, whose efforts at uncovering the True Cross are told in another Old English poem, Cynewulf's *Elene*.

46 Szarmach makes this point well: '[The Rood's] narration becomes in effect its own *titulus*, describing what the dreamer is presumably perceiving as art (as if on the walls) and offering the more or less full *historia* that explains all that is seen.' In a footnote, Szarmach gives evidence, from an article by Elizabeth C. Teviotdale, for *tituli* in Anglo-Saxon art, both Latin and vernacular ('*The Dream of the Rood* as Ekphrasis', p. 286). Importance of captions (*superscriptio, inscriptio*) becomes apparent in the story from *Libri Carolini*, in which two identical pictures receive a diametrically opposed treatment because one of them is labelled Venus, the other Mary. *Libri Carolini*, IV, 16 (PL 98, *c*.1219), quoted and translated in Władysław Tatarkiewicz, *History of Aesthetics*, II, *Medieval Aesthetics*, trans. R. M. Montgomery (Warsaw: Polish Scientific Publishers, 1970), p. 100.

47 Szarmach, '*The Dream of the Rood* as Ekphrasis', p. 287.

48 For a fascinating look at interaction between stone, metal, and text in relation to these two physical artefacts and the lyric, see Seeta Chaganti, 'Vestigial Signs: Inscription, Performance, and The Dream of the Rood', *PMLA*, 125 (2010), 48–72. Chaganti summarises her argument thus: 'Rather than construct a historical narrative linking these verse manifestations ... I shall ultimately read all three as containing vestiges of one another, each existing both inside and outside the time of the others' (p. 51).

49 Mercedes Salvador-Bello, *Isidorean Perceptions of Order: The Exeter Book Riddles and Medieval Latin Enigmata* (Morgantown: West Virginia University Press, 2015), p. 328. The 'polysemic term' that Salvador-Bello mentions is *beam*, 'tree, log, ship, and cross', identified as such by Francis A. Blackburn, in reference to Riddle 30a.

50 Roberta Frank, '*Beowulf* and Sutton Hoo: The Odd Couple', in Calvin B. Kendall and Peter S. Wells (eds), *Voyage to the Other World: The Legacy of Sutton Hoo* (Minneapolis: University of Minnesota Press, 1992), pp. 47–64; Emily V. Thornbury, '*Eald enta geweorc* and the Relics of Empire: Revisiting the Dragon's Lair in *Beowulf*', *Quaestio*, 1 (2000), 82–92.

51 Chaganti, 'Vestigial Signs', p. 60.

52 I borrow here Szarmach's definition ('*The Dream of the Rood* as Ekphrasis', p. 267).

53 Adijata Ibrišimović-Šabić, '*Kameni spavač*' *Maka Dizdara i ruska književna avangarda* [*Mak Dizdar's 'Stone Sleeper' and the Russian Literary Avant-garde*] (Sarajevo: Slavistički komitet, 2010), p. 66. 'Njegova glavna odlika sastoji se u tome da u centru pažnje više nije

Introduction: Powerful fragments 29

toliko sam umjetnički objekt, koliko pjesnikov doživljaj datog predmeta
... *Ekfrazisi* ovog tipa zapravo su modificirani tekst, tekst koji ne imitira, već stvaralački prerađuje ...' The translation is mine.

54 '... zaključak da se jedino riječju, govorom može do kraja razotkriti, dopuniti ili adekvatno prenijeti značenje i smisao nekog djela likovne umjetnosti. Bez posredništva riječi, stećak bi se pretvorio u nijemi i nepotrebni predmet, tuđ i nerazumljiv savremenom čovjeku, prijeteći zaboravom prošlosti' (p. 68).

55 Maria Fabricius Hansen, *The Eloquence of Appropriation: Prolegomena to an Understanding of Spolia in Early Christian Rome* (Rome: 'L'Erma' di Bretschneider, 2003), p. 14.

56 Arnold Esch, 'Spolien', *Archiv für Kulturgeschichte*, 51 (1969), 1–64, at 3.

57 Helen Saradi, 'The Use of Ancient Spolia in Byzantine Monuments: The Archaeological and Literary Evidence', *International Journal of the Classical Tradition*, 3 (1997), 395–423, at 395 (the Acropolis) and 421 (St Photeine). Saradi notes that in present-day Greece and Turkey 'antique *spolia* are still used in some houses, churches, and monasteries, especially in the countryside' (Ibid., 419).

58 Sobin, *Ladder of Shadows*, p. 13.

59 Dale Kinney, 'The Concept of Spolia', in Conrad Rudolph (ed.), *A Companion to Medieval Art* (Oxford: Blackwell, 2006), pp. 233–52, at 233.

60 Beat Brenk, 'Spolia from Constantine to Charlemagne: Aesthetics versus Ideology', *Dumbarton Oak Papers*, 41 (1987), pp. 103–9, at 105.

61 Ibid., p. 109.

62 Martin Irvine, *The Making of Textual Culture: 'Grammatica' and Literary Theory, 350–1100* (Cambridge: Cambridge University Press, 1994), p. 311; Esch, 'Spolien', pp. 50–1.

63 Esch describes the competitive cross-Mediterranean *spolia* shuffle wittily: 'Karl der Große und Aachen, die Spolie als Ausweis seiner Ansprüch gegenüber Byzanz, die Spolie gleichsam ein "in Teilstücken transferiertes" Rom – Rom transferiert nach Aachen, Rom transferiert aber auch in die (geographische wie politische) Gegenrichtung, nach Byzanz, Byzanz wiederum in Teilstücken transferiert nach Venedig, wenn schon nicht (das bekannte, wenngleich apokryphe Projekt von etwa 1220) das ganze Venedig transferiert nach Byzanz' [Charles the Great and Aachen: the *spolia* as a demonstration of his claims against Byzantium, the *spolia*, so to speak, a Rome transferred in pieces – Rome transferred to Aachen, and also Rome transferred in (geographical as well as political) opposition to Byzantium, Byzantium in turn transferred to Venice, if not yet (as in the well-known albeit apocryphal project of around 1220) all Venice transferred to Byzantium] (my translation)] (pp. 50–1).

64 Ilene H. Forsyth, 'Art with History: The Role of Spolia in the Cumulative Work of Art', in Christopher Moss and Katherine Kiefer

(eds), *Byzantine East, Latin West. Art-Historical Studies in Honor of Kurt Weitzmann* (Princeton: Department of Art and Archaeology, Princeton University, 1995), pp. 153–62, at 155 (origin of the fragments), 158 (*culminatio*).
65 Nicholas Howe, 'Rome: Capital of Anglo-Saxon England', *Journal of Medieval and Early Modern Studies*, 34 (2004), 147–72. Later reworked and printed in his *Writing the Map of Anglo-Saxon England* (New Haven: Yale University Press, 2008), pp. 101–24.
66 Tim Eaton, *Plundering the Past: Roman Stonework in Medieval Britain* (Stroud, Gloucestershire: Tempus, 2000). Illustrations number 32 (p. 73) and 64 (p. 119). Hexham Abbey, built in the seventh century, has a twelfth-century addition called Wilfred's Church, but most of the Roman *spolia* was incorporated by the Anglo-Saxons (p. 11).
67 St Peter from Bradwell-on-Sea is featured on the cover of Eaton's book, and in the colour plate (number 3).
68 Richard Morris, *Churches in the Landscape* (London: J. M. Dent and Sons, 1989), p. 72.
69 Eaton, *Plundering the Past*, p. 157.
70 Ibid., pp. 68–9; the translations as given there.
71 Previous scholars' excessive zeal in applying Augustinian exegesis to all Anglo-Saxon texts has recently come under scrutiny. Leslie Lockett warns us not to assume 'that Augustine's opinion on a given topic, or a watered-down version thereof, was the "default" opinion for any early medieval individual'. Leslie Lockett, *Anglo-Saxon Psychologies in the Vernacular and Latin Traditions* (Toronto: Toronto University Press, 2011), p. 214. In these three paragraphs, I am not making such an assumption. I do not privilege Augustine's thinking in this chapter or anywhere else in the book, but rather offer it as one of many possible, suggestive frameworks. We do not have, as Lockett says, 'any reason to think that the typical Anglo-Saxon poet or homilist or hagiographer had access to a patristic library of the calibre of Bede's or Ælfric's' (p. 181), but I do mention Bede and Alfred, who interacted with Augustine's works, later in the chapter. See below for Alfred's introduction to his translation of Augustine's *Soliloquys*.
72 Augustine, *On Christian Teaching*, trans. R. P. H. Green (Oxford: Oxford University Press, 1997), pp. 64–5. The scriptural refrences are added by Green. The Latin reads: 'Sicut enim Aegyptii non tantum idola habebant et onera gravia quae populus Israel detestaretur et fugeret sed etiam vasa atque ornamenta de auro et de argento et vestem, quae ille populus exiens de Aegypto sibi potius tamquam ad usum meliorem clanculo vindicavit, non auctoritate propia sed praecepto dei, ipsis Aegyptiis nescienter commodantibus ea quibus non bene utebantur, – 145. sic doctrinae omnes gentilium non solum simulata et superstitiosa figmenta gravesque sarcinas supervacanei laboris habent, quae unusquisque nostrum duce Christo de societate gentilium exiens debet abominari atque devitare, sed etiam liberales disciplinas usui veritatis aptiores et quedam morum praecepta

utilissima continent, deque ipso uno deo colendo nonnulla vera inveniuntur apud eos.' Augustine, *De doctrina christiana*, ed. R. P. H. Green (Oxford: Oxford University Press, 1996), p. 124.
73 Augustine, *On Christian Teaching*, p. 65; Augustine, *De doctrina*, p. 126.
74 Augustine, *On Christian Teaching*, p. 66; Augustine, *De doctrina*, p. 126.
75 James L. Kugel and Rowan A. Greer, *Early Biblical Interpretation* (Philadelphia: Westminster Press, 1986), pp. 133–4. Typology, 'understood as relating old to new', is often confused with allegory, 'understood as relating earthly to heavenly' (ibid.).
76 *The Oxford Dictionary of the Christian Church*, ed. F. L. Cross, 3rd edn rev., ed. E. A. Livingstone (Oxford: Oxford University Press, 2005), pp. 1660–1.
77 William S. Babcock, 'Harrowing of Hell', in Everett Ferguson (ed.), *Encyclopedia of Early Christianity*, vol. 1 (New York: Garland, 1997), pp. 509–11, at 511 ('widely adopted...') and 510 (the list).
78 Edited by Krapp and Dobbie and called *The Descent into Hell* (in *The Exeter Book*, pp. 219–23).
79 See S. A. J. Bradley's introduction to his translation of *The Descent into Hell* (*Anglo-Saxon Poetry: An Anthology of Old English Poems in Prose Translation* (London: J. M. Dent, 1982), p. 391).
80 K. M. Openshaw, 'The Battle between Christ and Satan in the Tiberius Psalter', *Journal of the Warburg and Courtauld Institutes*, 52 (1989), 14–33, at 19. She gives the illustration as plate 8a.
81 These definitions come from Joseph Bosworth and T. Northcote Toller, *An Anglo-Saxon Dictionary* (London: Oxford Press, 1954).
82 Karl Tamburr, *The Harrowing of Hell in Medieval England* (Woodbridge: Boydell & Brewer, 2007), p. 1.
83 Definitions and etymology from George Sherman Lane, 'Words for Clothing in the Principal Indo-European Languages', *Language*, 7 (1931), 3–44, at 10.
84 Most recently in Phyllis Portnoy, '*Laf*-Craft in Five Old English Riddles (K-D 5, 20, 56, 71, 91)', *Neophilologus*, 97 (2013), 555–79.
85 Ibid., p. 556.
86 Included among them is Virgil, who pillaged Homer, Ennius, and others. Irvine, *The Making of Textual Culture*, p. 147 (from whence the quote); also see Hansen, *The Eloquence of Appropriation*, pp. 168–9.
87 Irvine, *The Making of Textual Culture*, p. 242
88 Ibid., pp. 277, 515 (n. 24).
89 The text and translation come from ibid., p. 436. Alfred elaborates on, and brings into the vernacular, the convention of *sylva* (*hyle* in Greek), the forest of classical authors from which one gathers materials for his text, known to such luminaries as Isidore of Seville, Aldhelm, and Boniface (p. 437).
90 Tilghman, 'On the Enigmatic Nature of Things', p. 22.

91 Seamus Heaney and Robert Hass, 'Sounding Lines: The Art of Translating Poetry/ Seamus Heaney and Robert Hass in Conversation', February 1999, http://repositories.cdlib.org/cgi/viewcontent.cgi?articl e=1019&context=townsend, accessed 15 March 2017, pp. 1–2.
92 R. M. Liuzza (trans.), *Beowulf* (Petersborough, ON: Broadview, 2000), p. 31.
93 Haruko Momma, 'Old English Poetic Form: Genre, Style, Prosody', in Clare A. Lees (ed.), *The Cambridge History of Early Medieval English Literature* (Cambridge: Cambridge University Press, 2013), pp. 278–308, at 279.
94 This inspiration, in the case of Momma, was noted by Tiffany Beechy in her review of Lees's volume https://scholarworks.iu.edu/journals/ index.php/tmr/article/view/18571/24684, accessed 15 March 2017. Tolkien's allegory comes from his famous essay '*Beowulf*: The Monsters and the Critics' (1936), partially reprinted in Daniel Donoghue (ed.), *Beowulf: A Verse Translation*, trans. Seamus Heaney, (New York: Norton, 2002), pp. 103–29, at 105–6.
95 Amy Papalexandrou, 'Memory Tattered and Torn: *Spolia* in the Heartland of Byzantine Hellenism', in Ruth M. Van Dyke and Susan E. Alcock (eds), *Archaeologies of Memory* (Oxford: Blackwell, 2003), pp. 56–80, at 61.
96 Michael Roberts, *The Jeweled Style: Poetry and Poetics in Late Antiquity* (Ithaca: Cornell University Press, 1989), pp. 145–6.
97 Hansen, *The Eloquence of Appropriation*, p. 119 (mixing of styles); 178 (coherence, pauses).
98 Ibid., p. 178.
99 Roberts, *The Jeweled Style*, p. 146.
100 For a call to uncover a 'contra-modern aesthetic' that encompasses both medieval and post-colonial works, and an example of such an endeavour, see Ananya Jahanara Kabir, 'Towards a Contra-Modern Aesthetics: Reading the Old English *Andreas* Against an Image of the Virgin of Guadalupe', in Nils Holger Petersen et al. (eds), *Signs of Change: Transformations of Christian Traditions and Their Representation in the Arts, 1000–2000* (New York: Rodopi, 2004), pp. 31–50. For brilliant explorations of the links between Mediterranean medieval and post-colonial American hemispheric literatures and music, see María Rosa Menocal, *Shards of Love: Exile and the Origins of the Lyric* (Durham: Duke University Press, 1994).
101 Irvine, *The Making of Textual Culture*, p. 426.
102 In medieval material culture, relics might appear in reliquaries and crosses made with *spolia* 'in the form of ancient gems, cameos, or seals' (Hansen, *The Eloquence of Appropriation*, p. 153).
103 Sobin, *Ladder of Shadows*, pp. 1–2 (his italics). Though the writer here speaks of 'the thousand years that [his] study touches upon' (from the third to the thirteenth centuries), it is clear from the foreword by Michael Ignatieff that much of this desire for transfiguration also characterises Sobin himself (see, for instance, p. xx).

1
Encyclopedic miniatures: Combinatory powers of loot in the Exeter Riddles

Introduction: Part-to-the-whole, part-to-part, part-to-itself

The Exeter Riddles stand apart from much of the surviving poetic corpus in Old English because of their range of tones and the sheer variety of their subjects. They appear in three clusters in the Exeter Book, a late tenth-century miscellany of verse that includes, to mention only the best-known texts today, *The Ruin, The Wanderer, The Seafarer, The Wife's Lament,* and *The Husband's Message.* Many of the artefacts and concepts presented in the vernacular enigmas have not been witnessed elsewhere. The riddles are encyclopedic in their method and subject matter.[1] 'The extreme heterogeneity of the compilation'[2] is evident from proposed and largely accepted solutions that involve natural phenomena, weapons of war, all matter of everyday tools, nautical equipment, food, alcoholic beverages, sexual references, birds and other animals, musical instruments, scriptorium paraphernalia, even the problematic biblical patriarch Lot and a one-eyed seller of garlic. The Exeter Riddles commonly focus on appetites hidden in texts like *Beowulf* that avoid references to the twinned temptations of food and sex,[3] and they may hold hints to stylistic registers of Old English vocabulary other than the predominant high poetic idiom.[4] Whereas other Old English texts, verse as well as prose, avoid giving detailed descriptions of artefacts, the riddles describe material culture enigmatically but accurately enough for many of the clues to add up to a convincing solution. They present a markedly different side of war, domestication, and production, as they give voice to the downtrodden, enslaved, and unrooted, featuring exploited plants and animals, women and Welsh slaves, even if only in a few lines that could give way to a 'safe' solution in the end.[5] Critics have repeatedly turned to the riddles in order to illuminate lived realities of Anglo-Saxon England,[6] especially those of the monastic orders and ordinary people. Without these texts, we might even have concluded that the early English had no sense of humour other than the stoic, dying-in-battle type or dark understatement.

The Exeter Riddles expose and problematise many cherished binaries in Anglo-Saxon scholarship. We desire to find glimpses of Anglo-Saxon everyday life so stubbornly denied us in other literature from the period, but we may find artistic transformation of that life rather than conventions of realist fiction or photographic reportage (mediated representations, as well). We grapple with orality and literacy, with vernacularity and Latinity, in an attempt to calibrate these important factors in relation to the enigmas. We see reverberations of an aristocratic way of life in riddles describing the feasts and battles, warriors like those in heroic verse carving out a space within the monastic culture. Or we imagine monks reshaping their early Germanic vernacular literary culture to uphold the lifestyle of intellectual investigation and religious devotion in a transition from 'tribal' to 'scribal'.[7] Scholarly fashions change, as we invoke transhistorical folk or early medieval Latin enigmatic traditions to help us situate and interpret the Exeter Riddles.[8] I would go beyond saying that these varied, miniature texts engage with both larger traditions in Anglo-Saxon England while being recognisably a separate body of work: I would say that they variously encourage and challenge attempts to place them in both frameworks, whether they translate Latin *enigmata* or, more commonly, reshape the material from them. The riddles display awareness akin to the self-consciousness of other vernacular early medieval English work that exhibits features possible only in the mother tongue,[9] but they go even further since they mark their difference from other Old English verse.

The relationship of a part to the whole – a fragment to the framework – is implicated in such discussions on more than one level, as scholars struggle with textual boundaries between individual enigmas or connections between them and other poems in the Exeter Book, such as *The Husband's Message* that comes immediately after Riddle 60 ('Reed') in the manuscript.[10] I will mention below passages where I suspect the riddles hint at themes from poems from different codices, such as *Beowulf* and *Exodus*; though direct links cannot be established, because of the shared poetic vocabulary and our lack of knowledge of exact literary-historical connections, alluding playfully to epic verse would not seem too alien to the enigmas.

Beside part-to-the-whole, the dynamics of part-to-part and part-to-itself consistently emerge attended by doubling and

Encyclopedic miniatures

accumulation. Within the compilation the riddles form particular clusters, by physical proximity and/or thematic resemblance, so that we can speak of implement, ornithological, scriptoria, sexual, and other sets of riddles.[11] Some of them appear coupled, such as the oyster and crab (77 and 78, as solved by Salvador-Bello); some delight in double entendre. Some of them would require a pair of solutions, such as Riddles 29 ('Moon and Sun'), 42 ('Cock and Hen'), or 43 ('Soul and Body'). Others have two related but distinct concepts expressed by the same word in Old English, such as *ac* for 'oak' and 'ship' (Riddle 74).[12] Some of them have actual doubles or triples, with apparently identical solutions, such as Riddles 12 and 72 ('Ox'); 14 and 80 ('Horn'); 25 and 65 ('Onion'); 40, 66, and 94 ('Creation'); and 26, 92, and 95 ('Book/Bible'). While clusters and pairings may aid decoding of individual texts, a grand organising structure behind the compilation would go counter to the genre as 'the topics of consecutive riddles must not be too closely related or else the game is spoiled!'[13] The collection needs to create the dual effect by suggesting an entire world, orderly and meaningful, and yet refusing to give us an illusion of having a complete control over its resplendent poetic mystery.

It is apt that the enigmas constantly frustrate our attempts to contain them in distinct categories, for this type of resistance inheres in their very nature. James Paz writes, 'these riddles are designed ... to force the reader or listener to question the conceptual categories they take for granted, to force us to ask what we mean when we say something is dead, especially when that thing is nonhuman'.[14] In invoking and complicating such binaries as past/present, present/future, oral/literate, Germanic/Latinate, heroic/monastic, local/global, micro/macro, textual/visual, animate/inanimate, and overt/covert, the Exeter Riddles parallel important effects that I argue *spolia* have. *Spolia*, too, prompt the readers or observers to interrogate the ready-made categories. Moreover, a number of Old English enigmas prominently feature examples of plunder, revealing their participation in a similar poetics. Self-consciously recycled artefacts become coherent when fixed in a larger, new context, but at the same time gesture towards something outside of it, temporally, spatially, and existentially. They enable startling changes of scale. *Spolia* interconnect while remaining distinct. They bespeak the dangers of survival and accumulation. A sense of loss and a feeling of excess inhere in them side by side.

In the remainder of the chapter, I will first focus on Riddles 14 ('Horn'), 20 ('Sword'), and 29 ('Moon and Sun') to uncover a new thematic cluster within the collection that suggests, taken together and through its individual components, multiple and shifting dimensions of plunder. Then I will move on to three enigmas that display the impulse to accumulate quite ambiguously. On one hand, Riddles 49 ('Bookcase/Oven') and 40 ('Creation') feature the speakers who, despite the uplifting solutions, underline bound, debased, down-to-earth realities of hoarding. On the other hand, Riddles 60 ('Creation') and 95 ('Book') suggest ways of escaping, the former by keeping only the broadest contours of its subject and the latter by teasingly foregrounding the fleeting nature of text. Riddle 40 is a close rendition of Aldhelm's 'De Creatura', and Riddle 60 is a version of Riddle 40, a transcreation of a translation. Interactions within the Old English literary tradition and between it and its Latin counterpart provide another type of spoliation. In all these cases, the riddles betray intense consciousness of craft and creativity, showing that the act of creation links makers and artefacts, humans and non-humans alike, through its exhilarating, dangerous energy.

A sketch of the plunder cluster: Riddles 14 ('Horn'), 20 ('Sword'), and 29 ('Moon and Sun')

Riddle 14 speaks of a thing that changes its appearance and function, being ornamented and deprived of its contents, sometimes kissed, other times calling men to battle or feast, travelling over sea and land, and hanging on the wall. Scholars agree that the solution is horn in its different incarnations as a body part of an animal, a drinking vessel, and an instrument.[15] The text describes an object that starts off as plunder and can easily become plunder again. After it grows on a bovine's head, someone takes it from its owner, the animal. What is strange in the riddle is that the thing is caught in cycle of war from the very beginning. The cow or bull wields it as 'a weapon' to protect itself or to attack, a 'warrior' by nature. The cycles are indicated by the repeated *hwilum* [at times], ten times in the poem of nineteen lines, giving a rhythm to narration.[16] Sometimes it appears in quick succession, once each in four adjacent lines (3–6). About a mid-point through the riddle, in line nine, the horn explains what happens to it in its incarnation as a drinking vessel. After someone, presumably another warrior, at a feast like those in Anglo-Saxon heroic verse, drinks its contents in one go, the horn says, 'ic bordum sceal, / heard, heafodleas, behlyþed[17] licgan' [I must lie on the table, hard, headless, robbed (i.e., of drink)]. This image paints drinking in warlike colours.[18] A bovine's life and a drinking party are not a respite from battle, precious moments to provide contrast from fighting; they are themselves a kind of battle. The speaker's headlessness might bring to mind decapitations in other Old English poems such as *Beowulf* and *Judith*, where heads of adversaries function as trophies. The horn's status as a piece of plunder is central to its existence as well as to the riddle, near the centre of which the word *behlyþan* occurs (line 10 out of 19; 'to deprive, despoil' [*DOE*]). Its position in the text is key in another way because it comes after the sixth instance of *hwilum* and the brilliant, equivocal clue 'hard and headless'.[19] The horn becomes plunder continuously, at every turn: not just when it is taken from the animal on which it grew, and not just in battle in the usual way warriors seize booty, but also when men swallow alcoholic draughts from it. Riddle 14 resembles many other Exeter Riddles that recast ordinary situations in a menacing, dangerous light. The object suffers when it is emptied and placed down on a table (since it does not have a stand). Its displacement sounds painful. Once removed from its immediate organic context, the head of an animal, it undergoes constant transformation and seeks a stable environment. At the end of the riddle, the instrument originating in plunder and repeatedly experiencing becoming plunder aptly protects plunder. The last clue to the identity of the speaker is that 'hwilum wraþum[20] sceal / stefne minre forstolen hreddan, / flyman feondsceaþan' [I sometimes have to protect with my voice that which was stolen from angry men, to make the hostile enemy flee] (17–19). Cycles of robbery, in which the speaker participates as an object and an instigator, constitute the subject of the riddle in both senses of the word, the topic and the thing itself.

The poem intertwines these moments of spoliation, of stripping, of loss, with instances of the horn's ornamentation, dressing, accumulated value. In the presentation of two opposite scenes, both of which are true at the same time, Riddle 14 brings to mind the cross sometimes covered with jewels, sometimes with blood, the speaker of the enigmatic *The Dream of the Rood*. Neither the horn nor any other thing can match the transcendent power of the rood,[21] but its portrayal does offer a parallel. Just as the cross remains essentially the same in its various embodiments, whether the relic of the True Cross, a cruciform pendant on a necklace, or an internalised sign, the horn preserves its shape whatever happens to it, whether the warriors kiss it, drink from it, put it down, carry it on a horse or a ship, or blow it to call to a feast or battle. Once it is removed from the animal which had carried it, it seems to be in ceaseless motion, portable and attachable. Stripped or enrobed in precious metals, the speaker of Riddle 14 does not lose its subjectivity. One of the rare adjectives that refers to the horn in the poem, *heard* [hard] is central for our understanding of the object's immutability. '[H]eard, heafodleas' [hard, headless] is a telling pair: even separated from its source, the horn does not totally give in. It has a consistent role to play, whatever the context. Its shape communicates its usage; though it yields to plundering, to baring, and ornamentation, it never loses its function as a container. Its emptiness fills, with liquor that 'meaðða sum ... beaghroden' [some maiden ... ring-adorned] pours in its bosom ('minne gefylleð ... bosm') (8–9), or with breath, figured as treasure, that it takes 'of sumes bosme' [from somebody's bosom] (15). Not coincidentally, Riddle 14 hints at the flows of nature in those two images of the full becoming empty and the person expending air to blow forcefully into the instrument. The usage of the same word *bosm* [bosom] for the interior part of the horn and the blower connects the two, rendering them into containers, for drink or breath. Bosoms, whether of people or ships, often carry material wealth, as famously in *Beowulf* when the Danes push Scyld's corpse off to sea: 'aledon þa leofne þeoden, / ... on bearm scipes ... him on bearme læg / maðma maenigo' [then they laid down the beloved lord in the bosom of a ship ... many treasures lay on his breast] (34–5, 40–1).[22] Our speaker the horn contains treasure without and within. Humans take from it, and it takes from them. Both people and objects are caught in the rhythms of life, ornamentation and deprivation, plenitude and void. They rise and fall like a body breathing or a boat on the waves, wear armour to perform their function and lose it when they are stripped after a defeat. These rhythms correspond to the cyclicality communicated by the repeated temporal adverb, *hwilum* [at times].

The give-and-take nature of the horn tells a story of the human community served by the object. A degree of tenderness comes through when the speaker refers to people whom it serves, carrying even a tinge of sexual charge, not unexpected in the Exeter Riddles. The horn reports that a 'geong hagostealdmon' [young warrior] beautifies it; that men kiss it; that it calls *folcwigan* [folk-fighters] to war; that a young woman wearing splendid jewellery fills it with libations; and that it takes someone's treasured breath away.[23] All the expressions bespeak admiration, demonstrating the horn's enjoyment of the aristocratic warrior world that it helps to maintain. It may even love the people. In its acknowledgement of pain and embrace of overlordship, Riddle 14 could readily fit the dynamic that Jennifer Neville reveals in the 'implement riddles', at once upholding the master-servant relationship and laying bare its costs.[24] The horn moves, but only when attached to its owners or to their other possessions, that is to say, its expanding meanings are always read back into human interaction. And yet, in its many manifestations, the horn easily survives its various masters. Warriors die in battle; however noble and young they may be, their enemies are harmful (-*sceaþan* in *feondsceaþan*). The horn's material persistence enables it to praise those who had ennobled it and to lament their passing implicitly as the riddle moves between the speaker decrying its own condition and that of its companions in the world of men. The celebrations and bloody conflicts of the aristocratic class, their travels over land and sea, their artistic endeavours all concentrate on the humble speaker, flexible to a large degree but resistant at its organic core.

Likewise, *spolia* function in cycles, are taken from one context and integrated into another, but their attraction comes from their ultimate stubborn hardness and unwillingness to remain within the temporal frames of their mortal users. Robert DiNapoli argues that the horn 'insinuates itself into the very heart of the culture that has produced it and re-aligns all the ceremony and dignity of that culture around itself', thus serving as a subtle mask for the poet who similarly shapes and maintains the culture from which he comes.[25] A poem depends for its meaning on the culture that helps produce it, especially its audience, those who will respond to it, but it also carries potential to transcend the original framework, to gesture towards future uses. The preponderance of references to plundering in the enigma indicates a heightened awareness of the practice, its occurrence in cycles and human intertwining with their loot. Riddle 14 expresses both appreciation and ambivalence of the aristocratic activities that depend on, transform, and help circulate appropriated material culture.

Riddle 20 consists of two parts: the first containing assertions of material value of the object within the heroic setting of wars and celebrations and its deadly work in killing warriors, and the second featuring laments about its inability to beget children. It presents us with a speaker who describes its predicament, at least in the beginning, much in the same way as does the horn of Riddle 14. The most common solution is 'sword'.[26] The narrator opens the text by saying that it is 'on gewin sceapen' [shaped for/in struggle],[27] before revealing its relationship to its wielder, its beloved lord ('frean minum leof', 2). Again, we see a certain intimacy between objects and their owners. People need things to carry out their lifestyles, but things also need people to live on in the world. Like the horn, the sword delights in its outer appearance. It closely describes its ornamentation: it is 'fægre gegyrwed' [beautifully ornamented], its garments are variegated and it carries a jewel kept in place by metallic filaments (2–4). That jewel, through its name, *wælgim* [slaughter-gem] (4), demonstrates how intertwined the deadliness is with martial beauty. Moreover, the sword acts as a miniature of the hoard, displaying the power of its lord through the additive, ostentatious, precious materiality of its decoration.

It is not surprising that the weapon invokes 'hondweorc smiþa, / gold ofer geardas' [the handiwork of smiths, gold over lands/ dwelling-places] (7–8), which metonymically stand for two poles of civilisation, craftspeople and aristocrats. *Geard* suggests a cultivated place, where art takes over nature,[28] appropriately enough since a metalworker in forging a sword bends ore to his will. The back and forth between the battlefield and feast-hall is not the only dynamic in Riddle 20, as another area of constant, cyclical exchange comes through, that between the workshop and the court, the producers and the consumers. The sword helps the warrior acquire plunder, much like a warrior aids his lord. By the same token, the lord endows the sword with treasure as he would reward a thane for his service. 'Cyning mec gyrweð / since ond seolfre ond mec on sele weorþað' [A king adorns me with silver and treasures and honours me in the hall] (9–10). Cyclicality, however, does not always guarantee a happy outcome. 'At times' (*hwilum*, the key adverb in Riddle 14) appears immediately after the sword's meditation concerning its labour and reward to signal instability. The weapon's owner controls it, keeps it, or deploys it, depending on his desire. The sword's anxiety is most striking at this point, when it takes on the guilt of murderous humans. While the horn brings together 'folcwigan' [folk-fighters] albeit to war, the sword tears them apart: 'Oft ic oþrum scod / frecne æt his freonde' [I often cause one friend to hurt the other fiercely] (15–16). The speaker of Riddle 20 seems to depend on its lord for as long as it is not 'freed in battle'; after being liberated, it acquires agency and creates havoc.[29]

Another, more surprising, point of distinction between the object and the human user occurs after the middle of this longish enigma. Unlike warriors whose deaths can be avenged by their sons, the weapon cannot have children. More precisely, according to the speaker, if it engages in war, it will stay without an heir. Swords can have 'heirs' when they are broken down, their metals melted and reshaped, their ornamentation recycled. Spoliation here has parallels with sexual reproduction. A child lives on taken from its parents' immediate surroundings, but it is always linked with them, in appearance, temperament, or some other way. A certain resemblance remains. The sword of Riddle 20 points out that it cannot serve two masters, aristocratic warfare and heterosexual intercourse. In the lines in which the weapon laments its fate, its similarity to as well as difference from the phallus emerges. The Exeter Riddles famously offer several 'dirty' enigmas with innocent enough solutions (for example, Riddle 25 'Onion' or Riddle 44 'Key,' with the penis clearly suggested). Here, however, the sword is a brutal caricature, a travesty of the sexual organ that helps create life whilst giving pleasure. It not only kills men who would otherwise be able to have sex with their (female) lovers, but also takes men away from women, to war or even to other men.[30] Patrick J. Murphy expands the possibilities for the woman's anger further, as he says that it 'could be explained by any number of unfortunate incidents: swords can slaughter enemies and friends, husbands and wives, children as well as kings'.[31] The sword's master's fulfilment in war takes place of his satisfaction at home.[32]

Another, complementary reason for the woman's rage would combine the two meanings of *wæpon*. Phyllis Portnoy argues that the line 'ic ... / wonie hyre willan; heo me wom spreceð', usually translated 'I ... decrease her desire; she speaks insults to me' (32–3), could be additionally construed as 'I ... curtail her will; she speaks insults to me', to suggest the female character's resistence to wartime rape by the speaker-as-a-phallus and her subsequent murder by the speaker-as-a-sword.[33] Portnoy further points out that the sword and the woman echo each other, since the polysemic Old English word *laf* ('remnant' meaning widows and heirlooms) can refer to them both, concluding that 'linguistically as well as notionally, the poem's supposed female abuse of the male subject can also be seen as the reverse'.[34] *Laf*, as I discuss in the Introduction, has close connections with *spolia*. Things and people, especially women, can constitute plunder. Portnoy meditates on whether the Anglo-Saxon audience of Riddle 20 would read compassionately the woman's complaint at the end of the text (as it now survives) or view it in amusement. Much, of course, depends on whom we imagine and privilege as the audience of these enigmas and how varied we allow it to be. Portnoy's conclusion, drawing on other scholarly writing about 'dirty' riddles, states that the 'clean' solution of the sword does not allow for any criticism of sexual violence. This critic's and others' assumption that the 'clean' solution can safely dislodge any 'dirty' suggestions would work against the complexity and artfulness of the Exeter Riddles.

An expression of ambivalence may be at play here. Brian McFadden appeals to the late tenth-century context of the Viking attacks to read obscene riddles not as offering final containment, but expressing the period-specific uncertainty: '... the inability to contain certain riddles in single solutions acknowledges the possibility that a verbal solution to the text, like a political, military, or ecclesiastical solution to the affairs of the day, might not have been possible'.[35] If we remember that the raiders are usually also rapists, whatever the specific historical moment, the mirroring of the sword and the woman in Riddle 20 would prompt the question of whose sword and whose wife. The riddle contains no possessives, so either character could belong to any side or, indeed, could move – be forcibly taken – from one side to another. Like a *spolium* harnessed to uphold a new structure because of its difference, or a piece of plunder that signifies its new wearer's triumph and its own Otherness, a double entendre needs to preserve its tinge of danger in order to remain in use. If it is being deployed, it can always turn against its deployer. Both the sword and the wife do not hold back, at least verbally.

Whereas in Riddles 14 and 20 the speakers focus on real-life situations that produce plunder, the word 'plunder' works in a different way in Riddle 29. There, the narrator speaks of two creatures, one building a home from spoils and the other ousting it and seizing those goods. 'Moon and Sun' is almost universally accepted as the solution.[36] Another important distinction between the enigmas discussed above and Riddle 29 is that in the latter the speaker is not the solution, but rather someone who observes the two heavenly bodies. The scene of aristocratic battle with which the text opens works as a riddlic distraction. The moon is called 'lyftfæt leohtlic, listum gegierwed' [a shining air-vessel masterfully ornamented] that carries 'hornum bitweonum ... huþe to þam ham of þam heresiþe' [between its horns ... plunder home from the war journey] (3, 2, 4). A ship filled with booty and presumably adorned with previous instances of spoils so that it shines, the earth's satellite steals light in a type of battle to display it. The horns could signify the points of the crescent alongside pointed structures on elaborate wooden boats. The *Dictionary of Old English* registers both the astronomic ('each of the pointed extremities of the moon') and more general meanings ('projecting object resembling a horn, a horn-shaped or horn-like projection'). They would connect to the horn in Riddle 12 that, as we have seen, at once constitutes a despoiled object, invites soldiers to despoil, and protects the spoils of its owners. The repetition of the same word *huþe* (2, 4, 9) underlines the importance of the concept for Riddle 29. The cyclicality of war – the production of *spolia*, its display, and loss – metaphorically describes everyday cycles of nature, the moon's ascent at dusk and descent at dawn. As in Riddle 14, the speaker uncomfortably intertwines peacetime and wartime, and, because of the masculine gender of moon in Old English,[37] the opening image could have a threatening charge. Yet 'air' (*lyft-*) makes it obvious that these are not earthly terms. (Deadly aerial warfare has not yet been invented.) The celestial body's motion bespeaks elegance and lightness, evident, for instance, in the alliteration on 'l' in line three. As Roberta Frank writes, Old English poetry delights in images of lightness, including in Riddle 7 ('Swan') where the subject is silent while heavy and earthbound but sings when aloft.[38] Riddle 29 points out through lexis and phonology that the moon's plunder is not heavy and material but the lightest and most immaterial of phenomena: the light itself.[39]

Despite its grammatical gender, the moon resembles a nesting bird, or the burrowing animal of Riddle 15 who fights to protect her young ('Vixen' or 'Badger'), because it intends to construct a bedroom inside the fortified city. This warrior is not conventionally masculine. Bedrooms are feminine, not typically heroic places, like the 'bride-bower' (*brydbur*) in which Hrothgar sleeps with his queen while Beowulf guards Heorot from the inside (920–4). We grasp the creature's creative impulse in these lines. In addition to despoiling, the moon builds: it 'walde hyre ... atimbran' [wished to construct for itself ...] (5). It is an artist, as indicated by the adverbial phrase 'searwum asettan' [to set down with skill] (6). It is an active creator, unlike the speakers of Riddles 14 and 20, who depend on others for their adornment. The moon as an unconventional warrior artist attempts to create an abode from its booty, as underlined by the riddle's use of distinctly architectural terms like *atimbran* [to construct] and *byrig* [enclosure]. In only a few lines, the literal spoils of war and art-historical *spolia* come together, in the familiar, paradoxical pattern of material impact and elusiveness.

While the speaker of Riddle 29 describes the moon as *wiht* [creature], who carries its plunder *wundorlice* [wonderfully], he calls the sun 'wundorlicu wiht / ... seo ...' [a wonderful creature / ... that one (fem.) ...] (7–8). He thus makes a distinction as well as hints to the audience that the sun, gendered feminine in Old English, is stronger, shines brighter, than the moon. 'Gif hit swa meahte' [if it could be so] (6) indicates uncertainty about the moon's powers. The sun behaves like a powerful warrior, takes away the moon's plunder, and sends it away. This last detail sounds like a reference to exile because the satellite is called *wrecca* [a stranger, an exile] (10), except, in an unexpected twist, the moon goes home. Religious readings of the riddle that claim it also depicts God and Lucifer – with Lucifer being exiled from his old home in heaven to his new home in hell – could explain this conundrum. The suggestion of Harrowing of Hell nicely complements my *spolia*-centred reading.[40] One may also remember the scene from the embedded narrative of Hildeburh in *Beowulf*, where the Danes take the brother-less, husband-less, son-less, and doubly home-less Hildeburh 'home' from Frisia (after she attempts to create an image of bonding between two sides of her family at the funeral pyre).[41] The masculine moon once again would take on what looks like a feminine role in a heroic epic. But, interestingly, as the moon escapes, it does not do so in complete submission, but with strife (*fæhþum*) (11). A warlike escape seems like a concept in place only in the Old English *Exodus*, a poem abounding with such paradoxes about which I have more to say in Chapter 2.

As we have seen above, Riddle 20 ends with a more conventional gendered drama, perhaps a tragicomedy, of a scolding woman attacking a lamenting, impotent, though still trenchant sword. Riddle 29, on the contrary, concludes with the triumph of the sun and the resignation, restored dignity, and resilience of the moon. The repeated adverb *forð* in lines 11 and 13 communicates the urgency and elusiveness of the lesser celestial body. A moving lyricism pervades the last three lines of the Riddle 29. Line 12 in particular communicates the delicate balance between the moon and the sun, the night and the day, the up and the down: 'Dust stonc to heofonum, deaw feol on eorþan' [Dust rose to heavens, dew fell on the earth]. Scholars find this verse confusing because of the simultaneity of action and the baffling mention of the dust. One could venture an explanation by observing that Riddle 29 does not always describe the events in a linear fashion, but occasionally attempts to capture the duality of night and day. Beneath the calmness of these lines, we may still imagine a battle scene, with dust that the feet of warriors have stirred rising and their 'dew', that is blood, dropping on the ground.[42]

While the triumph of the day, of the sun, signifies a triumph over obscurity, it lasts for a limited time only. What everyone knows, what everyone experiences (the sun that is known to all the earth-dwellers), has a mysterious side, too. The statement 'Nænig siþþan / wera gewiste þære wihte sið' [afterwards, no one among men knew the creature's journey (i.e., where it went)] (13–14) sounds like the passage in *Beowulf*, where no one knows who takes the load of Scyld Scefing, the treasure-laden vessel on which his corpse lies. If that intertextual reference is indeed operative, then, in the spirit of cyclicality that characterises the plunder cluster, the riddle ends where it begins, with an invocation of a splendid ship full of spoils at the moment after the sun has taken the plunder back from the moon. An instance of the famed Anglo-Saxon envelope pattern, the opening and closing with an image of plunder would provide metatextual moments par excellence. The imprinting of that motif on nature, on creation itself, breaks down the binaries repeatedly undone by the Exeter Riddles and by instances of *spolia* in other Old English poems: of divine and human creation, female and male, peace and war, alive and dead, known and unknown.

Lowly accumulation: Riddles 49 ('Bookcase/Oven') and 40 ('Creation')

The speaker of Riddle 49 introduces a creature that, although deaf and speechless, consumes something more valuable than gold. The solution could be either an oven that bakes bread or a bookcase that contains more spiritual nourishment, or both.[43] In this section, I will entertain both possible responses at once, keeping in mind Winfried Rudolf's plea for 'a meaningful dialogue' between 'co-existing solutions accumulated in [the] poem'.[44] Although quite in keeping with a number of riddles within the collection, the harsh, condemnatory tone of this text appears perplexing, transcending the mere need to disorient the reader seeking to solve the enigma. The narrator describes the object as deaf and mute from the beginning, and calls its activity, whether baking or storing, swallowing: 'se oft dæges swilgeð / þurh gopes hond gifrum lacan' [that often swallows daily useful gifts by means of a servant's hand] (2–3). A parallel might emerge with one of the now most canonical riddles, Riddle 47, of the bookworm who likewise swallows without growing any wiser. Riddle 49 could form a cluster with others dealing with the scriptorium, its processes, tools, and uses or misuses. Mercedes Salvador-Bello explains that 'Exeter section 5A', in which she places both 47 and 49, deals with the production, preservation, keeping, and destruction of 'written culture'.[45] I would like to add to her assessment that this culture is insistently portrayed in material terms, as a life-cycle of books. Far from unequivocally praising wisdom to be gained from manuscripts, the cluster draws attention to darker undercurrents behind creation and circulation of knowledge.[46]

The question of problematic tone remains. While we may accept the arguments of scholars like Salvador-Bello who see a parody of an unaccomplished reader in Riddle 47,[47] it is harder to argue that a bookcase should gain something from the venerable tomes it houses. It swallows, but does not digest; more than that, it protects rather than breaks apart. The quality underlying the object's usefulness becomes a basis of its apparent criticism. On the other hand, if the other solution is also operative, swallowing represents an ironic means of deflection: the oven swallows first in order that we may swallow later; it does not grow or develop from the act so that we may do exactly that afterwards. Individually, it takes in a multitude of loaves to serve a multitude of people with no benefit to itself. Two possible solutions intersect in the problem of appetite, the potential danger of accumulation of materials or matter widely accepted as positive, indeed essential to human development.

Increased temporal awareness in Riddle 49 connects it to the plunder cluster I discuss above. Like those enigmas, the poem is interested in transformation. Once again, the speaker underlines the repeated action with such adverbs as *oft* and *hwilum* [at times]. Production of food or circulation of books would then occur regularly. The process continues as the speaker describes the solution of the riddle. Textual distribution and resulting 'feeding' on texts presumably happen through the creation and circulation of the enigmas themselves. Riddle 49 recognises the labour behind knowledge or nourishment, without which either would not be possible, even though it is the creators (kneaders, authors) and consumers (eaters, readers) who usually receive attention, not those delivering volumes or operating kitchen equipment. At the same time, this recognition seems tortured. The text constantly presents the servant as a creature of darkness – 'se wonna þegn, / sweart ond saloneb' [the dark servant, swarthy and dark-faced/nosed] (4–5) – to indicate his racialised (Welsh?) appearance and his usually obscured position, but also to add moral condemnation to him, and not only to the bookcase or oven, both contraptions with dark interiors. The man servicing the object becomes tainted by contact, by association. Obscurity is a common motif in the collection of poems that necessarily play with hiding and disclosure because of their genre. Seven riddles later, in Riddle 57, the subjects, likely swallows, are similarly thrice darkened, though they create an uproar rather than stay silent: '[þ]a sind blace swiþe, / swearte salopade' [they are very dark, swarthy, dusky-coated] (2–3) and 'hlude cirmað' [they chirp loudly] (4). The riddles describe concepts that in their darkness both stand out and stay hidden, that can speak in perplexing ways or be unable, even refuse, to speak, all qualities that *spolia* also share.

Yet Riddle 49 shows that the two characters complement one another, a phenomenon which hints at yet another thematic cluster, the riddles that pair servants with their implements (like Riddle 52 with a Welsh captive woman and a yoke of oxen or tools). They can each function thanks to the other. The servant moves within his designated space of a kitchen or library while the object stands fixed to the ground (*eardfæstne*) (1). Movement designates a certain level of liberty, yet we should not forget that it is still relative: he is compelled to move to deliver the goods to his superiors. Being a thane, by definition, the man has a lord, whereas the oven or bookcase stands alone (*anne*) (1), possibly to indicate its central yet isolated position. While the object is singular, so is the servant, but the beneficiaries of their labour are plural. What goes in and out of the thing – items providing physical, intellectual, or spiritual nourishment – are 'golde dyrran / þa æþelingas oft wilniað, / cyningas ond cwene' [dearer than gold, which princes, kings, and queens often desire] (6–8). The economic basis of a society as imagined in Old English texts such as *Beowulf*, the precious metal of gold emerges in several riddles, including Riddle 14, as a shorthand for material and aesthetic worth. Yet it pales in comparison to the necessity of bread or the value contained in manuscripts, though the latter may be gilded, as we learn from another riddle (Riddle 26, 'Book'). From the work of one labourer – or several undifferentiated labourers – and the containment of one contraption, many members of royalty get to read or eat. In only eleven lines, the poem thus sketches a sophisticated network of interdependencies of a thing and a servant, of a servant and a master, of a thing and a master.

The speaker seems to understand that he himself takes part in that network. On one hand, possibly in order to disorient the would-be solvers, he does not count himself among those whom the object serves, using 'them' (*him*) rather than 'us' to refer to the people who benefit from the 'mute one' (9). Such distancing fits well with the form of a third-person riddle. Whereas in first-person enigmas the objects speak, describing themselves, their sorrows and joys, in their textual counterparts that begin with 'I saw' or 'I know', someone else, someone human, speaks of them and frames them for our observation.[48] On the other hand, the narrator of Riddle 49 says that he will not name the subject 'nu gen' [yet] (8), which means that he associates himself with the unspeaking swallowing thing for all his condemnation of it. He knows what its name is, what it does, and he will be silent like it, though only for a moment. Even though openly criticised in Riddle 49, silence and swallowing do not need to be unambiguously bad in the world of Exeter enigmas. Jordan Zweck maintains that in the context of Riddle 47 ('Bookworm'), '[s]wallowing is a necessary, if also incomplete, step to learning', alluding to the familiar monastic trope of *ruminatio*. She goes on to claim that silence is productive rather than destructive – indeed, that it generously enables 'space for other silenced bodies' and unrecorded sounds to register.[49] Talking about Riddle 49, Zweck argues that the transformation of the riddler becomes possible through the quietness of the swallowing bookcase.[50] By keeping silence, even momentarily, the speaker allows his audience to fill the gaps with their words. We all share the same location: the field of an intellectual exercise, the manuscript page. The next-to-last line connects not only the speaker and the subject, but also both of them with the audience. It provides an indication of spatial proximity of the three: the dark, ignorant, unspeaking creature does its swallowing 'here' (*her*) (10).

Riddle 49 reveals a complex relationship that material fragments have with motion. On one hand, their identity depends greatly on their portability, as evident in Riddles 14 and 20. Books or loaves require distribution to provide nourishment, but they come from a ground-bound structure and have to be fixed in a particular place to be consumed properly. Horns and swords likewise circulate, acquiring more power through their travels. Still, these tools need to be attached to a person or a space (the wall on which horn sometimes hangs) to fulfil their function. Their movement is not unlimited. While the objects may yearn to be released, they realise that their continued existence necessitates closeness and attachment to humans.

Riddle 40 does not hint at goods produced and circulated in bulk, but another type of agglomeration. It consists of multiple pairs of oppositions that invoke many things and beings from nature, human-built environments, and even classical mythology. Critics agree that the speaker – who describes itself as easily frightened and braver than a fierce boar, better smelling than spikenard and fouler smelling than a swamp, younger than a newborn and older than the earth itself – is Creation.[51] The text is a fairly close but not rigid translation of Aldhelm's 'De Creatura', the riddle that concludes his collection of Latin *enigmata*. Salvador-Bello notes that Latin collections conventionally end with Creation riddles, presenting a concept that includes all the subjects that came up in earlier texts.[52] She even speculates that Riddles 40 and 66 came at the end of previous compilations of Old English enigmatic poems.[53] The Exeter Book seems to have possessed no fewer than three Creation riddles. In addition to the ones already mentioned, there is Riddle 94 that survives in fragmentary form. If we take Creation riddles as miniature hoards that contain every enigma that comes before them (analogous to the Creation, which encompasses every created being and thing), the collection would then function as a hoard of hoards. The riddlemaster's mode of operation reflects well this expansive impulse. As noted by Erin Sebo, unlike the more restrained Aldhelm, the Old English poet 'sees every image as an opportunity to give full rein to his powers of description. The riddle becomes a frame for his lively and abundant observations and experience of the world.'[54] The sense of abundance is communicated in many ways, often accompanied by a sense of anxiety. Sebo observes that the vernacular poem has an 'overall sense of a gentle and affectionate mutuality between Creator and created', but at the same time that it erases humans and presents them only in utter fragmentation, in the image of hair, eyelashes, and eyebrows falling off presumably in old age (lines 98–104).[55]

The translation not only blends together the opposing scales like the original, but it also varies between the distant and the proximate, the classical references and more domestic phenomena closer to the world described by most of the other riddles in ways that Aldhelm, writing in a full Latin mode, does not. For instance, the following passage that takes four lines in the original doubles in size in the vernacular.

> Dulcior in palato quam lenti nectaris haustus
> Dirior et rursus quam glauca absinthia campi.
> Mando dapes mordax lurconum more Ciclopum,
> Cum possim iugiter sine victu vivere felix. (31–4)[56]
> [I am sweeter on the palate than a taste of smooth nectar; yet again, I am more bitter than the grey wormwood in the field. I ravenously gulp down meals in the manner of gluttonous Cyclopes, although I can equally well live content without food.][57]

The Old English version is expansive, one-upping the original, fittingly in a scene that speaks about extravagant consumption.

> Ic eom on goman   gene swetra
> þonne þu beobread   blende mid hunige;
> swylce ic eom wraþre   þonne wermod sy,
> þe her on hyrstum   heasewe stondeþ.
> Ic mesan mæg   meahtelicor
> ond efnetan   ealdum þyrse,
> ond ic gesælig mæg   symle lifgan
> þeah ic ætes ne sy   æfre to feore. (58–65)
> [I am even sweeter on the palate than the honeycomb blended with honey. Yet I am more bitter than the wormwood, which grows here grey in the woods, may be. I can eat more mightily and feed as much as an old giant, and I can live content at a feast even if I should never eat again in (my) life.]

Instead of one splendid verb signifying eating, we have two ('mesan ... ond efnetan'). The second of them has two parts, *efen* 'exactly, just' (*DOE*) and *etan*, as if to underline the abundance. The nectar comes down to earth in the image of an overflowing honeycomb (lit., 'bee-bread'), which could form a link to previous texts in the compilation, such as Riddle 27 ('Mead') that mentions bees, honey, and mead. Wormwood is closer to the speaker and the audience, as well, '*here* in the woods' rather than 'in the field' (emphasis added). *Cyclopes* becomes *þyrs*, a noun that translates mythological creatures like Orcs, Colossi, and, indeed, Cyclops, as well as refers to a monster geographically nearer Anglo-Saxon England, Grendel (*Beowulf*, line 426).[58] But the most interesting expansion involves the last line, when the speaker describes being happy at a *symbel* – a word that suggests epic or elegiac poetry, since it appears in *Beowulf*, *Judith*, and *The Wanderer* – but without eating, an activity implied but never mentioned in verse other than the riddles.[59]

Riddle 40 pays particular attention to small creatures, especially invertebrates living close to the ground. Faster than the speaker, we learn, are the snail, the rain-worm, and the fen-frog ('snægl ... regnwyrm / ... ond fenyce') (70–1). And then the poem explains, 'Is þæs gores sunu gonge hrædra, / þone we wifel wordum nemnað' [The son of dung whom we call beetle is faster in moving (than I)] (72–3). One poetic translation into Modern English emphasises the lowliness of the creature by translating *gor* as 'shit'.[60] Quite apart from its slow movement, the dung beetle creating a large ball of excrement readily becomes an image of disproportional accumulation. Not coincidentally in this line, the speaker aligns itself with the audience, bringing the humans into the ambit of Creation for the first time, when it refers to the animal by the name that 'we' use. Aldhelm does not use the first-person plural though he, too, underlines the uncanniness of the animals: 'and yet the nasty earthworm and the slug and the slow swamp-turtle and the black beetle, offspring of stinking dung, all outpace me in a race more quickly than the telling'.[61] Again, Riddle 40 brings the dung beetle closer to the audience.

Three lines down, we encounter another distinctive small being: 'leohtre ic eom micle þonne þes lytla wyrm / þe her on flode gæð fotum dryge' [I am much lighter than the little insect that walks here on water with dry feet] (76–7). Bosworth and Toller show that the word *wyrm* can vary widely in scale in Old English, meaning both 'a serpent, reptile' and 'a creeping insect, worm'.[62] It appears frequently in the surviving corpus. Riddle 47 describes its book-nibbling vermin as a moth and a worm. The dragon in *Beowulf*, another *wyrm*, is a guardian of the cursed hoard of treasure. This type of animal signifies both loss and abundance, two ideas crucial for the notions of spoliation and hoarding.[63] Insects, worms, and dragons represent destruction, as they leave behind visible devastation. They also are either very large or quite small and appear in large quantities, in swarms, overwhelming people in both cases. Aldhelm says, straightforwardly: 'I am lighter than a feather to which (even) a pond-skater yields.'[64] Having created an image when his Latin origin has a phrase, the vernacular translator also grounds the little creature in our space by using 'here'.

If we agree with A. M. Juster, that Aldhelm's concluding enigma 'replicates the feel of a classical satire in order to summarize and expand the messages of the preceding riddles',[65] then Riddle 40's difference from its predecessor – prosodically, stylistically, lexically – stands out even more. Far from subsuming everything in the collection, the first Creature riddle in the Exeter Book dramatically signals its distinctiveness, sprawled through its 110 lines. Spoliation on more than one level becomes evident in an Old English translation of an Anglo-Latin enigma that itself plunders the classical textual tradition.

Extraction and expansion: Riddle 66 ('Creation')

Riddle 66 is considerably shorter than its source, Riddle 40 (ten times longer), and its source's source, Aldhelm's 'De Creatura' (nearly eight and a half times longer). The speaker emphasises its ubiquitous reach in space, whether terrestrial, marine, or supernatural, hinting at its identity as Creation.[66] The text appears elegant and rather uncluttered. It contains with one small exception only macro elements such as heavenly bodies, landscape features, and the two opposed unearthly dwelling places, heaven and hell. The text concerns itself almost exclusively with wide, seemingly empty spaces. The first five lines are connected by comparatives, as the speaker claims to be larger, smaller, brighter, and swifter ('mare ... læsse ... leohtre ... swiftre ...') than the middle-earth, the handworm, the moon, and the sun (1–3). What begins in a fundamental opposition of size, an establishment of shifting scales, continues not in a list of other crucial binaries, but in a series of images of lightness and speed.[67] Like the riddles of the Exeter Book, Creation is all-encompassing but also fleeting; while it inheres in everything, it resists capture. The handworm appears as the only living being (borrowed from Riddle 40, line 96) because it permits a human measure of smallness before any reference to individual beings disappears from the text.

Startlingly, the only live creature in the text has to be taken out. It does not matter what type of a vermin Riddle 66 refers to, perhaps a subcutaneous parasite,[68] but that it is one associated with hands, the body parts most closely suggestive of creation. Indeed, in Riddle 40, the afflicted person's extraction of the parasite is an example of ingenuity: 'se þe hæleþa bearn ... searoþoncle, seaxe delfað' [one that the children of men ... dig out with a knife, with cunning thought] (96, a passage with no equivalent in the Latin).[69] Except for the worm, nobody appears to dwell on earth, but the speaker does mention 'engla eard' [the residence of angels] (8), populating only one, supernatural, place. Creation slightly humanises itself when it describes how it embraces the seas and the bosom of the earth ('þes foldan bearm') (3–4). In the very last line the non-individualising speaker reveals that it has a self by saying that it fills the earth and the sea 'side mid me sylfum' [amply with myself] (10). The subject is on the move. From the middle of the text until the signature imperative in the last half-line, the challenge to the reader to name it, Creation uses active verbs only: 'ic hrine ... / underhnige ... ofestrige ... / wide ræce ... / gefylle ...' [I touch ... go down ... rise above ... spread widely ... fill]. In this manner the enigma communicates God's omnipresence and his creation's status as 'a dynamic force; an action constantly taking place as well as an *opus*'.[70]

Encyclopedic miniatures

As much as Riddle 40 delights in hoarding, Riddle 66 invokes large swaths of space without ever overwhelming the reader with details; whereas the former gives us a whale, more than one pig, several invertebrates, flowers, seaweed, and incense, the later only has the tiniest handworm. For an Old English poem it is fairly plain, especially if we can remember how many of the riddles, like 14 ('Horn') and 29 ('Moon and Sun') discussed above, delight in ornamentation. The speaker of Riddle 66 does not wish to hold anything or anyone down, but moves swiftly, 'swiftre þonne sunne' [swifter than the sun] (3). The sun makes sense for this analogy because it marks at once recurrence and passing of time, rejuvenation of Creation and its inconstant nature. In response to the luscious accumulation of Riddle 40, Riddle 66 gives us an exhilarating, fast-paced erasure through wide-open spaces in every direction.

Riddle 95 ('Book'): Fleeting text

The final Riddle 95 presents a speaker that underlines its desirability among the humankind, its ability to impart knowledge, and its occasional elusiveness from those who seek it. This enigma does not speak about creation at large, but rather about textual production, of a book, perhaps of riddles.[71] It begins with the subject speaking about its utmost value. Unlike the manuscripts or loaves in Riddle 49 ('Bookcase/Oven') destined for the consumption of royalty that value them more than gold, the speaker in Riddle 95 proudly proclaims that it appeals to and stays with a wide range of ranks: 'Ic eom indryhten ond eorlum cuð, / ond reste oft[72] ricum ond heanum, / folcum gefræge fere wide' [I am noble, known to earls, and I often rest among the rich and the lowly, familiar to the folk I travel widely] (1–3). The subject's transience comes to the fore in those lines. The book or its content rests, but not forever; it seems to have an urge to move. The following passage, challenging to parse, has most direct relation to plundering: 'ond me fremdes ær freondum stondeð / hiþendra hyht' (4–5), which I take to mean 'and a joy/hope of plunderers stands on me, previously estranged from friends'. The convoluted syntax underlines the message of having to pick apart words and rearrange them, as in a riddle.

I draw on Williamson for the translation of the passage as well as the interpretation of the phrase 'hiþendra hyht' as gold. Williamson further takes the verb 'to stand' to mean 'to shine'.[73] I would suggest that 'standing' of gold on a lavish manuscript could additionally suggest its detachable nature. *Hyht*, which means both expectation and delight, felicitously illustrates the effect of *spolia*; people desire to have the precious metal because it brings them pleasure. In the period of Viking invasions, when the heathen warriors plundered books not for their contents but for their precious ornaments, one would be aware of the detachability of gold and gems from a book cover. The book seems to attract treasure to itself, since the speaker says that the joy of plunderers stands on it 'gif ic habban sceal / blæd in burgum oþþe beorhtne god' [if I should have glory in the cities or bright goods] (5–6). *God* [good] sounds very much like *gold*, which provides a clue to the mysterious kenning, or miniature riddle, solved by Williamson. Within human enclosures, the *byrig*, the book acquires reputation and worth. As much as the subject of Riddle 95 enjoys attention of people, occasionally it escapes them. They may now seek its tracks very much ('Þeah nu ælda bearn …/ lastas mine / swiþe secað') (10, 11–12), but it hides its traces at times ('ic swaþe hwilum / mine bemiðe') (12–13) from anyone. The near identicality between *swiþe/swaþe* connects the idea of repeated action or great desire with tracks. Temporal play, familiar to us from other riddles, is evident in the adverbs *nu* and *hwilum*. *Nu* indicates immediacy of the readers longing for meaning in books – those 'ælda bearn' [children of men] looking for signs are us attempting to solve the riddle – and *hwilum* signifies the frequent slipperiness of texts. Unlike medieval Latin riddle collections mentioned by Salvador-Bello, the Exeter compilation does not conclude with a Creation enigma that takes in everything created, either accumulating like Riddle 40 or cutting through like Riddle 60. Appropriately, the last riddle hints at an object that is generally desired and elusive, physically manifest and often invisible.

Notes

1 Winfried Rudolf argues that riddles as a genre 'impart encyclopaedic knowledge concerning the properties and the classification of things; they inspire logical reasoning, but most importantly, they teach rhetorical flexibility on various levels'. Winfried Rudolf, 'Riddling and Reading: Iconicity and Logogriphs in Exeter Book Riddles 23 and 45', *Anglia*, 130 (2012), 499–525, at 499. More specifically, in *Isidorean Perceptions*, Mercedes Salvador-Bello attempts to demonstrate an Isidorean encyclopedic rationale behind the organisation of the Exeter Riddles. Though much of her discussion is illuminating, as will become obvious from my citations of it in this chapter, Salvador-Bello often assumes a particular type of orthodoxy on behalf of the authors and engages in repeated compiler- and scribe-blaming.

2 Salvador-Bello, *Isidorean Perceptions*, p. 287.
3 For a brief explanation of their relation, see Rudolf, 'Riddling and Reading', p. 521.
4 Salvador-Bello, *Isidorean Perceptions*, p. 346 (*plægan* and *hæmedlaces* in Riddle 42), 358 (*geac* 'cuckoo ... suggesting a wayward student', in Riddle 9; *moððe*, 'bookworm' in Riddle 47); Heide Estes, *Anglo-Saxon Literary Landscapes: Ecotheory and the Environmental Imagination* (Amsterdam: Amsterdam University Press, 2017), p. 165 (*swifan*, 'to stick', the ancestor of Chaucer's *swyve* 'had already acquired a sexual connotation in Old English').
5 Scholars have identified proto-Marxist and environmentalist concerns not far under the surface. See, for example, Jennifer Neville, 'The Unexpected Treasure of the "Implement Trope": Hierarchical Relationships in the Old English Riddles', *The Review of English Studies*, 62 (2011), 505–19; Estes, *Anglo-Saxon Literary Landscapes*, pp. 145–75, especially 171; and Corinne Dale, *The Natural World in the Exeter Book Riddles* (Cambridge: D. S. Brewer, 2017). Edward B. Irving, Jr, mines the Riddles for evidence of suffering in war of women, servants, and young soldiers that the works like *Beowulf* passes over, 'the darker side of those bright exhilarations of combat and slaughter that infuse heroic poetry' ('Heroic Experience in the Old English Riddles', in Katherine O'Brien O'Keeffe (ed.), *Old English Shorter Poems: Basic Readings* (New York: Garland, 1994), pp. 199–212, at 210).
6 John D. Niles finds 'the bric-a-brac of daily life' in the riddles alongside clues to 'how the Anglo-Saxons thought and felt about the basic elements of their life-world'. John D. Niles, *Old English Enigmatic Poems and the Play of the Texts* (Turnhout: Brepols, 2006), pp. 52–3.
7 Dieter Bitterli, *Say What I Am Called: The Old English Riddles of the Exeter Book and the Anglo-Latin Riddle Tradition* (Toronto: Toronto University Press, 2009), p. 168.
8 Bitterli and Salvador-Bello focus on the Latin traditions, and Murphy acknowledges them and extensively uses transhistorical folk analogues (from later England but also Ireland, Russia, and the United States). Patrick J. Murphy, *Unriddling the Exeter Riddles* (University Park, PA: Pennsylvania State University Press, 2011).
9 Roberta Frank has argued that Old English biblical verse takes inspiration from Latin etymologising of scriptural names and supplies paronomasia only possible in the vernacular 'with an alliterative inevitability lacking in the Latin'. Roberta Frank, 'The Unbearable Lightness of Being a Philologist', *The Journal of English and Germanic Philology*, 96 (1997), 486–513, at 493.
10 I take the numbering and texts from Krapp and Dobbie's edition (*The Exeter Book*).
11 Neville, 'The Unexpected Treasure of "The Implement Trope"'; Audrey Meaney, 'Birds on the Stream of Consciousness: Riddles 7 to 10 of the Exeter Book', *Archaeological Review from Cambridge*,

18 (2002), 120–52; Laurence K. Shook, 'Riddles Relating to the Anglo-Saxon Scriptorium', in J. Reginald O'Donnell (ed.), *Essays in Honour of Anton Charles Pegis* (Toronto: Toronto University Press, 1974), pp. 215–36; Mercedes Salvador-Bello, 'The Sexual Riddle Type in Aldhelm's Enigmata, the Exeter Book, and Early Medieval Latin', *Philological Quarterly*, 90 (2012), 357–85.

12 John D. Niles, *Old English Enigmatic Poems and the Play of Texts*, p. 35.

13 Wim Tigges, 'Snakes and Ladders', p. 110.

14 Paz, *Nonhuman Voices*, p. 79.

15 Williamson (ed.), *The Old English Riddles*, p. 170. See the definitions of *horn* in *DOE*.

16 Patrizia Lendinara, 'Aspetti della società germanica negli enigmi del Codice Exoniense', *Antichità germaniche*, 1 (2001), 3–41, at 35.

17 I restore this manuscript reading, following Williamson. Krapp and Dobbie take Trautmann's emendation *behlywed* [protected], making the meaning 'von Brettern geschützt' [protected by boards] (*The Exeter Book*, p. 329).

18 The end of the riddle does not, then, definitely mark the end of the battle and the beginning of the feast ('la fine della battuta e l'inizio del banchetto', in Lendinara's words) ('Aspetti', p. 35). The speaker blends the two activities throughout. Lendinara identifies a strong ambivalence towards conventional heroism in the Riddles, and explains it by characterising the society that gave rise to the collection as a transitional one, where new and old (monastic and heroic, Christian and Germanic) values coexist, clash, and overlap (p. 41).

19 DiNapoli discusses the expression, calling it 'another perfectly realised bit of riddlic misdirection' and associating it with the larger phenomenon of 're-ordering of cognitive priorities and assumptions' in Anglo-Saxon verse. Robert DiNapoli, 'In the Kingdom of the Blind, the One-Eyed Man is a Seller of Garlic: Depth-Perception and the Poet's Perspective in the Exeter Book Riddles', *English Studies*, 81 (2000), pp. 422–55, at 441–2.

20 Although the manuscript reads *wraþþum*, both Krapp and Dobbie and Williamson emend to *wraþum* with no further explanation in the endnotes. I do not disagree with this decision, but I do find the sonic fierceness of the double thorn appropriate here.

21 DiNapoli notes that the transformation of the Rood is completely redemptive, unlike the more troubled objects in the riddles, like the inkhorns (from Riddles 17, 18, and 93) ('In the Kingdom of the Blind', p. 426). Jonathan Wilcox claims that the unsettling power of a typical riddle subject lasts much shorter and is, upon the subject's revelation as an everyday object, less dignified than the Rood (in reference to the rake of Riddle 32). Jonathan Wilcox, '"Tell me what I am": The Old English Riddles', in David F. Johnson and Elaine Treharne (eds), *Readings in Medieval Texts: Interpreting Old and Middle*

English Literature (Oxford: Oxford University Press, 2005), pp. 46–59, at 49–50. While I generally agree with Wilcox, I contend that the unsettling power can remain even after the solution: once seen as a loyal plunderer, the rake may not be easily reinscribed as a simple farm implement.

22 The word here is *bearm*, not *bosm*, but their meanings overlap, signifying not just the breast but also the lap and bringing up notions of embrace and enclosure (see both in *DOE*). I cite *Beowulf* from R. D. Fulk, Robert E. Bjork, and John D. Niles (eds), *Klaeber's Beowulf and the Fight at Finnsburg*, 4th edn (Toronto: University of Toronto Press, 2008).

23 For a discussion of Riddle 14 and others that feature aspects of human development, as theorised in the early Middle Ages, see Harriet Soper's study, 'Reading the *Exeter Book* Riddles as Life-Writing', *The Review of English Studies*, 68 (2017), 841–65 (pp. 859–60 on *hagosteald*).

24 'The Unexpected Treasure of the "Implement Trope"'.

25 DiNapoli, 'In the Kingdom of the Blind', p. 444.

26 Williamson (ed.), *The Old English Riddles*, p. 193. Williamson also mentions two other solutions championed by Trautmann and Kay respectively: 'hawk' or 'falcon' and 'double entendre "sword" and "phallus" with an emphasis upon the latter' (ibid.).

27 I take this double translation from Phyllis Portnoy, '*Laf*-Craft in Five Old English Riddles', p. 564. She explains the second possibility thus: '"shaped *in* strife" (that is, made in the forge)'. This would be another way in which the poet connects the smith's workshop with the battlefield: just the act of production of weapons is sufficiently violent to suggest their deadliness.

28 *DOE* gives the following definitions: 'dwelling-place, enclosure; home, abode'; 'country, region, district'; and 'fence, hedge'.

29 Corinne Dale's analysis of Riddle 83 ('Ore') offers some fascinating parallels. The ore suffers as it is extracted, melted, and beaten into coins, but once released into the world in form of money it can have deeply negative effects. Dale aptly depicts its disturbing, elusive presence, which resonates with the manner in which treasure works in *Beowulf*, 'Humans, it is implied, do not know where the coin goes after a transaction, and thus the coin can be said to pass out of human control. Although human beings usually play the dominant role in the human-nature relationship, here the ore is able to resist the mastery of humans and lay bonds on them ...' (*The Natural World*, p. 139).

30 Chris Bishop reminds us that the sexual riddles in the Exeter Book often figure the act of coitus as a battle, and ingeniously points out that '[i]f the *wunderlicu wiht* does not care for [þ]*æs compes*, a struggle with women, then perhaps he prefers [þ]*æt compes*, a struggle with men'. Chris Bishop, 'Ambiguous Eroticism in the Exeter Book', *Journal of the Australian Early Medieval Association*, 2 (2006), 9–22, at 13.

31 Murphy, *Unriddling the Exeter Riddles*, p. 214.
32 Irving offers the solution of 'Testosterone' ('Heroic Experience', p. 206).
33 Portnoy, '*Laf*-Craft in Five Old English Riddles', p. 566.
34 Ibid., 569.
35 Brian McFadden, 'Raiding, Reform, and Reaction: Wondrous Creatures in the Exeter Book Riddles', *Texas Studies in Literature and Language*, 50 (2008), 329–51, at 333.
36 Williamson (ed.), *The Old English Riddles*, p. 226.
37 In its old-fashioned, lyrical moments, Modern English genders the moon and the sun in exactly opposite terms. Kevin Crossley-Holland translates this riddle by calling the former 'she' and the latter 'he', thus erasing the unusual, interesting gender dynamic in the original. Kevin Crossley-Holland (trans.), *The Exeter Riddles: Revised Edition* (London: Enitharmon Press, 2008), p. 32.
38 Frank, 'The Unbearable Lightness', pp. 493–4.
39 The pun is there in Old English, as well. See *leoht-lic* in Bosworth and Toller, *Anglo-Saxon Dictionary*.
40 Patrick J. Murphy, *Unriddling the Exeter Riddles*, pp. 126–32.
41 For this parenthetical insight I am indebted to Jordan Zweck.
42 *Deawig-feþera* [dewy-feathered] refers to the birds of battle, such as ravens (*DOE*). The Old Norse kenning *valdögg*, translated by Geir T. Zoëga as 'the dew of the slain', denotes blood. See his *Concise Dictionary of Old Icelandic* (Oxford: Clarendon, 1926).
43 Williamson notes these possibilities alongside 'falcon-cage' (first suggested by F. Dietrich) and 'pen and ink' (by Laurence Shook) (*The Old English Riddles*, p. 289). He seems to lean towards the solution 'book'. However, he states that '[g]iven the uncertainties [such as the exact meaning of the word *gop* in line 3], it seems wisest to list the solution as "uncertain"' (p. 290).
44 Rudolf, 'Riddling and Reading', p. 521. He is discussing here Riddle 45, another bread-related text (usually solved as 'Dough/Phallus' to which he adds 'Ishmael unborn – Christ unborn').
45 Salvador-Bello, *Isidorean Perceptions*, p. 366.
46 Martin Foys has recently tended to these undercurrents. He argues that Riddles 47 and 48 ('Chalice') flow into one another, separated in the manuscript by only a *punctus*, a minuscule dot-like medieval punctuation sign (p. 21). He puts forth that '… the enigmatically doubled text of Riddle 47/48 … strains to solve its own cultural riddle, a dynamic, recursive tension born of the high status accorded to human artifice, and its lowly place within a divine order. Riddle 47/8 uneasily marks the precarious condition of the textual production of intellectual expression, and then identifies the theological incentive to reaffirm the necessity of such production's survival' (p. 23). Martin Foys, 'The Undoing of Exeter Book Riddle 47', in Graham D. Caie and Michael D. C. Drout (eds), *Transitional States: Cultural Change, Tradition,*

and Memory in Medieval England (Tempe: Arizona Center for Medieval and Renaissance Studies, forthcoming). Available as a pre-publication draft on https://hcommons.org/deposits/item/hc:10515, accessed 23 June 2018.
47 Salvador-Bello, *Isidorean Perceptions*, p. 357.
48 Craig Williamson speaks of the third-person riddles as 'riddles of description' in which a human observer describes a non-human creature in human terms (*The Old English Riddles*, p. 26). In Riddle 49, we find an even more complicated dynamic: a human speaker observes a non-human (bookcase/oven) working with a human (servant) and discusses the former in human, and the latter in a combination of human and non-human, ways.
49 Jordan Zweck, 'Silence in the Exeter Book Riddles', *Exemplaria*, 28 (2016), 319–36, 329 (*ruminatio*), 331 (generous enabling).
50 Ibid., p. 326.
51 Williamson (ed.), *The Old English Riddles*, p. 265.
52 Salvador-Bello, *Isidorean Perceptions*, pp. 336, 342.
53 Ibid., p. 389.
54 Erin Sebo, 'The Creation Riddle and Anglo-Saxon Cosmology', in Gale R. Owen-Crocker and Brian W. Schneider (eds), *The Anglo-Saxons: The World through their Eyes* (Manchester: British Archaeological Reports, 2014), pp. 149–56, at 150.
55 Sebo, 'The Creation Riddle', p. 151.
56 I cite the Latin edition of Pitman. Aldhelm, *The Riddles of Aldhelm*, ed. James Hall Pitman (New Haven: Yale University Press, 1925).
57 I use Lapidge's translation of Aldhelm. Michael Lapidge and James L. Rosier (trans.), *The Poetic Works* (Cambridge: D. S. Brewer, 1985).
58 Bosworth and Toller, *Anglo-Saxon Dictionary*.
59 For more on this avoidance, see Hugh Magennis, *Anglo-Saxon Appetites: Food and Drink and their Consumption in Old English and Related Literature* (Dublin: Four Courts Press, 1999).
60 '& the weevil, burrowing through/ the shit that spawned him, always shall outpace me', trans. David Wojahn. In Greg Delanty and Michael Matto (eds), *The Word Exchange: Anglo-Saxon Poems in Translation* (New York: Norton, 2011), p. 311.
61 Again, the translation is Lapidge's. The Latin original reads, 'Lumbricus et limax et tarda testudo palustris/ Atque, fimi soboles sordentis, cantarus ater/ Me dicto citius vincunt certamine cursus' (Pitman's edition, ll. 37–9).
62 Bosworth and Toller, *An Anglo-Saxon Dictionary*.
63 Foys emphasises loss when he reads the *wyrm* as 'a classic Old English formulation of human regression for both spiritual failing and corporeal decomposition' ('The Undoing of Exeter Book Riddle 47', p. 19)
64 That is, 'Sum levior pluma, cedit cui tippula limphae' (l. 41).
65 A. M. Juster (trans.), *Saint Aldhelm's Riddles* (Toronto: University of Toronto Press, 2015), p. xix.

66 This is another universally agreed-upon solution (Williamson (ed.), *The Old English Riddles*, p. 333).
67 Williamson states that 'this "creation" riddle is shorter than its predecessor and less bound to the recurrent notion of paradoxical pairs' (ibid.).
68 Williamson (ed.), *The Old English Riddles*, p. 274. Aldhelm has 'the thin worm which bores through corpses' ('Et minor exiguo, sulcat qui corpora, verme …').
69 Conversely, Foys sees the speaker of Riddle 40 humbling of human aspirations in this passage, as it underlines people's skill in 'heal[ing] themselves by inflicting wounds' ('The Undoing of Exeter Book Riddle 47', p. 11). The Old English enigmas generally speak of artistic creation, intellectual development, and physical pain together, at once admitting the suffering and need for it.
70 Erin Sebo, 'Hopkins and Early English Riddling: Solving *The Windhover?*', *Colloquy: Text, Theory, Critique*, 21 (2011), 25–37, at 33.
71 Williamson, who solves the riddle as 'book', lists a number of other proposed solutions, among them: 'wandering singer', 'moon', 'riddle', 'soul', and 'prostitute' (*The Old English Riddles*, pp. 397–9).
72 I remove the semicolon that Krapp and Dobbie place here in their edition.
73 Ibid., pp. 398 ('hiþendra hyht'), 400 ('to stand'/'to shine').

2
Architecture of the past and the future: Transformative potential of plunder in *Exodus*[1]

Introduction: Multiple focuses of a quite distinctive poem

The Old English *Exodus* survives solely in Oxford, Bodleian Library, MS Junius 11, a compilation of vernacular biblical verse that contains three other texts: *Genesis* and *Daniel*, based on the Old Testament stories, and *Christ and Satan*, developed from the New Testament materials. Even in this, most immediate context, the poem stands out. While it occupies the space expected chronologically, *Exodus* appears stylistically and structurally different from its neighbours and even the rest of the surviving corpus of Anglo-Saxon verse. R. M. Liuzza writes that it has 'some of the most dazzlingly inventive language of any Old English poetry ... and is ... notoriously difficult'. Daniel G. Calder and Stanley Greenfield note the difficulty, yet call the work 'one of the most stirring and exciting of Old English poems'.[2] Some of the exciting challenge comes from lively imagination and closeness of focus. *Exodus* takes up only a fraction of its scriptural source, as it provides a foreshortened narrative of the events before the flight from Egypt, some consideration of the time spent by the Israelites in the desert before reaching the Red Sea, the moment of the Crossing, and not much after the arrival on the shores of the Promised Land. As described, the storyline would seem relatively straightforward, but the poem also gestures towards other significant points in the Bible, independent from the story of Exodus. There are two so-called digressions, the 'patriarchal' (which tells of Noah's Flood, Abraham's near-sacrifice of Isaac, and Solomon's construction of the temple), and the 'homiletic' (which looks ahead to the tumult that will lead to the Judgement Day).[3] Most interestingly for my concerns in this book, *Exodus* adds more elements either dramatically expanded from the source, such as a series of *byrig* [cities or enclosures] and the shape-shifting pillar that protects the Israelites on their journey, or not easily identifiable from any scriptural context, such as the mysterious African woman who appears at the end of the poem. Such moments of expansion that carry within themselves a degree of mystery reveal the poem's awareness of itself as a translation in several senses of the word.[4]

Scholars have applied various combinations of exegetical and historical approaches to the text. Typology, a kind of textual spoliation mentioned in my Introduction, is a common key to interpreting the Old English *Exodus*. According to it, Noah, Abraham, Isaac, Solomon, and Moses, the patriarchs that appear in the poem, all foreshadow Christ, while the structures associated with Noah and Solomon, the Ark and the Temple respectively, typify the Church. Allegory provides another helpful religious framework. Allegorically, the Israelites wandering in the desert stand for Christians lured by earthly delights, with their enemy, the Pharaoh, being the Devil, the world, or sin. The Crossing of the Red Sea represents the baptism that enables the soul to move towards the Promised Land, namely, heaven.[5] Heroic motifs, the consideration of which complements spiritual readings, include the extended, energetic battle scenes and depiction of the fleeing Israelites as an army obedient to Moses, their leader. The Old English *Exodus* also seems to highlight questions of cultural difference and historic awareness. T. A. Shippey diagnoses the poem with a certain proto-nationalism, concluding that it is very 'worldly' because it is very English.[6] Nicholas Howe argues that the work 'forces the reader to confront it as a narrative of history' and engages with memories of the Anglo-Saxon migrations to Britain.[7]

While reading an Old Testament tale about the salvation of the Israelites, we may recall Andrew Scheil's statement that Jews and Judaism function in Anglo-Saxon society as a 'distorted mirror, [a] Rorschach blot', because Christianity, unable to push away its Jewish foundation from its core, 'in talking about Jews ... talks about itself'.[8] A different Other, more removed from the self, Egyptians would by that scheme work as shorthand for an enemy closer to early medieval England, the dispossessed indigenous Britons.[9] These interpretations are generally convincing, but what happens if we introduce the third element, the African/the Ethiopian and even the nameless group inhabiting the desert, in the space between the two opposed points, Pharaoh's realm and the Promised Land? Critics have noted that the poem associates the Israelites with the sea and the Egyptians with the land, but how is either related to the other two elements, the air and the fire? What happens when the sea turns into the land? Though the exegetical readers could fit the shape-shifting pillar into the edifice of the Church or explain the African woman among the Israelites as a symbol of the Church gathered of all nations, at the moment when these two phenomena enter the scene, the poet's handing of them appears rather in agreement with Cary Howie's formulation that '[i]n order for other people and things to "emerge," we must in a sense "merge" with them: not in an appropriative fashion, nor in the sense of a *reductio ad unum* ...'.[10] As the text whose leitmotiv is legible to every believer (an escape, a release from slavery) invites the readers to loosen up the hard distinctions, it encourages them to meditate on objects that are either *spolia* or *spolia*-like. Even in the wildest flights of imagination, the *Exodus* poet fixes his gaze on the concrete, mysterious fragment that belongs to a greater architectural or narrative framework that stands outside the reach of the poem.

'Afrisc meowle' [African woman]

Spolia embodies duality well for it belongs neither fully to the new context nor to the older one from which it has been taken, but rather combines the two to yield something else. One, more literal example, the unexplained figure of the African woman, emerges at the end of *Exodus*, surrounded by despoiled Egyptian corpses, herself possibly part of the plunder from another time. She descends from neither of the two opposing groups, being neither Israelite nor Egyptian. Her association with treasure and lineage appears unexpectedly:

> Þa wæs eðfynde   Afrisc meowle
> on geofones staðe   golde geworðod.
> Handa hofon   halswurðunge,
> bliðe wæron,   bote gesawon,
> heddon herereafes –   hæft wæs onsæled.
> Ongunnon sælafe   segnum dælan
> on yðlafe   ealde madmas,
> reaf ond randas;   heo on riht sceodon
> gold ond godweb,   Iosepes gestreon,
> wera wuldorgesteald.   Werigend lagon
> on deaðstede,   drihtfolca mæst. (580–90)[11]
> [There, on the ocean's shore, an African woman was easily found, adorned with gold. (The women) lifted neck ornaments with hands, they were joyful, they saw relief, they took in the spoils of war; the fetter was untied. On the leavings of the waves, they began to divide

by standards the leavings of the sea (or: they, the leavings of the sea, began to divide ...), old treasures, garments, and shields. By right they divided the gold and fine textile, Joseph's property, glorious possessions of men. The defenders lay in their place of death, the greatest of people.]

I will return to the passage after some observations on the continuous female presence in *Exodus*, the meaning of 'Africa' in Anglo-Saxon England, and potential parallels with Wealhtheow in *Beowulf*. To begin contextualising the 'Afrisc meowle', let us look at the significant role that women play in the poem across its various temporal layers. During the crossing of the Red Sea, the poet brings us backwards into the story of Noah's flood. Abraham, he points out, is the ancestor of Moses's people: 'Him was an fæder, / leof leodfruma, landriht geþah' [They had one father, the beloved originator of people (who) received the right to the land] (353–4). Lineage and continuity are invoked at the same time as storytelling; the author's self-consciousness manifests itself in establishing a correspondence between two types of propagation, sexual and textual. While in the lines above, the masculinist, patriarchal note predominates – as men beget sons with no mention of women – the Noah's ark features a promise of a rich future with both (traditional) genders present: 'On feorhgebeorh foldan hæfde / eallum eorðcynne ece lafe, / frumcneow gehwæs, fæder ond moder / tuddorteondra, geteled rime ... snottor sæleoda' [In the life-saving of earth, the wise seaman had counted by number the eternal remains of all earth-kind, each of the first generations, fathers and mothers, producers of descendents] (369–72, 374). Following such a statement, the reader soon realises that women have been there all along, in the group fleeing from Egypt, when they appear on the other shore, singing songs of praise.

Their presence among the Israelites comes in sharp contrast with the exclusively masculine composition of the Pharaoh's army. Unnecessarily for heroic poetry, the author of *Exodus* points out that the Egyptian army is entirely male: 'Hæfde him alesen leoda dugeðe / tireadigra twa þusendo / [...] forðon anra gehwilc ut alædde / wæpnedcynnes wigan æghwilcne / þara þe he on ðam fyrste findan mihte' [He had chosen a troop of men, two thousand glorious ones [...] and so led out each one of them, each warrior of weapon-kind, whom he could find at that time] (183–4, 187–9). The first part of the compound *wæpnedcynn* signals not just weapons as attributes of manhood, but also the genitals.[12] In a work abounding with images of being cut off, separated, and trapped as signs par excellence of divine punishment, the enemy troop's isolation from their wives, even as the context warrants it, seems especially noteworthy. When the Egyptian troop drowns, the poet reports that no one is left, not even a messenger to announce 'the greatest tidings of sorrow' ('beallospella mæst') to the warriors' wives ('hæleða cwenum') (511–12).

The African woman provides a contrast to both groups: she is at once connected to the Israelites and separate from them. Thus, she functions as an architectural *spolium*. She does not belong to an identifiable nation. While she probably comes from another story, biblical or otherwise (since the Old English poem is unlikely to have invented a character with such a specific, distant designation), we are still not sure which narrative to connect her to. A safe assumption is that she is *not* one of the Pharaoh's tribe. Fred C. Robinson explains that '[l]exically *Afrisc meowle* is an accurate enough rendering of *aethiopissa*, for the standard geographical authorities of the period make it clear that *Aethiopia* is an African nation', before adding that the late ninth-century Anglo-Saxon translator of Orosius interprets Aethiopia as 'Affrica'. He further observes in a footnote that not much was known about Ethiopia in early medieval England other than that it was to the south of Egypt.[13] Mary B. Campbell writes that 'no continuous corpus of travel accounts' in the Middle Ages treats the continent in any detail: 'Egypt … was a part of Asia, and Ethiopia was legend alone.'[14] A casual glance at the Old English corpus reveals that the word *Africa* and its derivations *Africanas* and *Africanus* occur only in translated texts. Orosius mentions Africa three times, once as the place where the fame-hungry Alexander the Great wishes to travel after his conquests (but his servants poison him before he can go). According to the Old English *Martyrologium*, St Augustine, having spent his days 'on Africa londe', is buried, with honours, in the city of Sardinia, the locale that the Saracens plunder or ravage. These contexts, however interesting, do not help us situate the *Afrisc meowle* any better. The English adjectival form, *Afrisc*, is unique to *Exodus*.[15]

Furthermore, we do not know what position she will occupy in her recently acquired context, as a foreigner among the Chosen People. Her foreignness and gender mark her as a possible possession as well as a symbol of the Israelite lineage's strength and future global expansion. To envision this function of the *Afrisc meowle*, one need only compare her to Wealtheow, Hrothgar's wife in *Beowulf*.[16] Wealtheow, whose name likely means 'foreign slave', is invested in propagating her new family line and culture partly because of her remoteness from her own motherland.[17] The queen's prominence demonstrates the king's superiority because he can marry whomever he desires, regardless of her origin or prior status.[18] On a different but related note, her presence might also point to her lord's ability to love even those rather different from him, geographically and/or socially, including his thanes.[19] The African woman provides a surety of continuation for the Israelite bloodline, and functions as a sign that the kings in Exodus – Moses and God – transcend socio-cultural boundaries through their fervent, inclusive love, the love that reveals itself in accumulation of material and human resources through time and space.

We can now return to her placement in the poem for more clues. Her lack of grounding in a specific place signifies vibrant possibility in juxtaposition to the unmoving dead bodies of the doomed army. She is not trapped. She is alive while the Egyptians are dead, and she puts on their jewellery. We find her, along with her company, at the shore, 'on yðlafe' [the leavings of the waves], the border between the sea and the land (586). Though she is neither Israelite nor Egyptian, the African woman finds herself in a group of rejoicing Israelite women. She is a part of the Chosen People then, perhaps even Zipporah, Moses's Ethiopian wife, or Miriam.[20] But because of the moment when she appears, she becomes associated with the plundered treasure formerly belonging to the Egyptians. *Exodus*, a text that persistently meditates on diverse kinds of remnants, aptly concludes with a reiteration of what remains after the Crossing: salvaged people and objects indicative of the intertwining of self and Other. Both the despoiled ornaments that the 'Afrisc meowle' has put on herself and the larger group of the Israelites can, grammatically and otherwise, be designated as the 'leavings of the sea' (*sælafe*) because they have survived the tumultuous voyage (585). The rather liminal place on which they – the treasures, the textiles, the precious seed from which the Sacred History develops – stand has a similar description: 'leavings of the waves' (*on yðlafe*) (586).[21] In the most literal way, the gold, garments, and shields constitute plunder. The African woman takes up the power and splendour of Egypt by clasping on *halswurðunge* [neck-ornaments] together with her Israelite girlfriends. Power of all nations, including Ethiopia and Egypt, flows to strengthen the Chosen People on their way to salvation, but the differences between the individual peoples cannot be completely erased in order to make the inter-ethnic fortification visible.

Even now, in its ringing conclusion, the poem will not leave behind material traces of the Other that constitute the triumph of its heroes. At the moment of separation from the drowned enemy, and one final instance of the contrast between the upright winners and the reclining losers, the poet instantaneously reminds his audience of the past interaction between the two groups. The objects are marked as 'Iosepes gestreon' [Joseph's property] rightfully belonging to the 'seafarers'.[22] The Israelites do not just despoil the Egyptians; they take back what the Egyptians had taken from them. And yet the reader may wonder what meanings the artefacts must have accrued in their captivity. The poem does not end with reclaiming of what the Pharaoh's followers had appropriated from their 'guests'. In the very last lines, the Old English *Exodus* gazes back upon the body of the foes, which breaks the surface of the sea and the text: 'Werigend lagon / on deaðstede, drihtfolca mæst' [the protectors lay in their place of death, the greatest of nations] (589–90). This may well serve as a final triumphalist statement. They were the greatest among earth-dwellers, but God is still greater; the enemy's superiority only enhances one's own achievement in conquering him. But the scene also echoes other supremely elegiac moments earlier in the poem, abundant with words denoting materiality: the ones in which the *hoard*-guardians perish (35), the arms of the laughter-*smiths* are fettered (43), and the joys of the *hall* vanish (36); or the ones in which the poet imagines the Egyptian women not receiving any news of their husbands' downfall because the herald died with the rest of the army (511–12).[23] In other words, at this junction in the text, with the faces of the Israelites turned towards the Promised Land, the 'burh ond beagas, brade rice' [the cities and rings, the broad kingdom] (557), the poet nevertheless effects one last flashback.

The concluding image repeats a pattern that has been established in the poem, as we will see below. People and possessions cluster around elusive enclosures, as the plundered enemies – previously defined by their role of safekeeping cities and hoards – still hold onto the title of the greatest nation, even while being severed from their homes and fixed in their deaths.

Burh [A city, enclosure]

This backwards glance at the time when only a forwards glance would be expected persists throughout the poem in the image of a city, enclosure, *burh*. According to the *Dictionary of Old English*, the word *burh* means: 'A. fortified enclosure, fortification; A1. stronghold, fortress, citadel; A2. fortified dwelling, estate, manor' and 'B. town; B1. fortified town; generally, town or city …'. The term, judging by these definitions, focuses on the enclosing, either the structure that encloses, or that which is enclosed by it. Studies of Anglo-Saxon toponyms have shown that the early English referred to a number of structures by that noun, 'from an ancient pre-English earthwork or encampment to a Roman station or camp, to an Anglo-Saxon stronghold, fortified house or town'.[24] By the time the Junius 11 manuscript was compiled, in the early eleventh century, *byrig* (pl.) had acquired a particular resonance. These structures functioned as forts to rebuff Viking advances as well as 'regional economic centres for the exchange and manufacture of commodities',[25] a development that began in late ninth-century Wessex before spreading elsewhere a century later. Archaeology shows that *byrig* grew in population and diversity in the late tenth century, with the evidence of imported pottery indicating growing cosmopolitan tastes of the inhabitants.[26]

For a poem inundated by the sands of the desert and the waves of the sea, *Exodus* engages frequently in meditations on various permutations of the urban landscape. Taken individually, many of these instances may not appear remarkable, but, as a whole, they bear witness to a powerful poetics invested in the construction and transformation of cities. I will discuss some of these 'city' moments on their own as well as examine them as a manifestation of the larger tendency of the text to blend, much like *spolia* does, two or more distinct components such as two opposing sides (the Israelites and the Egyptians), human beings and physical objects, or the natural world and the world of craft. These fusions, as manipulated by our author, help create the nuance and wonder that sustain the story of a conflict between God's people and his enemies. In *Exodus* the *burh* emerges as something shifting, hard to define, peculiar, yet concrete and universal.[27]

We encounter *burh* for the first time in line 38, in the compound *burhweardas* [city-guardians], meaning the Egyptians. The narrative part of our poem begins with a brief but suggestive account of the destruction of the enemy's first-born.

> Þa wæs ungeare   ealdum witum
> deaðe gedrenced[28]   drihtfolca mæst,
> hordwearda hryre   (heaf wæs geniwad):
> swæfon seledreamas   since berofene.

Hæfde mansceaðan æt middere niht
frecne gefylled, frumbearna fela,
abrocene burhweardas. Bana wide scrað,
lað leodhata, land ðrysmyde
deadra hræwum – dugoð forð gewat.
Wop wæs wide, worulddreama lyt,
wæron hleahtorsmiðum handa belocene,
alyfed laðsið leode gretan,
folc ferende – freond[29] wæs bereafod.
Hergas on helle (heofon þider becom)
druron deofolgyld. (33–47)
[Then, as an ancient punishment, the greatest of nations was drowned utterly, to death. Lamentation for the fall of hoard-guardians was renewed, joys of the hall perished, all treasure gone. In the middle of the night, the destroyer of men slaughtered horribly many first-borns, broken city-guardians. The killer, the hostile human-hater ranged widely; the land darkened with dead bodies; the troop went forth. Weeping was widespread, world-joys little. The hands of the laughter-smiths were tied; a hateful journey (was) allowed to welcome the people. With the folk leaving, friends/relatives were bereaved. Armies (were) in hell, heaven came down there, idols fell.]

The ancient punishment strikes a society with a prominent culture that resembles those powerfully depicted in *Beowulf* and *The Wanderer*. With the hoard-guardians perishing, treasure is gone, and with it, the 'joys of the hall' (35–6). At midnight, the deadly angel slays the first-born, who are either identified as or joined with the 'city-guardians' (38–9). The poem, interested in, even obsessed with, imagining multiple temporal layers at once, envisions 'infidel' infants as future maintainers of their culture. If one distinguishes the first-born from the city-protectors, as J. F. Vickrey does, the crushed *burhweardas* can refer to the idols mentioned nine lines below, by the compound *deofolgyld* [lit., devil-worship].[30] The downfall of the hoard-guardians, or several generations of the Egyptians, would then parallel the destruction of city-guardians, or the artefacts worshipped as gods for protection. In this episode we have a fusing of objects and people, around an urban core, a *burh*. The destruction of the first two results in the dissipation of the third. God shows his wrath by breaking and scattering a nation's material culture in addition to murdering its descendants. Manipulation of architectural and sculptural features, either by modifying or erasing them, invariably accompanies any political and military overtaking, but '[e]ven when the monuments are gone and the artifacts looted, the images, memories, and heroic stories associated with them carry on'.³¹ Rather than simply delighting in ruination, *Exodus* memorialises it, harnessing the charge of any attendant triumphant and elegiac energies.

Urbicidal action does not merely punish those striving against the lord. It also lets loose the Chosen People from a place to which they had had several ties, not all of them negative. Many have remarked on, and been confused by, the *Exodus* poet's ability to present occasionally the point of view of the doomed antagonists without either warning or further comment. In the passage above, we learn that 'the hands of the laughter-smiths' were fettered (43) and 'friends or relatives' (both expressed by *freond*) bereaved (45). Some editors, refusing to allow for a momentary shift of perspective, quickly emend *freond* to *feond*, 'enemy'. Laughter-smiths, possibly meaning 'entertainers',³² would belong to the same courtly culture as the hoards and city-guardians. *Freond* live close to one another. Additionally, kinship relations could be understood as constituting a *burh*; later, as the Israelites leave Egypt in ruins, the poet calls them a *mægburh*, literally 'a family-enclosure' or 'a city of kinspeople'.

Sympathetic expressions like 'laughter-smiths' and 'friends/relatives' when applied to Pharaoh's people do not only attempt to capture their feelings, but also to intimate how the 'guests' might have felt. Other parts of the poem, too, indicate that the *Exodus* poet is well aware of varying types of interactions that the Israelites might have had with the Egyptians. In line 144, for instance, the author tells us that the current Pharaoh had forgotten how his father obtained his treasure thanks to the Jews. Consequently, the poem would not find it inconceivable that the Chosen could feel sympathy for the doomed, if only for the mode of life that they still shared.

As the work moves towards its conclusion, more cities are promised to Moses's folk. God enables the break with Egypt through his attack on the enemy's offspring, settlements, and belongings, but he does not enjoin the Israelites to give up worldly joys altogether. They will have earthly fulfilment elsewhere, in the land of Canaan, where, as Moses announces after the Crossing, they will possess 'burh ond beagas, brade rice' [cities and rings, a broad kingdom] (557) and even 'beorselas beorna' [beer-halls of men] (564). In juxtaposition to this promise of financial and physical security, the fall of the Egyptians seems all the more painful. When the sea comes down on the enemy's army, no one from the host remains, not even a messenger to 'bodigean æfter burgum bealospella mæst, / hordwearda hryre, hæleða cwenum' [announce to the warrior's wives in the cities the greatest tidings of sorrow, the fall of hoard-guardians] (511–12). Further disintegration awaits the *byrig* deprived of their protectors: women who had presumably lost their children earlier now lose their husbands. Depending on one's point of view, the tone could be just as easily elegiac as triumphant. In either case, the message is expressed through manipulation of *byrig*. The poet mentions in the same breath the 'cities', 'hoard-guardians', and, a little less explicitly, the lineage. The imagery stays the same as in the previous scenes of urban destruction for the Egyptians and comfortable future flourishing for the Israelites.

Exodus also activates more spiritual though no less complicated readings of the *burh* image. The only city mentioned by name is Etham in the borderlands, around which the righteous troop made camp under Moses's command, marking the third of the five stations through which they passed (63). What the place signifies depends on whether one reads it in *malo* or in *bono*. Willem Helder summarises: 'Etham is a figure of the devil's fortress, but in a typological sense it becomes the city of the great King.'[33] The poet intertwines the spiritual and the secular, much as he does everything else. Etham's designation as a *burh* does not come from the Bible. Peter J. Lucas proposes that the Celtic phenomenon of border-area trading posts growing into towns might be behind this particular reference.[34] Thus, more fusion with the *byrig* at its centre may occur: the area outside of Egypt may hint at the lands beyond the limits of Anglo-Saxon England, those adjacent to it as well as those separated from it by land and sea.

Even more mysterious settlements appear in the desert landscape before the Israelites reach Etham. They move, as noted above, in a *mægburh* [family-enclosure], meaning that they remain in a type of a city after leaving behind the civilisation of the Egyptians. The *mægburh* comes upon more *byrig*. Moses leads his people through 'fæstena worn, / land ond leodgeard [MS leod weard][35] laðra manna, / enge anpaðas, uncuð gelad ...' [a number of fortresses, lands and people-enclosures [people protections] of hostile men, narrow paths, unknown roads ...] (56–8). Finally, they encounter the enigmatic *guðmyrce* [warlike border-dwellers]. Their identity seems unknown, like that of the African woman at the end of the poem, but it is clear that they are neither Israelites, nor Egyptians, nor Ethiopians,[36] who will appear later. For all that, they inhabit *mearchofu* [borderland courts] (61). The blending of natural and human-made, unfamiliar and familiar, elusive and contained, common to *spolia*, appears in these lines; the 'narrow paths' and 'unknown roads' could have their origin in natural formations as well as human endeavour.

The poet broadens the vision at this moment, as he does in many others, including the ending with the enigmatic African woman amidst plunder. But now, rather than move between the Egyptians and the Israelites, with momentary shifts of perspective, he introduces a third side. Although uninvolved in the central conflict, that side exhibits crucial marks of a recognisable civilisation shared by the doomed and the saved: warfare, protective architecture, and demarcation of frontiers and passageways. The first two elements produce *spolia* quite easily, while the second provides spaces for encounters between self and Other. The details such as the invocation of the *guðmyrce* may not have direct bearing on the narrative in the long run. I would nevertheless argue that they enrich it by intimating that other tales emerge at a particular juncture, other people and settlements, most of which the Old English *Exodus* cannot address.[37] Still, the invocation of the *lyfthelm* [air helmet] that covers the land of the 'warlike border-dwellers' flows smoothly into the prolonged depiction of *wederwolcen* [weather cloud] that shields and guides the Hebrews on their journey – an essential image for the poem.

When they go around the settlement of the border-dwellers in the desert, the Israelites completely avoid the land of the Ethiopians. (If the woman at the end of the poem is indeed Ethiopian, they must have included her in their community on some other occasion.) The group turns northwards because 'wiston him be suðan Sigelwara land, / forbærned burhhleoðu, brune leode / hatum heofoncolum' [they knew that the land of the Ethiopians was to the south of them, its *burh*-slopes burned and the people brown because of the hot heaven-coals] (69–71). Here we can observe the same poetic strategy that I liken to spoliation and exhibition of *spolia*, merging of people with treasure under a broad enclosure. At this moment we have an even more subtle fusion, on the level of a single compound, which intertwines a natural protection with an architectural one. *Burh* appears in *burhhleoðu* instead of *beorh* [hill, mountain]. Lucas remarks that 'A[nglo-]S[axon] scribes sometimes associated or confused *beorh*(-) and *burh*(-)' and gives examples from other texts. The same compound, he continues, occurs in line 449, spelled more conventionally as *beorhhliðu* in reference to the walls of water from the Red Sea that crash on the enemy troops.[38]

James H. Wilson identifies the pun *burh*/*beorh* in line 132, when the Israelites are shown spreading over *beorgum* as they strike a camp by the Red Sea; he sees the two images of 'hill' and 'fortified place' strengthening 'the notions of endurance and security', often for ironic effect.[39] Soon enough, having seen the Pharaoh's army approach, the exiles huddle 'æfter beorgum in blacum reafum, / wean on wenum' [on hills, dressed in black, expecting sorrow] (212–13). If *beorh* recalls *burh*, revealing Moses's people's exposure to the elements, the robes of mourning stand in contrast to the bright treasure passing over to the Israelites from the dead Egyptians at the end, including *godweb* [fine weavings] (588). By drawing attention to the association between *burh* and *beorh*, the poet yokes together the powers of human and divine artifice. He indirectly poses the question of what it would be like to live on a *beorh* as if in a *burh*, for mountains, like cities, can be exposed to the elements. The *Sigelware* appear not as exotic monsters, but another *burh*-dwelling *leod* [people], the noun that occurs nine other times in *Exodus*, seven times designating the Israelites and twice the Egyptians.

Though we cannot know what kinds of treasure the *Sigelware* keep in their *burhhleoðu* [mountain- or city-slopes] from the poem's casual reference to them, their name reflects their possessions. J. R. R. Tolkien explains the first component, *sigel*, in this way:

> On one hand we have a word *sigel* used in runes and verse with the sense 'sun'. On the other we have *(a) sigel*, a round jewel or golden ornament, possibly neuter and distinct from *(b) sigel (sigele)*, a necklace, and probably *(c) sig(e)le* of similar sense, associated in the passage where it is best evidenced with *beag* [ring] ...[40]

For the words under (b) and (c) he claims origin, 'or at least their principal origin', in Latin *sigillum*, plural *sigilla*, 'a small image or figure, the impress of a stamp or seal'.[41] The Anglo-Saxon term for Ethiopians reflects the climactic and mineralogical condition of their land: the sun's intense heat turns them dark, while the learned tradition of Isidore and its more popular offshoots like the Old English *Wonders of the East* associate them with various precious stones.[42] Their burnished skins recall a specific quality of forged metal, as we see the *brun* [brown or gleaming] sword in *Beowulf* or 'brune helmas' [burnished helmets] in *Judith*.[43] The different enclosure-people-valuables compilations, those elusive collections of *spolia* and *spolia*-like objects, that move rapidly across the Old English *Exodus* are in contrast as much as in parallel with one another. Being dark people in the wilderness, the Ethiopians could easily be relegated to the status of the gentiles awaiting the baptismal destruction of the devil to join the Church;[44] according to such interpretations, the Israelites for all their unaware anticipation of Christianity are in a similar position, as are all unbaptised peoples. But the allegorical readings too often elide specificity of images or suppress their strangeness. The Ethiopians differ from the *gyðmyrce* since they are better known and described more clearly. Furthermore, unlike the mysterious border-dwellers and the Israelites, they can survive in a hostile, sun-scorched landscape without special provisions like the sheltering cloud.

One final, inimitable city that appears in *Exodus* results from divine action. During the scene of the parting of the Red Sea by Moses, the Israelites witness an unprecedented and never-again-repeated instance of urban construction. It is soon followed by devastation, when the Egyptians attempt to pursue them across the passageway. Moses speaks:

> Hwæt, ge nu eagum to on lociað,
> folca leofost, færwundra sum,
> hu[45] ic sylfa sloh and þeos swiðre hand
> grene tacne garsecges deop.
> Yð up færeð, ofstum wyrceð
> wæter on wealfæsten. Wegas syndon dryge,
> haswe herestræta, holm gerymed,
> ealde staðolas, þa ic ær ne gefrægn
> ofer middangeard men geferan,
> fage feldas, þa forð heonon
> in ece tid yðe þeccað. (278–88)
>
> [Behold, the dearest of peoples, you are now witnessing with your own eyes a certain awe-inspiring wonder, how I myself struck the ocean's deep with a green token and this right hand. The wave is rising up, the water rapidly making a wall-fortification. The pathways are dry, the grey marching roads, the opened sea, the ancient foundation which I have never heard men step on anywhere on earth, the bright/variegated fields which waves will cover from now on into eternity.]

Moses tames the hostile landscape with God's help, even incites it to turn into a more human habitation, to become an artist itself. The Lord's might transfers to his prophet, then to the elements: after being struck with Moses's powerful rod, the water rushes to create ramparts. Whereas earlier we saw many fortifications in the wasteland, 'fæstena worn' (56), by which the leader led his tribe, now we are asked to imagine the sea becoming an urbanised desert.

Architecture of the past and the future 75

The paths around the previous *byrig* were unknown and narrow, but the newly revealed grey marching ways appear safe and broad. The phrase describing them, *herestræta*, suggests roads paved with stones, like Roman roads in Britain. However, they are *hasu* coloured, a word that ranges from 'pale-grey brown' over 'grey-red' to 'yellow/ yellow orange'.[46] The paths clearly show an overlap between the artificial and the natural, since the poet calls them 'fage feldas' [bright/variegated fields] (287). Elsewhere in the Old English poetry, *fag/fah*, 'particoloured ... stained ... shining', an Anglo-Saxon adjective for treasure par excellence, refers to horses, dragons, tessellated floors and pavements, something stained by blood and sins, and weapons (*DOE*). Apart from its unplumbed riches, the city-in-the-sea resembles the previous instantiations of *byrig* because it does not remain visible for long. The dried-up greyish ancient sea-bottom is allowed to sparkle for a short while before the waves cover it for eternity, locking it in place. The many fortresses of the unknown tribes and the burned slopes of the Ethiopians appear, disappear, and the readers move on, along with the Israelites. However, the images are not lost forever: a memory of them remains to inform and enrich the encounters with similar phenomena in the text, enabling parallels to be drawn. With the Red Sea City so far we have the elusive *burh* with its foundations, ramparts, and passageways functioning as valuable artefacts at the intersection of the elements (the sea, the earth, and the air).

People figured as treasure are also present in the scene. Most literally, there are the followers of Moses. Additionally, the Israelites about to cross the Red Sea contain in them multitudes, all the humankind to come, including Jesus himself. When the crossing begins, the poet of *Exodus* launches into the so-called patriarchal digression, the first part of which describes Noah transporting the 'maðmhorda mæst' [the greatest of treasure-hoards] across the waves (368). Enclosed in the 'bearm scipes' [the bosom of the ship][47] are fathers and mothers beyond count, along with every kind of a seed, that is, whatever is needed to preserve humankind and the flora and fauna of the earth (375). When the sea destroys the doomed in the main, exodus frame (as it also does in the story of Noah), we learn that 'randbyrig wæron rofene' [shield-protectors were shattered] (464) and 'wigbord scinon. / Heah ofer hæleðum, holmweall astah...' [battle-bucklers shone, high above the warriors, the sea-wall rose...] (467–8). After shielding the Israelites with its ramparts, the sea-turned-warrior employs the same architectural elements to deprive the enemy of their shields. The formerly protective enclosure, snatched from the ocean, comes down on the Egyptians, cutting them off from their families and possessions. In this way, the symbolically powerful demolition of *byrig* happens twice.

The *byrig* in the poem are each distinct from the other: the destroyed city of the enemy; the kinship enclosure of the Israelites; the mountain-city; the barely mentioned forts of hostile tribes which Moses and company manage to avoid; the City of God hovering almost imperceptibly over the Chosen; the wave-fortifications that protect the intricately ornamented paths when the Israelites pass but crash down on the Egyptians. They are associated with financial and geneaological proliferation or ruin, with the very continuation of life: the hoard-guardians who are the *burh*-guardians; the wealth which resides in those travelling with Noah and Moses; the potential for abundance from Ethiopia; the foe's armour floating on the surface. Throughout his work, the poet of the Old English *Exodus* invites us to seek out and meditate on the many guises of *byrig*, the wonders he has created to recall 'handweorc Godes' [God's handiwork] (493).

A shape-shifting pillar

The same *spolia*-like dynamic is at work in a smaller but equally multifold image that could be taken as paradigmatic for the poem, even as a figure for it. When the Israelites travel through the desert, a peculiar formation emerges to protect them against the sun's deadly rays. While it has roots in the Bible, it receives extraordinary elaboration in the Old English *Exodus*:

> Þær halig God
> wið færbryne   folc gescylde,
> bælce oferbrædde byrnendne heofon,
> halgan nette hatwendne lyft.
> Hæfde wederwolcen widum fæðmum
> eorðan ond uprodor efne gedæled,
> lædde leodwerod, ligfyr adranc,
> hate heofontorht. Hæleð wafedon,
> drihta gedrymost. Dægsceades hleo
> wand ofer wolcnum; hæfde witig God
> sunnan siðfæt segle ofertolden,
> swa þa mæstrapas men ne cuðon,
> ne ða seglrode geseon meahton,
> eorðbuende ealle cræfte,
> hu afæstnod wæs feldhusa mæst,

Architecture of the past and the future

siððan He mid wuldre geweorðode
þeodenholde. Þa wæs þridda wic
folce to frofre. Fyrd eall geseah
hu þær hlifedon halige seglas,
lyftwundor leoht; leode ongeton,
dugoð Israhela, þæt þær Drihten cwom
weroda Drihten, wicstæl metan.
Him beforan foran fyr and wolcen
in beorhtrodor, beamas twegen,
þara æghwæðer efngedælde
heahþegnunga Haliges Gastes,
deormodra sið dagum and nihtum. (71–97)
[There holy God shielded the people against the terrible heat; he covered the burning heaven with a board, the hot sky with a holy net. The storm-cloud had evenly divided earth and heaven with its enfolding reaches; it led the host of people; the fire, sky-bright with heat, was drowned. Heroes looked out in astonishment, most gleeful of troops. The protection of the sun-shield went over the clouds. Wise God had stretched the sail over the pathway of the sun, so that the men did not know the mast-ropes, nor could the earth-dwellers see the sail-yard, for all their skills, how the greatest of tents was set up, when he honoured with his glory those steadfast to their lord. Then the third camp was made, a consolation to the people. The whole army saw how the holy sails rose high above, light/bright air-wonders. The men, the weathered Israelites fighters, recognised that the lord had come there, the lord of the hosts, to mark off their camping ground. Before them went fire and cloud in the bright sky, the two beams, each of which was in high service of the holy ghost, evenly divided the journey of the noble-minded heroes by day and night.]

The shape-shifting pillar continues and modifies the larger dynamic of presenting people in terms of treasure, while framing both humans and valuable objects within an elusive enclosure. At first, 'the greatest of tents' seems opposed to *byrig*. Not only does it not have the same grounding as a citadel (its wings/sails flutter in the air), but it is also frequently presented as a single – albeit constantly changing – object, a fragment from a larger structure rather than the structure itself. Furthermore, the pillar's inscrutability stands out immediately. The 'storm cloud' forcefully embodies duality more than Etham with its potential double resonance as the City of God and the dwelling-place of the devil. Whereas before, the poet leads us, like his hero Moses, along past the ramparts of the mysterious desert tribes, here he makes us dwell on the enigma of the pillar by spinning out a lengthy description. The Israelites cannot understand how 'the greatest of tents was set up', how its constituent parts add up, largely because the 'ship' comes from the future in which they unknowingly participate. It is a *spolium* from the Christian time: the pillar with its accessories can signify the body of Christ in the tomb and resurrected,[48] the complementary meanings of the two-part Scriptures,[49] the Ship of the Church foretold by Noah's Ark, as well as the poem itself.[50]

Still, we can observe that the metamorphosing artefact shares some traits with the peculiar *byrig* created by the *Exodus* poet. First, it divides the space to protect the people; it contains them, projecting, from above, an extension onto the third camp of the Israelites. The pillar's designation as a 'feldhusa mæst' [the greatest of tents] fuses the natural, *feld* [field], and the human-made, *hus* [house], as does the term *burhhleoðu*. Like the temporary city in the Red Sea (and the African woman at the end), the *wederwolcen* [storm-cloud] appears at the intersection of the elements, drawing its strength from their energy. It glides on the invisible sea, flutters in the air, and comes down before the perplexed and thankful voyagers in two forms as cloud (itself a combination of water and air) and fire. In its many transformations the pillar follows the actions of the *byrig*. Despite its shape-shifting, the object remains recognisably protective and generative, at least for the Chosen.

We can turn to Gaston Bachelard for clues on how a vigorous metamorphosis of fragmentary images relates to the narrative of descent and liberation. After using our dynamic imagination to 'develop a feeling for aerial phenomena', we will perceive 'a real *verticality*'. In Bachelard's terms, this is 'no empty metaphor [but] a principle of order, a law governing filiation, a scale along which someone can experience the different degrees of a special sensibility'. Within that imagination, clouds occupy a special place, because their contemplation makes us face 'a world where there are just as many forms as there are motions. Motion produces form, forms are in motion, and motion constantly deforms them.'[51] If horizontality betokens progression (the move from one land to another) and change (the prone body of the vanquished or the flattened walls of the sea-city), then verticality reveals a central organising principle embodied in the pillar that, regardless of its transformations, holds the world together. It brings God's presence down to the earth, leading from the children of Israel up to Jesus, their descendant.

Seen less abstractly, the burning upright column recalls Moses's green rod with which he hits the Red Sea to begin God's temporary urbanising project (281), along with other rods scattered through the text.[52] Still, before we embark on an enthusiastic journey with the phallus for our guide, we should remember that the 'sail-yard' is at other times called a net, a board, and a sail. They represent nurturing or captivating surfaces that might recall the feminine principle, for example, the Virgin Mary, who enfolds the Word after being filled with the Holy Ghost, the divine shaper served by the pillars of fire and cloud in *Exodus*. Just as the invocation of the border-dwellers and Ethiopians prepares the stage for the African woman's appearance, so, too, do the complexly gendered resonances of the pillar anticipate the woman in the background of the epic, at once in the heart of the poem's affairs, as a companion to the man, and remote from it, as a figure that the text can only partially illuminate.

In any case, the metamorphosing pillar allows for a staggering number of interpretations. One only needs to look at the meticulously assembled Table 6 in Miranda Wilcox's essay on 'the cloud-tent-ship conceit' in *Exodus* to feel a sense of wonder, even awe, at the potential of multiplicity embodied by the object. To illustrate the '[i]ntegrated metaphorical network' at play in the passage, Wilcox lists biblical passages and characters along with less explicitly religious concepts grounded in the everyday of Anglo-Saxons, a sea-faring people ('deck', '[net]-like pattern', 'canvas cloth').[53] The table takes over more than half a page, and its sheer size produces something akin to the power of *wrætlic*, as recently analysed by Peter Ramey and Irina Dumitrescu, the combined sense of materiality, impressiveness, creativity, craft, and terror.[54] *Wrætlic* and riddlic go hand in hand. The African woman, the enclosure, and the shape-shifting pillar, for all their ontological difference, could act as clues to a macro-riddle with multiple solutions (*spolia*, the Church, a site for gathering of peoples). The signature blending of the opposites in the riddles, which creates their essential disorientation-by-paradox, provides a productive lens for other poetry. However, unlike the biblical verse, the riddles do not consistently have the comfort or containment of an ultimate religious explanation for a Christian reader.

But these greater associations are not available to the characters caught in the narrative. Nevertheless, not knowing each intricate detail of the artefact's make-up or its typological resonances does not pose a problem for the Israelites. They can grasp the ultimate meaning of the phenomenon seemingly without much difficulty: 'leode ongeton, / dugoð Israhela, þæt þær Drihten cwom / wereda Drihten, wicsteal metan' [The men, the weathered Israelite fighters, recognised that the lord had come there, the lord of the hosts, to mark off their camping ground] (90–2). The utmost simplicity breaks through after singularity expressed through enigmatic imagery and *hapax legomena* (such as *færbryne* [terrible heat]; *bælc* [board]; *wederwolcen* [storm-cloud]). Not only is the same noun for the lord repeated twice, contrary to the usual practice in Anglo-Saxon poetry,[55] but it has the attribute *wereda* [of hosts] the second time, *werod* being one of the most frequently used words in *Exodus*.[56] If the *byrig* in the desert show ultimate commonality of civilisation among different groups of people, this transparent vocabulary upholds the same way of life.

Potential skaldic effects in the description of the *beam* might make early medieval audiences reflect on the cultural, especially aesthetic, values they share with those in their midst and on the other side of the North Sea. As the African woman indicates that the Israelites did not only pass by strange settlements but also interacted with the people from them, this particular *objet d'art* shows how far Scandinavians could reach into the Anglo-Saxon imagination. In one of her attempts to diagnose the 'skaldic tooth' of the audience of *Exodus*, Roberta Frank has written of the shape-shifting pillar, demonstrating that many of the most puzzling words used to describe the artefact (the tent, net, sail, board, and cloud) mean 'shield' in 'the skalds' metalanguage'. According to Frank, such compatibility in poetic devices bears witness 'to the possibility of interchange between pagans and Christians in the Germanic North'.[57]

At the heart of that interchange is a *spolium* or a *spolium*-like object, a concrete fragment that cuts through the conventional boundaries. The pagan Danes who settled in the Derbyshire region of England delighted in 'a prolific display of stone monuments', including crosses, a phenomenon that certainly 'arose from the context of two cultures in contact'.[58] Keeping in mind the readings that interpret the *beam* as the cross, we could imagine our 'storm-cloud' to be one such sculpture set in motion. The *Exodus* poet, by focusing his attention on such enigmatic yet rich images as an African woman and a single, resplendent pillar, beside a series of shifting cities, demonstrates his awareness that an artefact is that which passes between various peoples, surviving for the ages because it shapes the peoples through whose hands it passes, and by whom it is, in turn, shaped.

Notes

1. Parts of this chapter appeared, in different form, in Denis Ferhatović, 'Burh & Beam, Burning Bright: A Study in the Poetic Imagination of the Old English Exodus', *Neophilologus*, 94:3 (2010), 509–22.
2. R. M. Liuzza (trans.), *Exodus*, in Joseph Black et al. (eds), *The Broadview Anthology of British Literature*, vol. 1 (Peterborough, ON: Broadview, 2006), 101–9, at 101. Daniel G. Calder and Stanley Greenfield, *A New Critical History of Old English Literature* (New York: New York University Press, 1986), p. 212. The text's difference has been recognised from an early time. Levin Schücking even speculated that *Exodus* is the only remaining trace of a lost poetic school. Levin L. Schücking, *Untersuchungen zur Bedeutungslehre der angelsächsischen Dichtersprache* (Heidelberg: Carl Winters, 1915), 16–17.
3. I take these convenient terms from Phyllis Portnoy, 'Ring Composition and the Digressions of *Exodus*: The "Legacy" of the "Remnant"', *English Studies*, 4 (2001), 298–307.
4. For more on this point, see Denis Ferhatović, '"Life's Interpreter for the New Millennium": On Three Poetic Translations of the Old English Exodus', *Forum for Modern Language Studies*, 50 (2014), 233–44, at 233.
5. For a comprehensive account of spiritual readings, see Malcolm Godden, 'Biblical Literature: The Old Testament', in Malcolm Godden and Michael Lapidge (eds), *Cambridge Companion to Old English Literature*, 2nd edn (Cambridge: Cambridge University Press, 2013), pp. 214–34.
6. T. A. Shippey, *Old English Verse* (London: Hutchinson University Library, 1973), pp. 154.
7. Howe, *Migration and Mythmaking*, p. 107.
8. Andrew Scheil, *The Footsteps of Israel: Understanding Jews in Anglo-Saxon England* (Ann Arbor: University of Michigan Press, 2004), p. 334. For more on this dynamic, especially in relation to imagined architecture, see Kathy Lavezzo's chapter 'Sepulchral Jews and Stony Christians: Supersession in Bede and Cynewulf', in her book *The Accommodated Jew: English Anti-Semitism from Bede to Milton* (Ithaca: Cornell University Press, 2016), pp. 28–63. Lavezzo argues that in Cynewulf's *Elene*, Constantine's mother Helena's intense relationship with Judas reveals 'the contradictory nature of supersession as an ideology that embraces the materiality it claims to trump and, conversely, proves anxious over the spirituality it purports to embrace' (p. 57).
9. See John Hermann, *Allegories of War: Language and Violence in Old English Poetry* (Ann Arbor: University of Michigan Press, 1989), p. 78; and Ann Savage, 'The Old English *Exodus* and the Colonization

of the Promised Land', in Wendy Scase et al. (eds), *New Medieval Literatures*, 4 (Oxford: Oxford University Press, 2001), 39–60.
10 Howie, *Claustrophilia: The Erotics of Enclosure in Medieval Literature* (New York: Palgrave, 2007), p. 33.
11 I cite Lucas's edition. Peter J. Lucas (ed.), *Exodus*, rev. edn (Exeter: University of Exeter Press, 1994). Other editions, like Krapp's, emend 'Afrisc meowle' to 'Afrisc neowle', intending the phrase to mean 'prostrate Egyptian'. *The Junius Manuscript*, ASPR 1 (New York: Columbia University Press, 1931). Even without the emendation, the African woman's state is questioned; for example, Sarah Novacich reads her as dead, a female body as a site of masculine textual readings. Sarah Novacich, 'The Old English *Exodus* and the Read Sea', *Exemplaria*, 23 (2011), 50–66, at 64.
12 On the same pun in Riddle 20, see Chapter 1.
13 Fred C. Robinson, 'Notes on the Old English *Exodus*', *Anglia*, 80 (1968), 373–4.
14 Mary B. Campbell, *The Witness and the Other World: Exotic European Travel Writing, 400–1600* (Ithaca: Cornell University Press, 1988), p. 3.
15 *Old English Corpus*, s. v. *Africa* and *afrisc*.
16 Some critics have already drawn this parallel. See, for instance, Robinson, 'Notes on the Old English *Exodus*', p. 378.
17 Patricia Ingham, 'From Kinship to Kingship: Mourning, Gender, and Anglo-Saxon Community', in Jennifer C. Vaugh (ed.), *Grief and Gender: 700–1700* (New York: Palgrave, 2003), pp. 18–31, at 21. The distance seems considerable if we read *wealh* as Welsh, for Wealhtheow would then have moved to Denmark for Hrothgar. For a slightly different, though admittedly tentative, etymologising of Wealhtheow as 'Cnut's Norman captive', see Helen Damico, *Beowulf and the Grendel-Kin: Politics and Poetry in Eleventh-Century England* (Morgantown: West Virginia University Press, 2015), pp. 226–7.
18 Thomas D. Hill, 'Wealhtheow as a Foreign Slave: Some Continental Analogues', *Philological Quarterly*, 69 (1990), 106–12, at 108.
19 Stacy Klein, *Ruling Women: Queenship and Gender in Anglo-Saxon Literature* (Notre Dame Press, 2006), p. 115.
20 Robinson, 'Notes on the Old English *Exodus*' (Zipporah); Ellen E. Martin, 'Allegory and the African Woman in the Old English *Exodus*', *Journal of English and Germanic Philology*, 81 (1982), 1–15, esp. 10–15 (Miriam).
21 The second part of both compounds is *laf*, also mentioned in my Introduction and Chapter 1.
22 John F. Vickrey writes suggestively that '[i]t is reasonable … to ask whether *godweb*, or perhaps both *gold* and *godweb*, along with *Iosepes gestreon*, might allude to Joseph's renowned garment and acquisition, his coat of many colors'. '"Exodus" and the Robe of Joseph', *Studies in Philology*, 86 (1989), 1–17, at 13.

23 Steven F. Kruger writes that, in addition to providing triumphalist irony, '... the poem's final lines also function more sympathetically, expressing a certain elegiac sadness'. 'The poet', he continues, 'suggests, for the last time, the common humanity of Israelites and Egyptians, and, in so doing, calls to mind the Egyptians' human potential for good.' 'Oppositions and Their Opposition in the Old English *Exodus*', *Neophilologus*, 78 (1994), 165–70, at 169.

24 Barrie Cox, 'The Pattern of Old English *burh* in Early Lindsey', *Anglo-Saxon England*, 23 (1994), 35–58, at 35. Cox adds that in 'post-Conquest names' the word denotes 'a castle or ... market town'.

25 Grenville Astill, 'Community, Identity and the Later Anglo-Saxon Town: The Case of Southern England', in Wendy Davies et al. (eds), *People and Space in the Middle Ages, 300–1300* (Turnhout: Brepols, 2006), pp. 233–54, at 235.

26 Astill, 'Community, Identity and the Later Anglo-Saxon Town', p. 248.

27 In her article on 'the idea-complex' of the hall in Old English poetry, also sometimes called *burh*, Kathryn Hume demonstrates 'an impressively divergent array of attitudes' towards the image of the hall, and warns the critics not to reduce this variety to 'simple formulas of consistent outlook and interpretation'. Kathryn Hume, 'The Concept of the Hall', *Anglo-Saxon England*, 3 (1974), 63–74, at 74.

28 I restore the manuscript reading. Lucas emends to *gedrecced*.

29 I have changed Lucas's *feond* back to the manuscript reading *freond*. I present my rationale below.

30 Joseph K. Vickrey, '"Exodus" and the Tenth Plague', *Archiv für das Studium der neueren Sprachen und Literaturen*, 210 (1973), 41–52, at 44.

31 Pamela Karimi and Nasser Rabbat, 'The Demise and Afterlife of Artifacts', *Aggregate*, http://we-aggregate.org/piece/the-demise-and-afterlife-of-artifacts, accessed 18 December 2016.

32 For more on 'laughter-smith' and other similar expressions, see E. G. Stanley, 'Wonder-Smiths and Others: *Smið* Compounds in Old English Poetry – With an Excursus on *Hleahtor*', *Neophilologus*, 101 (2017), 277–304.

33 Willem Helder, 'Etham and the Ethiopians in the Old English *Exodus*', *Annuale Mediævale*, 16 (1975), 5–24, at 8. Helder uses Augustine's commentary on Psalm 34 to reach this conclusion.

34 Lucas (ed.), *Exodus*, p. 84.

35 *Leodgeard*, 'country, lit., people-enclosure' is a common emendation (Grein's suggestion followed by Irving and Lucas) of *leod weard*.

36 Irving writes, 'It is impossible to tell whether the poet had a specific tribe in mind ... there is no indication that the Guðmyrce are Negroes; they are certainly not the Ethiopians mentioned later and probably not the Nubians favored by Gollancz ...' (Edward B. Irving, Jr (ed.), *The Old English* Exodus (New Haven: Yale University Press, 1953), p. 71).

37 Brian Green claims that 'the multiple images of foreign lands, cities, and roads (56a–62b) serve to define Israelites as a people different from all other peoples of the world'. Brian Green, 'The Mode and Meaning of the Old English "Exodus"', *English Studies in Africa*, 24 (1981), 73–82, at 75. I prefer to see the urban multiplication in the landscape as a result of an intricate interplay of similarity and difference at work in the poem.
38 Lucas (ed.), *Exodus*, n. 70a, p. 87.
39 James H. Wilson, *Christian Theology and Old English Poetry* (The Hague: Mouton, 1974), p. 132.
40 J. R. R. Tolkien, '*Sigelwara land*', *Medium Ævum*, 3.2 (1934), 95–111, at 104.
41 Ibid., p. 102.
42 Ibid., p. 106.
43 See *brun* 3 in the *DOE*.
44 Helder, 'Etham and the Ethiopians', pp. 11–13.
45 I restore the manuscript reading. Lucas emends to *nu*.
46 C. P. Biggam, *Grey in Old English: An Interdisciplinary Semantic Study* (London: Runetree Press, 1998), pp. 273–4, 291–3.
47 For more on bosoms and treasure, see my discussion of Riddle 14 in Chapter 1.
48 James W. Bright, 'The Relation of the Cædmonian Exodus to the Liturgy', *Modern Language Notes*, 27 (1912), 97–103, at 98.
49 Martin, 'Allegory and the African Woman', p. 6.
50 The classical literary analogy of 'ship: pilot/poem: poet' persists into the Middle Ages and beyond. This trope begins with Virgil and Horace, and continues with Anglo-Saxon authors writing in Latin. Aldhelm speaks of an unpractised poet creating his work as a sailor in a 'leaky boat', while Alcuin refers to the pitfalls of writing as 'sea-monsters'. Ernst Robert Curtius, *European Literature and the Latin Middle Ages*, trans. Willard R. Trask (Princeton: Princeton University Press, 1953), p. 129.
51 The italics are Bachelard's. Gaston Bachelard, *Air and Dreams: An Essay on the Imagination of Movement*, trans. Edith R. Farrell and C. Frederick Farrell (Dallas: The Dallas Institute of Humanities and Culture, 1988), pp. 10, 194.
52 For more on the rods, see Thomas D. Hill, 'The *virga* of Moses and the Old English *Exodus*', in John D. Niles (ed.), *Old English Literature in Context: Ten Essays* (Cambridge: D. S. Brewer, 1980), pp. 57–65; and Thomas N. Hall, 'The Cross as Green Tree in the *Vindicta Salvatoris* and the Green Rod of Moses in *Exodus*', *English Studies*, 24 (1991), 297–307.
53 Miranda Wilcox, 'Creating the Cloud-Tent-Ship Conceit in *Exodus*', *Anglo-Saxon England*, 40 (2011), 103–50, at 149.

54 Ramey, 'The Riddle of Beauty', pp. 477–81; Dumitrescu, *The Experience of Education*, p. 128.
55 Of course, a lack of variation is not unprecedented in Old English verse. Fred C. Robinson observes that 'something deep in the Anglo-Saxon tradition seems to relish both the metaphorical statement and the clarity which metaphor sometimes lack'. Fred C. Robinson, 'Two Aspects of Variation', in Daniel G. Calder (ed.), *Old English Poetry: Essays on Style* (Berkeley: University of California Press, 1979), pp. 127–45, at 137.
56 Lucas counts twenty-one instances as a simplex and one occurrence in a compound (Lucas (ed.), *Exodus*, p. 51).
57 Roberta Frank, 'What Kind of Poetry is *Exodus?*', in Daniel G. Calder and T. Craig Christy (eds), *Germania: Comparative Studies in the Old Germanic Languages and Literatures* (Cambridge: D. S. Brewer, 1988), pp. 191–205, at 194–5 (metalanguage), 201 (interchange).
58 Phil Sidebottom, 'Viking Age Stone Monuments and Social Identity in Derbyshire', in Dawn M. Hadley and Julian D. Richards (eds), *Cultures in Contact: Scandinavian Settlement in England in the Ninth and Tenth Centuries* (Turnhout: Brepols, 2000), pp. 213–35, at 213.

3
Animated, animating: Bringing stone, flesh, and text to life in *Andreas*[1]

Introduction: An apocryphal epic's many frames

As a story, the Old English *Andreas* appears extremely appealing. God sends the apostle Andrew to the island of Mermedonia to release Matthew who has been imprisoned by savage locals to be raised for food. The hero, protesting at first about the dangers of the journey, not the least being the culture shock,[2] boards the ship which, unbeknownst to him, has Christ at its helm. Jesus in sailor disguise questions Andrew on points of religion, especially his interaction with the Messiah himself. Soon the protagonist reaches the land of the cannibals, liberates Matthew and many others beside him, but shortly thereafter becomes the victim of the Mermedonians, who, goaded on by the devil, torment him in the cruellest ways. With the help of God, Andrew makes a pillar in his gaol cell split and issue forth a flood, punishing but also converting the aggressive heathens. The poem ends after the conversion has taken root, with the Church firmly established; only then can Andrew leave.

While the surviving textual context does help in reading *Andreas*, it also presents us with some tantalising problems. Its most immediate setting, the manuscript in which it exclusively survives, Vercelli, Biblioteca Capitolare CXVII, dating from the tenth century, contains religiously themed works, both in prose and verse. There are poems, two of them signed in runes by Cynewulf: *The Fates of the Apostles*, which lists their exemplary deaths, and *Elene*, an account of Constantine's mother Helen's finding of the True Cross. Others, like *Andreas*, are anonymous: the famed *The Dream of the Rood*, a vivid contemplation of the True Cross; *Soul and Body*; and a fragment of a homiletic poem. Prose homilies, twenty-three in number, that appear to provide 'penitential meditation upon themes familiar to A[nglo-]S[axon] spirituality', complete the rest of the codex.[3] In terms of its subject matter most generally, the poem fits well with the manuscript, but stylistically it stands out from the rest.

The sources that the *Andreas* poet might have consulted constitute another frame of reference for the poem. Scholars have singled out two other treatments of the apocryphal legend, one in Greek, another in Latin. The first, *Praxeis Andreou kai Matheian eis ten Polin ton Anthropophagon* (*Acts of Andrew and Matthew in the City of the Cannibals*) survives in a complete version in a manuscript from the ninth or tenth century, but it 'doubtless represent[s] an earlier redaction'.[4] How direct an influence it could have exerted on *Andreas* depends on one's assumptions about the linguistic abilities of the Anglo-Saxons. But even scholars who, like Robert Boenig, allow for a considerable knowledge of Greek in certain circles in early medieval England, agree that the Old English poet probably worked from a Latin text.[5] Hence, a now-lost version in that language must have been available, whose handling of the legend significantly followed *Praxeis*.[6] The *Recensio Casanatensis*, a complete Latin rendition of Andrew's adventures in Mermedonia, is extant in a manuscript two centuries after Vercelli.[7] Brooks briefly describes that version: '[t]he text of C, which is written in a most barbarous Latin, follows P in its main details, but there are differences which prove that C is not a direct translation of any extant texts of P'. Ultimately, no surviving version can be claimed as an immediate source for *Andreas*.[8] While one cannot prove that either *Praxeis* or *Casanatensis* was available to the author of *Andreas*, a comparison of their different treatment of a particular passage often yields valuable insight.

Many details in *Andreas*, from similar or identical compounds and phrases to entire scenes not attested in either of the two non-English versions occur also in other, less explicitly religious, Old English poems, most notably *Beowulf*, another traditional frame through which to observe *Andreas*. Beginning with A. Fritzsche in the late nineteenth century, scholars have debated the extent to which our poet is indebted to the creator of the famed Geat. Detecting influence becomes more difficult if one takes into account the conventionality of much Anglo-Saxon poetic expression. Still, certain linguistic units occur only in the two poems. I will cite only two examples here for the sake of illustration.[9] *Heah ond horngeap* [high and wide-gabled] occurs only in *Andreas* to describe the temple in Jerusalem (668) and in *Beowulf* in reference to Heorot (82). The flood-stricken cannibals are faced with a *meoduscerwen* [sharing out of mead] (1526); the Danes experience an *ealuscerwen* [sharing out (or: depriving) of ale] while listening to the noise of Beowulf's struggle with Grendel (769). Some critics seem convinced by the evidence of these echoes that the *Andreas* poet 'heavily plundered' parts of the other author's narrative, and that, consequently, reading of the former makes one feel 'haunted' by the latter.[10] Others find no reason to study *Andreas* 'as if it were a deliberate and feeble imitation of *Beowulf* (which it is not)'.[11] Reading the adventures of St Andrew in Mermedonia with one eye always on trans-Scandinavian heroic exploits might work to the detriment of the former work. Daniel G. Calder lists a sampling of rather unflattering adjectives that well-known Anglo-Saxonists have applied to our author and his text in the past: 'light-weight ... ludicrous'; 'a poetical dunderhead'; 'ludicrous', 'clumsy', 'incongruous'; 'risible'.[12] Other critics, like Calder himself, have defended them, especially in 'the past few decades'.[13] Aaron Hostetter says that *Andreas* belongs to 'a self-conscious avant-garde that confronts and consumes its past selves' and is 'a generic hybrid that has always rested uneasily in the Anglo-Saxon canon'.[14] Irina Dumitrescu finds citation, including of *Beowulf*, in rather unexpected settings, to be an integral component of the *Andreas*-author's sophisticated pedagogical programme.[15]

The fourth textual frame, more general than *Praxeis* or *Beowulf*, comes from Old English generic conventions, but here, too, complications arise. To which genre does *Andreas* belong? Most critics acknowledge its pronounced epic elements, but classify it as a saint's life. Fabienne L. Michelet, for example, divides the Old English saints' lives into two categories, the *passio*, in which the hero or heroine is martyred for the cause of faith, and the *vita*, where the protagonist 'accomplishes a real or a metaphorical martyrdom', with *Andreas* belonging to the former.[16] Yet the poem does not fit easily into either classification. Michael Alexander voices his agreement with Tom Shippey that the heroic handling and the exotic setting of the narrative overwhelm its hagiographic content.[17] Ivan Herbison finds that the author does not quite succeed at the task of translating the essentially romantic hero of the *Praxeis*, 'the figure of Andrew as the developing apostle', into the unchanging protagonist from a different genre, 'the idealised *imago Christi* of Christian hagiography'.[18] After noting the poet's 'tonal and generic experimentation', Hostetter opts for the designation 'hagiographic romance', claiming that *Andreas* is a forerunner of twelfth-century romances (such as Benoît de Saint-Maure's *Romance of Troy* and Marie de France's *Lais*) because of its narrative twists and turns.[19] Whatever expectations we derive from the context of the manuscript, from the two

Animated, animating

potential non-English sources, from *Beowulf*, or from genre analyses, the poem is bound to make us reassess and complicate them.

The startling visuality of *Andreas*

In this chapter, I present one more frame for seeing the Old English verse account of the adventures of St Andrew among the cannibals: that of the plastic arts, more specifically, of the stone artefacts that occur at particularly charged points of the narrative, the enclosure in which they do and do not fit, and of the stranger who moves among the objects. After a brief discussion of a particular type of critical response, I will turn to two distinct physical objects: the angel-sculpture miraculously animated by Jesus in a temple (as reported by the hero), and the marble pillar in Andrew's gaol cell from which the saint elicits a destructive yet cleansing flood. Though the angel and the pillar become detached from their immediate, architectural context to participate in the larger Christian history, their space within the new framework is far from certain. Between the two episodes of spoliation come the hero's *passio* and the narrator's self-interruption, both of which offer clues to the author's poetics of the concrete fragment. I will conclude the chapter with a consideration of the figure of Andrew in relation to the larger enclosure, the *burh* [city, enclosure] of the Mermedonians, which abounds in pieces of artful objects.[20]

The forceful imagery of *Andreas* has encouraged more than one scholar to make analogies with sculptures and paintings. Michael Alexander describes the culture shock, which, according to him, twenty-first-century readers of the poem experience. Alexander writes, '[Those readers] are likely to react as northern European protestants [*sic*] do to those Italian cathedrals which seem to have been faced with Neapolitan ice-cream, or to Bernini's statue of a sensually swooning St. Theresa receiving the stigmata.'[21] He refers to more painters when he praises certain moments of 'spiritual and physical tension' in the poem that resemble 'a sacred canvas of the Catholic Reformation of the late sixteenth century, such as some by Tintoretto or El Greco'.[22] Other critics draw parallels to more recent visual traditions. In the beginning of his article on the animated angel-figure whom Jesus sends to resurrect three Old Testament patriarchs from their tombs in *Andreas*, Penn R. Szittya admits that the episode evokes for him 'at once some of the more abstruse manifestations of medieval iconography and the paintings of Salvador Dali'.[23] Not only, then, does the text possess immediacy and extravagance that bring to mind more material artworks, but it also seems to anticipate masterpieces from contexts spatially and temporally remote from Anglo-Saxon England.

Animated angel-likeness

One of Jesus's miraculous deeds that Andrew narrates to the heavenly craftsman himself during the sea voyage involves the animation of a statue, a metapoetic image par excellence. The story goes as follows. The disciples come with their teacher to a temple, where the priests refuse to believe in Jesus despite the many signs that he shows to them. There, Christ catches a glimpse of

> ... wrætlice   wundor agræfene,
> anlicnesse   engla sinra
> ...   on seles wage,
> on twa healfe torhte gefrætwed,
> wlitige geworhte ... (712–16)
> [... artfully carved wonders, likenesses of his angels on the wall of the hall, on both sides, adorned brightly, beautifully crafted ...]

At this point, a comparison with Greek and Latin versions throws light on what is distinctive about the Old English poet. Unlike his earlier counterparts, the author of *Andreas* draws attention to the radiance of the artefacts. He speaks of them as likenesses rather than 'sphinxes' (*spingas*) as in *Paraxeis* and *Casanatensis* (8; 38).[24] They are carved in two previous texts, but only in *Andreas* does Christ, as quoted to Christ by the hero, give more extensive comment on their appearance; he describes the objects as having 'haligra hiw' [colour/shape of the holy ones] (725), that is marked through the power of a hand and 'awriten on wealle' [carved/incised on a wall] (726). It is not only that the 'barbarian' adds colour or shape and brightness where the late Roman only has 'marble' (37). *Awritan* means 'to write', 'to compose', 'to inscribe', and 'to draw', the latter meaning often in conjunction with the adverbial phrase "on wealle".[25] This particular verb brings to mind pictorial as well as literary ex- or im-pression.[26]

The Anglo-Saxon author shows his interest in many facets of artistic experience, and other multi-media moments follow. Jesus identifies the images as representations of the angel-kind found, he says, among city-dwellers in the enclosure ('mid þam burgwarum / in þære ceastre') (718–19), those engaged in *swegeldreamum* [sound-joys, music], the 'Cherubim et Seraphim'. Even though in these lines we can see the Latin source of the poem breaking through the surface in the conjunction *et*, the poet departs from the earlier renditions to emphasise the concrete and the crafted, notions already present in those other texts. The author of *Praxeis* inexplicably has Jesus interpret the sculptures as 'the type of the Cross', and then add that they look like 'the cherubim and seraphim in Heaven' (8–9). In *Casanatensis*, the Lord notes the resemblance of 'these creations of the hands of craftsmen' to 'the cherubim and seraphim, formed just as if they are of Heaven' (38).[27] In this scene in *Andreas*, Christ refers to Paradise as a fortress and its dwellers as citizens, underlining the civilised aspect of the afterlife. The arts feature prominently in that place, and the images that we see immobile (for the moment) on earth, live in the celestial abode, where they take part in another art, music. The figures on the wall remind Jesus of the heavenly scene in which the angels worship him through sound and he connects the images with their heavenly prototypes.

Divine meta-awareness continues. Uniquely among the versions of this episode, the Saviour in *Andreas* issues a command by describing himself issuing it (that is, Andrew describes him in that act). Christ addresses the sculpture indirectly, but rather ceremoniously, saying: 'Nu ic bebeode ... ðæt þeos onlicnes eorðan sece / ... ond word sprece, / secge soðcwidum' [Now I order this image ... to step down ... and speak in words, to utter truth-statements] (729–33), rather than exclaiming 'You sculpture ... separate yourself from the place in which you stand and come down from there ... in order that you might establish and make it known ...' (*Casanatensis*, 38).[28] The rhyme and assonance of *sece/sprece/secge* [seek/speak/say] underline the speaker's awareness of his speech as action/creation. Asking for detachment of an artefact from its immediate context so that it could fit itself in the largest context possible, that of the arc of Christian history, Christ first detaches himself for a moment from his own current position, to imagine a scene in Heaven, then, rather self-consciously, he performs his miracle. Whereas in *Praxeis* and *Casanatensis* Jesus demands of the likeness to proclaim to the unbelieving and idolatrous high priest whether the man in front of them is God or a mere human ('si ego sum deus aut homo') (58), in *Andreas* he judges it sufficient that the sculpture truly speaks 'hwæt min æðelo sien' [what my lineage is] (734). The implication is that, if an individual is placed in a greater story, then his role is instantaneously illuminated. When the angel-shaped sculpture, following its Lord's orders, leaps off the wall, the narrator Andrew calls it 'frod fyrngeweorc ... / stan fram stane' [a very old, ancient work ... stone from stone] (737–8). The statue's age, its inhabitation of a greater time-frame, enforces its power as does its unyielding materiality. '[H]lud þurh heardne' [loudly through the hard one] comes the voice (739), all the more strange and beautiful because of its concrete source. To those who had already made up their minds about Christ, the 'resolute' or 'stubborn' persons, the stone's behaviour seems, nevertheless, *wrætlic* [creative, intricate, mysterious, singular, artful, terrifying],[29] one of the key words also in *Andreas*.

Our poet does more than highlight the many levels of artifice at work in the angel-animation scene (by the angels, by Christ, by Andrew, by himself). He begins to ask what happens to the fragment outside of the enclosure. Once endowed with a loud voice, the artefact launches into a disquisition whose structure is familiar from the older versions. First, it attacks the priests for their mistaken beliefs; then it praises God in his role as the Creator, singling out three characters from the Old Testament (Abraham, Isaac, and Jacob). When the stubborn elders still refuse to acknowledge the miracles, which they attribute to magic, Christ orders the sculpture to seek and raise from the dead Abraham and his two sons. (This happens only in *Praxeis* and *Andreas*. In *Casanatensis*, Jesus judges the miracle of the moving statue sufficient and, following its speech, he commands it to assume its place again.) The author of *Praxeis* relates that, after hearing the Saviour's directions to seek the patriarchs in a particular locale, the animated sculpture 'immediately ... went into the country of the Canaanites into the field of Mamre, and he called out to the tomb just as God commanded him' (10). Not surprisingly for a text that imagines so intensely the landscape of Mermedonia and the seaway separating the island from the Holy Land, *Andreas* cannot resist dwelling a little on the journey undertaken by the artefact from the temple to Abraham's burial place. Andrew narrates to Christ:

> Ða se þeoden bebead þryðweorc faran,
> stan on stræte of stedewange,
> ond forð gan foldweg tredan,
> grene grundas, Godes ærendu
> larum lædan on þa leodmearce
> to Channaneum ... (773–8)
> [Then the Lord ordered the glorious work to go, a stone on the street, from its place, and proceed to cross the earth-way, green expanses, to carry out God's errand according to the instructions, onto the territories, into Canaan ...]

Much as in *Exodus*, where the poet hints at the demarcations, populations and architecture in the space between Egypt and the Red Sea (with which the poem is not immediately concerned), here we have an Anglo-Saxon poet providing us, however briefly, with some points of interest along the road travelled by the angel-likeness. There is the 'street', in anticipation of the paved roads of Mermedonia, which gives way to earthen paths, then verdant fields, to end with the lands claimed by people (*leode* [people, nation]; *mearc* [mark, border]) and a recognisable name. In contrast, Christ in *Praxeis* does not depict the landscape along the way but gives only the end-point with the necessary toponyms: '[G]o into the country of Canaan and go into the double cave in the field of Mamre ...' (10).[30]

Attention to the features in the landscape contributes to the larger themes in this passage. Though in both earlier works the animated sculpture speaks of God in his role as the creator, it is only the Old English poem that circles around the theme of divine creation. The Lord gives new life to the object crafted by artists in imitation of the synesthetic, heavenly joy. He sends the angel-likeness to run through natural formations that he, too, created, which are dotted by artefacts made, appropriated, and transformed by humans. We learn that the detached statue does what 'scyppend wera' [the shaper of men] ordains, that it travels 'ofer mearcpaðu' [over border-paths], until it comes to Mamre, 'beorhte blican' [shining brightly] (787–9). Once again, the narrator invokes God's creative power at this key moment along with natural or artificial passageways. It is as if the landscape and the object divinely set in motion draw energy from each other. The angel-harrower acquires radiance from its journey.

'This glorious work' repeats what Christ did to it. After it raises Abraham, Isaac, and the 'third prince' from their graves, it commands them to prepare for a voyage, 'het hie to þam siðe gyrwan' (795).[31] Their task is to make known to the people 'hwa æt frumsceafte furðum teode / eorðan eallgrene ond upheofon, / hwæt se wealdend wære þe þæt weorc staðolade' [who first, in the beginning, fashioned the all-green earth and the heaven above, who the ruler was who established that work] (797–9). Everything in the animated-sculpture scene holds forth on creation. An artistic *spolium*, an angel-likeness wrenched from its immediate architectural context, calls up the Old Testament heroes who themselves will be the spoils after Christ's Harrowing of Hell. Constance B. Hieatt sees this 'unorthodox episode' as one in the series of Harrowing parallels that climax with Andrew's release of Matthew (and many other captives) from 'the hellish Mermedonian prison'. She does not discuss the scene in much detail, remarking only that it serves as another link between Christ and Andrew because the apostle similarly employs a stone pillar later in the text, an episode to which I turn later.[32]

Back in the temple, the unbelievers react with horror to Abraham, Isaac, and Jacob's arrival. John Hermann provides the following commentary on the passage: 'Such narrative resurrection is a biological elaboration of textual processes of typology and sublation ... [t]he narrative invents the miracles which sustain and authenticate it.'[33] He further argues that the variation presented in the story is deceptive, since, with its many-sided reinforcing of the Christian message, it insistently stifles any dissenting voices, projecting them into the mouths of demonised Jews or Mermedonians or the devil himself. Judged by this view, *Andreas* appears to allow for a 'continuing series of representations', but only insofar as they terrorise the unbeliever with the orthodox teachings of the Church.[34] I would contend, however, that the *Andreas* poet, while writing a conversion narrative, does leave a window of possibility open. He does not completely erase hermeneutical distractions because, unlike Jesus, he does not '[æ]ghwylces [cann] / worda for worulde wislic andgit' [have a wise understanding of everything, of words in the world] (508–9). In *Praxeis*, the double-animation scene ends with Christ commanding both the artefact and the three patriarchs to return to their places (10). The Anglo-Saxon verse account offers no such closure. We are not even sure whether the statue stays in Mamre or goes back to the temple. Whatever the position of this particular work of art, it is not strictly fixed.

The poet's peculiar treatment of the animated-statue scene complicates the interpretation issued by patristic scholars. The stone object 'coming at the end of Andreas' account of the deeds of Christ' unites the events from the end of Jesus's life that are central for medieval Catholicism, 'the establishment of the rock of the Church, and the Resurrection of Christ', thus standing in for 'Christ himself, the *petra*, the *lapis angularis*, and *lapis vivus* ... any of the elect who make up the living walls of the Church ... and by synecdoche ... the Church itself'.[35] But then the disappearance of the artefact at the end of the passage becomes difficult to explain. Moreover, the end of Andrew's narrative to Christ does not correspond to the end of the poem, which concludes not even with the flood that comes from another stone to kill, cleanse, and resurrect (most of) the Mermedonians, but with Andrew singled out, sailing into the unknown. The narrative placement of the double-animation passage has crucial implications. The poet not only sends his message more effectively to the audience through a long concluding report that the protagonist gives to Jesus (and indirectly to his own followers), in which he 'embeds the direct speeches of the chief priest, of Christ, and of the stone itself', but he also communicates to them 'the way in which meaning can be transmitted by way of a discourse which is finally calling attention to its self-consciously self-reflexive nature'.[36]

Adding to this many-sided meditation Christ's indirect manner of giving commands to the sculpture, his need for the object to resurrect the patriarchs, and the artefact's journey across the green fields and the Old Testament figures' trek over many a *mearcland* [borderland], we may perceive that the poem distances us from any quick allegorical explanation. It rather highlights the readers' separation from the actors in the story and their separation from each other. We should additionally keep in mind that only one figure among many breaks off from the wall for a determined stroll in the Palestinian countryside; the poet does not explore the reactions of the other angel-likenesses on the temple's wall, but the possibility of their animation in the future remains.

The separability of the artefact, the Old Testament figures, the saint, and even momentarily the Saviour, present in the older version yet painstakingly elaborated by the *Andreas*-poet, does not appear as something lamentable. They all clearly participate in the larger spiritual history. Unlike the priests who refuse to believe, the ones who have 'brandhata nið' [blazing-hot hate] surging in their minds (768–9) and are 'morðre bewunden' [wound about with murder] (772), they have no moral taint. By not spelling out the links between the characters, the architecture, and the outside spaces, our poet places a challenge on the readers. Michael Chabon, in his essay on fan fiction and Sherlock Holmes, likens all writers to amateurs producing sequels to the works of their beloved authors. This statement applies particularly well to hagiographers handling adventure-filled apocryphal narratives:

> Though parody and pastiche, allusion and homage, retelling and reimagining the stories that were told before us and that we have come of age loving – amateurs – we proceed, seeking out the blank places in the map that our favorite writers, in their greatness and negligence, have left for us, hoping to pass on to our own readers – should we be lucky enough to find any – some of the pleasure that we ourselves have taken in the stuff we love: to get in on the game.[37]

The *Andreas* poet challenges us to play the game, to fill out 'the blank places in the map', to wonder about the space between Jerusalem and Mamre, what the angel sculpture looks like, and where it goes after resurrecting the patriarchs. Leaving gaps becomes one type of authorial strategy; another is to scatter the fragments in the forms of full characters, body parts, and shards of artefacts for the reader to assemble.

The body and the *burh*

I will soon discuss in some detail the *Andreas* poet's short metatextual excursus in the form of a self-interruption, in which, after voicing doubts about his storytelling thus far, he declares that he will, nevertheless, proceed telling 'lytlum sticcum leoðworda dæl' [in small bits, a portion of poetic words] (1488), a move identified by John M. Foley as a creation of a new genre.[38] But before this excursus comes the episode telling of the saint's disintegration and reintegration. God's demonstration of his awe-inspiring restorative power begins when the Lord enters the protagonist's cell and 'wordum grette / ond frofre gecwæð' [greeted with words, and spoke consolation] (1464–5) to the prisoner who has been mutilated unsparingly by the Mermedonians. Here is one more instance of the theme of healing speech common to *Andreas*. The Creator needs only to command his servant to use his body in its healthy completeness ('Heht his lichoman / hales brucan') (1466–7), freeing him from the humiliation of those he calls *searohæbbendra* [those who possess artifice/cunning] (1468), for the previously wretched man to arise and speak his thanks 'hal of hæfte' [whole/unharmed from imprisonment] (1470). Putting together what had been scattered, God's craft counters that of the heathens, while his words inspire Andrew's. A list of parts follows, so that we can clearly perceive the components that quickly merge into the new/old holy man. The process helps generate even more words of healing:

> Næs him gewemmed wlite,   ne wloh of hrægle
> lungre alysed,   ne loc of heafde,
> ne ban gebrocen,   ne blodig wund
> lice gelenge,   ne laðes dæl
> þurh dolgslege   dreore bestemed,
> ac wæs eft swa ær   þurh þa æðelan miht
> lof lædende,   ond on his lice trum. (1471–7)
> [His countenance was not disfigured, nor a hem of his garment quickly torn off, nor a lock from his head, nor a bone broken, nor

a bloody wound affecting his body, nor any kind/portion of injury from a gore-drenched gash, but through that glorious power, he was again as before, giving praise, and strong in his body.]

This passage enables us to begin to ascertain the *Andreas* poet's relationship with and hope for his own work in pieces. Fragmentation is associated with harm, but also with differentiation permitted by division, because the word *dæl* can mean 'part of speech', 'share, allotted portion', 'amount, quantity'.[39] This excerpt does more in remarking the transformation of the face and clothes of our hero than meticulously gather the bits whose loss Andrew laments some fifty lines earlier:

Ðu ðæt gehete þurh þin halig word,
þa ðu us twelfe trymman ongunne,
þæt us heterofra hild ne gesceode,
ne lices dæl lungre oððeoded
ne synu ne ban on swaðe lagon,
ne loc of heafde to forlore wurde,
gif we þine lare læstan woldon;
nu sint sionwe toslopen, is min swat adropen,
licgað æfter lande loccas todrifene,
fex on foldan. Is me feorhgedal
leofre mycle þonne þeos lifcearo! (1418–28)
[You commanded with your holy word, when you encouraged the twelve of us, that no fierce enemy would hurt us in a battle, no part of our bodies be abruptly torn off, neither sinew nor bone lie on the road, no lock from our heads be lost, if we pursued your lore. Now my sinews are ripped apart, my blood is poured out, my locks lie scattered on the ground, my hair on the earth. Parting from life is much dearer to me than this life of pain!]

Not only are the blood, bones, and hair re-invoked in the latter passage, but the connection between healing language and intact body is re-established. In a work where God regularly absconds upwards (for instance, after talking to Matthew in line 119), the ground comes to signify the hard realities of the world that trap humankind. Corporeal disintegration, difficult to accept on its own, borders on intolerable when it takes place on the ground. A dispersal of something formerly protected and intact is worsened by the fact that the individual strands of hair or pieces of bone rest on a surface that exemplified action and interaction: the tracks for human traffic (like the ones which the angel-sculpture trod), the soil from which life springs. Following on the path of God's narrative ('lare læstan') should strengthen the believer against falling behind and apart. The loss of each 'lices dæl' [part of the body], the author intimates, brings *feorhgedal* [parting from life] or desire for it all the closer.

The poet of *Andreas*, here as in the animation episodes, elaborates exuberantly on a detail or two that exist in the older narratives. In *Praxeis* the apostle merely reminds the Lord of his promise 'Not one of your hairs will perish', before asking him 'what has happened to my flesh and the hairs of my head?' (19); the Greek author shows no trace of the unflinching gruesomeness present in the Old English text, but neither does he mention Andrew's regeneration. According to *Casanatensis*, the hero laments, 'My hairs are plucked, scattered through the lanes, my flesh is torn up through the streets, my blood splattered'; he repeats God's promise that not even the smallest hair of his would perish (50);[40] but he experiences no physical healing, which prompts his cannibal detainers to conclude that '[s]ince his flesh and hairs are already destroyed, perhaps he will die in the night' (50–1), doubtless bewailing his diminished deliciousness.[41]

Like his character, the Anglo-Saxon poet puts forth the fragments in the hope that they might be integrated. He counts upon the audience as well as God to stitch them together. The author of *Andreas* wants his readers to see correspondences between the geographical space and the text, between his, God's, and the Mermedonians' deployment of the hero. When the cannibals drag the saint over the landscape, they inadvertently but inevitably mark a large portion of the island with the man's body. They lay the ground for the grand metamorphosis soon executed by the Creator. In the following passage, several distinct sets of imagery – weather, sound, the architecture, the disjointed body – all essential components for metapoetic reflection in Anglo-Saxon poetry, fuse with unparalleled vigour:

> drogon deormode   æfter dunscræfum,
> ymb stanhleoðo   stærcedferþþe,
> efne swa wide   swa wegas tolagon,
> enta ærgeweorc,   innan burgum,
> stræte stanfage.   Storm upp aras
> æfter ceasterhofum,   cirm unlytel
> hæðnes heriges.   Wæs þæs halgan lic
> sarbennum soden,   swate bestemed,
> banhus abrocen;   blod yðum weoll,
> haton heolfre. (1232–41)

[The bold, strong-hearted ones pulled (him) through mountain caves, round rocky slopes, as far as roads, the stone-paved streets, the ancient works of giants extended within the cities. A storm rose up in the stronghold-dwellings, an unlittle uproar of the heathens' army. The body of the holy man was tormented with painful wounds, drenched with blood, the bone-house broken. His blood welled in streams of hot gore.]

Brooks's response to those extraordinary details not found in the Greek and Latin versions (but evident in other Old English texts in more straightforward settings) bespeaks unwillingness to recognise the peculiar artistry of *Andreas*. Brooks notes that *deormode* and *stærcedferþþe*, 'otherwise laudatory adjectives', here apply to the Mermedonians, a phenomenon he associates with the poet's 'characteristic vagueness' in an endnote to l. 693. Similarly, he attributes the expressions 'the ancient work of giants' and 'the stone-adorned streets' to the author's misguided adherence to formulas. 'The idea [of Roman tessellated pavements] is foreign to the context here; the poet is perhaps using a formula inappropriately, if not consciously echoing *Beowulf*.'[42] Regarding the pair of 'otherwise laudatory adjectives', we can identify a momentary shift of perspective infused with a certain irony. Andrew's tormentors imagine that they are great; they have to be great to increase his torment and God's power in erasing the traces of it later. Unwittingly, they participate in the saint's passion, thus ultimately contributing to his, and his story's, greatness.

As for the ancient urbanistic features, the poet here demonstrates his awareness of history and the many forms that the island of Mermedonia took. These fierce adversaries do not inhabit a timeless void, an allegorised wasteland of evil. They take part in a recognisable civilisation marked by an engagement with the artefacts of others; they come from a textual tradition that takes pieces from here and there. It is not a wonder that Jesus the helmsman, a connoisseur of words and the world, calls the habitation of the cannibals a 'mæran byrig' [a famous city] (973). The structures are already in place, all that needs to happen is for an authorial presence to fill them with an appropriate spirit. And indeed, later on, God presents Andrew with Mermedonia transformed into a *locus amoenus*, a rarity in Anglo-Saxon literature, 'geblowene bearwas standan / blædum gehrodene, swa he ær his blod aget' [groves standing abloom, adorned with blossoms where he had shed his blood before] (1448–9).[43] Here the augmentation is small, a group of trees rather than one or several: in *Praxeis*, the protagonist's bits of hair and flesh become 'a great tree bringing forth fruits' (19), and in *Casanatensis* 'trees blossoming and bearing fruit' (50).[44]

Lytlum sticcum [In small pieces]

Although the divine craft that makes whole serves as a model for our poet, he worries about his own shortcomings. An interlude, unparalleled in the earlier versions or in the Old English literary corpus, follows the account of God's physical, psychological, and sartorial healing of his saint. It marks a new beginning with the exclamation *hwæt*, which also occurs in the first line of *Andreas*, but here *hwæt* precedes the first-person singular, not the plural. The poet foregrounds his own individuality from the very start:

> Hwæt, ic hwile nu   haliges lare
> leoðgiddinga,   lof þæs þe worhte,
> wordum wemde,   wyrd undyrne.
> Ofer min gemet   mycel is to secganne,
> langsum leornung,   þæt he in life adreag,
> eall æfter orde;   þæt scell æglæwra
> mann on moldan   þonne ic me tælige
> findan on ferðe,   þæt fram fruman cunne
> eall þa earfeðo   þe he mid elne adreah
> grimra guða.   Hwæðre git sceolon
> lytlum sticcum   leoðworda dæl
> furður reccan;   þæt is fyrnsægen,
> hu he weorna feala   wita geðolode,
> heardra hilda,   in þære hæðenan byrig. (1478–91)
> [Behold, I have now been proclaiming for a while in words, in poetic song, the unconcealed event, the holy one's lore, the glory of what he created. Much is (there) to say, exceeding my reach, a long-lasting study, what he endured in life, everything from the beginning; a man on earth more learned in the divine law, than I consider myself, must find (it) in his spirit/mind, he who knows from the beginning all the hardship of grim battles that he endured with courage. And yet, and still, we have to narrate further, in small pieces, a portion of poetic words; this is an ancient legend (of) how he suffered a great number of torments, fierce attacks, in that heathen city.]

The passage is more than 'a rhetorical disclaimer that [the poet] does not know the whole story of St. Andrew'.[45] It functions the way modesty topoi usually do:[46] in decrying his inadequate skill in verse-making, the author not only demonstrates how adequate it actually is, but he also draws attention to the act. Similarly, in disassociating himself from the saint, he establishes an association between himself and the famed character he makes his own. Lore (*lar*, 1478) means 'teaching' as well as 'a story'. The glory that Andrew works parallels the proclamation that the speaker makes, both of them radiant with revelation, as *worhte* [created] alliterates with *wordum* [words] and *wyrd* [destiny, event, becoming]. Moving towards the conclusion of his tale, with time rushing to its end, the narrator suddenly wishes to emphasise the length of the saint's suffering. He also speaks of his own difficulty with beginnings and sources, both possibly signified by *ord*. Seen from the point of origin, Andrew's passion seems unbearable, unmanageable, requiring a more knowledgeable yet still earthly person ('mann on moldan') to contain it, mentally and narratively.

We are in the midst of things, and, faced with intense pain and beauty, we are unable to make out the beginning or the end. Although the phrases such as 'glory that he worked' and 'the holy one' point indubitably to a happy outcome, readers are prompted to feel some discomfort and fear regarding both the poet who is (re-)creating the tale and the character who lives through it, even feels it inscribed on his skin.[47] Here we can perceive a modicum of awareness that the splendid additions and extrapolations, of which the poet is so enamoured, distract him from doing what a more grounded individual might do, focusing on the story as treated in holy writ.[48]

But the poet quickly regains his confidence or changes his performance. *Ic* turns into *we*, unstated but implied by *sceolon* [(we) have to], after a pair of contrastive conjunctions. Consideration of origins in time or other texts has brought him back to the inclusive plural referent of his opening: 'Hwæt, we gefrunan ...' [Behold, we have learnt ...] (1). Yet with a return to the unity of author and audience, held together by the same injunction – as he is compelled to keep talking about St Andrew, so are we, his listeners, commanded to spread the legend – we immediately hear about another instance of fragmentation. The narrator describes his poetic method as an assemblage of bits in opposition to the sweeping narrative that includes 'all'. The phrase 'lytlum sticcum' in reference to verse-making happens only here.

According to the *Concordance to Old English Poetry*, the word *stycce* [piece, portion] does not occur in any other poem. Body parts of humans or animals are often cut or torn or broken into *sticcum*. In one homily, Ælfric reports that the devils let a sorcerer go and, falling, he 'tobærst on feower sticcum' [broke into four pieces]; in one of her *vitæ*, St Margaret prays to God to protect her from the many dogs surrounding her that 'willeð minne lichamen to sticcan gebringan' [wish to tear my body to pieces]; from a prose translation of Exodus comes the instruction for making an offering: 'þone ram þu sniþst to sticcon; his innewearde & his fet þu legst uppan his heofod' [cut the ram to pieces, and place his innards and feet on his head].[49] In glosses, 'on sticca' corresponds to the Latin phrases such as 'in frusta' [in scraps] and 'in partes'.[50]

Further evidence comes from within the passage. The *hapax* compound *leoðword* [word/s of a poem (or a song)], implying in the same line that individual words make up poetry, carries a qualifier *dæl* [a portion, part] that can mean fragmentation as well as differentiation enabled by division. Another *hapax* follows, one that establishes continuity in discontinuity, *fyrnsægen* [an old legend/tradition] that can and does speak of a 'great many' trials and travails of our hero, if not 'all'. The interlude concludes with 'the heathen city', which takes us back to the setting of the story, the oppressive enclosure that, nevertheless, has a productive effect on verse-making. All the *spolia*-related elements that I have been following – the fragment, hero, *burh* – emerge in the metapoetic excursus.

How to do things with pillars

The passage before the self-interruption echoes many other charged moments in the work. It shows that the ultimate proof of a creator's efficiency, be he divine or mere mortal, is the ability to go beyond restoring the fragment to drawing out the whole from the part. The episode that follows the statement of the poetics of 'little pieces' has a similar effect. Here readers, along with Andrew, encounter a cluster of significant artefacts, from which the hero singles one out:

> He be wealle geseah   wundrum fæste
> under sælwage   sweras unlytle,
> stapulas standan   storme bedrifene,
> eald enta geweorc;   he wið anne þæra,
> mihtig ond modrof,   mæðel gehede,
> wis, wundrum gleaw,   word stunde ahof ... (1492–7)
> [He saw by the wall, within the walls of the building, unlittle columns, pillars standing, marvellously fixed, storm-beaten, old works of giants; mighty and brave, wise and marvellously sage, he held an assembly with one of them, lifted up a word at once ...]

Some important expressions that occur here echo those from the episode of the saint's outdoor passion: the same understatement *unlytle* refers to the pillars here and the noise there; 'eald enta geweorc' parallels 'enta ærgeweorc'; and *storm* surfaces unexpectedly again. Brooks protests that 'storm-beaten' is 'strictly inappropriate' because the columns are inside the prison.[51] Two solutions to this problem can be proposed. One is that the *sweras* in question are *spolia*, formerly outside supports of a building constructed by earlier inhabitants of the isle, which had been plundered by the Mermedonians. North and Bintley write that '... if any more material sense is to be made of [the condition of] the pillars ... these must be Roman spolia rather than the sort of prehistoric stonework that supports the dragon's barrow [in *Beowulf*]'.[52] This proposition accords with the echoes of the Harrowing perceived in the double-animation episode as well as with the strategic, self-conscious poetic despoiling of *Beowulf*.[53] It also works well with Boenig's suggestion that the 'great posts tightly wound' (his translation of 'wundrum fæste ... sweras unlytle') resemble 'Anglo-Saxon interlace design',[54] testifying further to a great visual-artistic awareness of the *Andreas* poet. The second, related solution requires more explanation. Daniel Tiffany's discussion of Old English riddles leads him to proclaim that

> the innate obscurity of matter in the history of physics, like the inscrutability of things in lyric poetry, betrays the inescapable role of language in depicting the nonempirical qualities – the invisible aspect – of material phenomena.[55]

Tiffany pursues the tight linking, even intertwining, of a poem's darkness with its materiality at various points in the history of lyric in English, from Anglo-Saxon riddles to Gerard Manley Hopkins, from T. S. Eliot's essays on Metaphysical poetry to Jorie Graham. He asks two questions, to which he already suggests an answer: 'Are there corporeal phenomena analogous to the qualities in language that we judge to be obscure?' and 'What precisely does obscurity yield in the act of reading – in the absence of clear, cognitive meaning – if not a sense, strange indeed, of poetic *materials*?'[56] Tiffany argues that poets from different periods and locations look for 'correspondences between the poem's nebulous body and certain amorphous bodies in nature ... a rainbow, a cloud of dust, a shadow, a storm ...' to depict that substance of things shot through with textual darkness.[57]

The group of pillars ravaged by storm acts as an acknowledgement by the text of its place in a long-standing history. *Andreas* is built on plunder. The power of poetry, and by extension of the word, seeps into the darkest of places; no interior cell is safe from the creative atmospheric pressure. If we recall that the noise of the cannibals helps produce the storm that fills up the fortified courts of Mermedonia in lines 1236–7, we can conclude that the poet makes a potentially uncomfortable connection between his endeavour and that of Andrew's enemies.[58] Depending on the transformative power of readers and scholars, of people more learned in the divine law, his efforts may turn to good. Like the island-settlement through which the cannibals drag the hero, the prison where they attempt to contain him features traces of the past that help to bring the story out of its most immediate surroundings. Both scenes also indicate that the tools for converting the 'well-known *burh*' are at hand; one only needs to know how to find and animate the artefact.

The protagonist carries out precisely those actions. More than selecting the *objet d'art juste*, Andrew knows how to prompt it into action by speaking to it properly. *Andreas*, for all its pyrotechnics and perceived incongruence, reveals an acute concern with voice, tone, and tongue. Proper rhetorical animation consists of positioning the matter from which the pillar is made into the larger narrative of Christian salvation. The hero apostrophises the stone as follows:

> Geher ðu, marmanstan,   meotudes rædum,
> fore þæs onsyne   ealle gesceafte
> forhte geweorðað,   þonne hie fæder geseoð
> heofonas ond eorðan   herigea mæste
> on middangeard   mancynn secan! (1498–1502)
> [O marble-stone, hear the counsels of the Lord, before whose face all creation becomes fearful, when they see the father of heaven and earth seeking humankind in the world with the greatest host!]

To wrench a flood out of a piece of marble, the saint implicitly asks it to remember that it, too, was created by the Measurer, who is defined by his power to create, and that it inhabits the world of *mancynn* between the earth and the sky. After mentioning the two elements, the air and the earth, to set the stage for the cataclysmic event to follow, the hero orders the pillar to issue large quantities of water: 'streamas …/… ea …/… wæter widrynig to wera cwealme, / geofon [MS heofon] geotende' [streams … a river … water wide-flowing to kill the men, a surging ocean [MS heaven]] (1503–4, 1507–8). The poet of *Andreas* draws a link between this part of the poem and the past water-journey of the protagonist through his emphasis on aquatic imagery.

God's creation and destruction seem constantly intertwined. First, we hear that the Lord's creation shudders before him because they know he can run them aground with his mighty army; then, we see the energy, the flow previously mastered by Christ to enable Andrew to arrive safely in Mermedonia, turn into a second Noah's flood. The hero desires a cumulative effect, for waves to become a river, a river an ocean, even, if we follow the manuscript reading, heaven. Whereas before, in the description of the 'stapulas ... storme bedrifene' [pillars ... storm-beaten] (1494) we had the storm as a symbol of the poet's all-pervading poetics of the obscure concrete, now we have the image of a fluid that threatens to fill out the space between earth and sky. The ensuing topsy-turviness famously brings to mind drowning in alcohol: the *meoduscerwen* [sharing out of mead] (1526), and 'biter beorþegu' [bitter beer-drinking] (1533). We may remember here Kenneth Gross's characterisation of Michelangelo's sculpture as the art whose 'virtual life ... might be seen to inhere less in its brilliant illusionism, its perfected mimesis of visible nature, than in the establishment of some link to a potency shared by the imagination of the artist, the processes of nature, and divine creativity'.[59] Such links persist in the most powerful passages in the poem, those sections that most unsettle the critics.

With cosmic specifications out of the way, the apostle can proceed to remind the marble swiftly of the honour that the Lord has lavished on it. Andrew pronounces the stone better than gold or treasure because the King wrote on it, 'wordum cyðde / recene geryno, ond ryhte æ / getacnode on tyn wordum' [promptly revealed mysteries with words and signified the right law in ten statements] (1510–12). The importance of words is underlined by the repetition of *wordum*, so ordinary yet forceful, forming a miniature envelope pattern around the themes of revelation (*cyðde*) and symbolism (*getacnode*). James W. Earl explains that 'the very stone on which God inscribed the ten commandments', now found among the Mermedonians in the shape of 'a foundational column under the city wall', that will provide the foundation for the 'new Church', functions as 'a boldly conceived symbol calling attention to the relationship of the Mermedonians to the Jews'.[60] The text indeed fuses these various architectural incarnations of stone, but it continues insisting, all along, on the stone's stoniness, the word's concreteness. From the allusion to 'tyn wordum' – separable, countable units – Andrew speaks only briefly of the immediate recipient of the commandments, Moses and his two kinsmen Joshua and Tobias (1513, 1516). The end of the speech acquires special prominence as it displays three crucial themes in *Andreas* commonly suggested by *spolia* – treasure, continuity, and artifice. 'Nu ðu miht gecnawan', the saint says, 'þæt

þe cyning engla / gefrætwode furður mycle / giofum geardagum
þonne eall gimma cynn' [Now you can acknowledge that the King
of the angels adorned you with gifts in the days of yore much more
than all the race of gems] (1517–19).

Such profound transformation through celebration of the material that creates and destroys is unparalleled in the Greek and Latin versions of the story. In *Praxeis*, only the reference to the Ten Commandments exists without any explicit naming of the Old Testament figures or comment about God's stone-decoration (20), whilst in *Casanatensis* the animated artefact, an 'erect marble column' with a statue on top, has no lofty origin and is even addressed as 'small' by Andrew (51–2).[61] The Old English poet envisions the marble-stone as a human-like actor, a member of a *cynn*, even of the divine *comitatus*, a gem which God has loaded with favours and decorated with his words in *longue durée*. Possible subtractions are as important as elaborations for an attempt to ascertain how the *Andreas* poet distinguishes himself. Edward B. Irving, Jr, notes that, while the stone-animation scene in the earlier accounts may appear more realistic because of the water-spewing statue atop the column, 'one may prefer the charming riddle-like quality in the Old English of talking to Stone in abstract'.[62] The riddle aspect of Anglo-Saxon poetics emerges once again, not confined to the riddles proper. Irina Dumitrescu even considers the poem to be 'composed of small riddles, metaphorically speaking, but in fact some passages function as riddles in a more concrete fashion'.[63]

With this insight, we could revisit Tiffany's list of 'certain, amorphous bodies in nature' that the poets consistently imagine their 'poem's nebulous body' to be, those rainbows, dust-clouds, and storms,[64] and add to them the flood that comes out of a storm-roughened marble column. The concrete touched and marked by air and liquid can turn into fluid at the right command. The statue ultimately helps Andrew turn the people away from *helltrafum* [hellish tents/pavilions] (1691); a transformed fragment takes up and conquers the entire heathen architecture. Having done its job, the stone pillar leaves the text – unless it figures, along with its possibly intertwined companions, in the construction of churches in the newly Christian Mermedonia.

The saint and the city

After the Mermedonians have been cleansed and converted, and the landscape Christianised with the foundation of the church and placement of a bishop, Andrew voices his intention to leave. This passage stands out amid declarations of spiritual victory because of its almost elegiac tone:

> Sægde his fusne hige,
> þæt he þa goldburg ofgifan wolde,
> secga seledream ond sincgestreon,
> beorht beagselu, ond him brimþisan
> æt sæs faroðe secan wolde. (1654–8)
> [He said that his mind was eager to go, that he wished to leave the gold-city, the hall-joy of men, and the precious treasure, the bright ring-hall, and would seek for himself a wave-breaker at the sea-shore.]

The saint senses that the time has come to quit not only the island, but also the world of humans. Interestingly, that world is depicted as a set of encirclements – a *beagselu* [hall forming a ring] contained within a *goldburg* [golden fortification] – that creates a particular feeling of elation ('secga seledream'). There is an implication that 'he will be voyaging ... out of life as well',[65] coupled with the image of breaking through the waves, natural formations often envisioned in Anglo-Saxon poetry as interlocked. Seeking exile and, by extension, death requires effort on the part of the hero; the desire for alienation and extinction of self has entered his mind, forcing him to look on his own for a ship that would take him back to the sea. Though we could imagine Andrew beginning to resemble the protagonist of *The Wanderer* or *The Seafarer* at this point, the author only hints at such an intertextual resemblance. We cannot follow the protagonist there: he is supposed to face death alone.

God, however, does not allow his warrior to depart just yet. The islanders lament Andrew's absence bitterly, and the Lord underscores his demand that the saint take a while longer to strengthen the commitment of the new believers with an architectural metaphor: 'him naman minne / on ferðlocan fæste getimbre' [construct my name firmly in their mind-lockers (hearts)] (1670–1). Andrew has to remain in 'þære winbyrig .../... salu sinchroden' [the city of joy ... (in) the halls adorned with treasure] (1672–3) for seven more nights before he can set off with God's blessing. During the 'seofon nihta fyrst', Andrew takes on a (re-)creator's role, adding to the heavenly structure that binds the Mermedonians to their Maker and each other. After the appointed time passes, the saint experiences the same longing to part from the *wederburg* [the weather-city] (1697) and embark on his final, mysterious journey. If we remember the place of storms in Anglo-Saxon poetry-making, we can conclude that Andrew takes his leave from the text as much as from the island of Mermedonia, both *loci* imagined as collections of artefacts enveloped in intense obscurity. Yet the hero is not the only character who departs from *Andreas* at this juncture:

> ongan hine þa fysan   ond to flote gyrwan,
> blissum hremig;   wolde on brimþisan
> Achaie   oðre siðe
> sylfa gesecan,   þær he sawulgedal,
> beaducwealm gebad.   Þæt þam banan ne wearð
> hleahtre behworfen;   ah in helle ceafl
> sið asette,   ond syððan no,
> fah freonda leas, frofre benohte. (1698–1705)
> [He began to prepare himself and to get ready for the sea, exulting in happiness. Once again he wished to seek Achaia on his own, where he would await the soul-parting, battle-death. For this the slayer would have no reason to laugh; rather, he set on a journey into the jaws of hell, and afterwards, stained and deprived of friends, partook of no relief.]

As in the previous excerpt, the poet singles the protagonist out. Implicitly, Andrew is contrasted with the crowd that sees him off. Their wailing gives way to praise of God when his ship leaves their sight. The individual vanishes from our poem, but not before he sparkles for a final split-second in his full complexity. He is filled with joy to travel to a place where he will await not only death, but death of a painful kind, an end comparable to that on the battlefield.

I would compare Andrew as a lonely, accomplished individual to his counterparts in *Judith* and *Beowulf*. In these three works, because of his or her very prowess at encountering the savage Other in 'intimate encounters', the heroic protagonist ensures '(for at least a certain amount of time) ... a more secure mead hall, community, or nation', but for the same reason, must remain outside of 'the newly secured space', into which he or she cannot be assimilated.[66] In lines 1698–1702 we see that immediately after the brief account of Andrew's journey comes a more bombastic mention of the devil's destruction figured as his voyage into the gaping mouth of hell. Of course, the author contrasts the two: their paths diverge. But the saint, too, seems 'freonda leas' [deprived of friends], since he has to do everything on his own once again. Further, as *beaducwealm*, the second compound referring to his death, implies a violent battle, we might ask with whom the hero fights, if the devil has already been dispatched to his appointed dwelling-place. The poet of *Andreas* leaves open the possibility that with Andrew's return to Achaia, the enemy of humankind does not disappear, that he follows the individual to his deathbed, and that the combat with the demonic ends only with one's final passing. If we agree with James W. Earl that 'Andrew is as much the converted as the converter',[67] we can also conclude that the act of conversion of oneself and others does not stop with the building of a church and hiring of a bishop. Neither can reinforcing the name of God in the hearts of the new faithful happen in the space of a week. Indeed, the acts of double construction, physical and psychological, must continue for as long as the world exists.

What impact does this realisation have on our poet and his poetics of 'little pieces'? Earl argues that the over-arching theme of *Andreas* is conversion: of Mermedonians, of 'the world at the end of time', and in 'its most personal sense [as] the strengthening of faith … so familiar to us in poems like *The Dream of the Rood* and, more interestingly, in the four Cynewulfian signatures'.[68] Whatever the poem's relationship to the runic signature in *The Fates of the Apostles*, its most immediate neighbour in the manuscript, *Andreas* does not end with the narrator's contemplation of his own conversion. Instead, the poet splits his conclusion in two. He presents us with an image of the individual, marked by his encounter with the demonic, travelling away, towards his death, and a final glimpse of a community praising unanimously the 'ece God eallra gesceafta' [eternal God of all creation], whose power and rule spread over the entire earth (1717–8).

Notes

1 Parts of this chapter appeared, in different form, in Denis Ferhatović, '*Spolia*-Inflected Poetics of the Old English *Andreas*', *Studies in Philology*, 111 (2013), 199–219.
2 'Ne synt me winas cuðe,/ eorlas elþeodige, ne þær æniges wat/ hæleða gehygdo …' [I do not know any friends, foreign warriors, nor am I acquainted with any heroes] (198–200). The Old English text comes from Brooks's edition. Kenneth R. Brooks (ed.), *Andreas and the Fates of the Apostles* (Oxford: Clarendon, 1961). Irving summarises Andrew's concerns wittily: 'he has no friends there, he cannot understand the language, he does not know the way, and anyhow an angel could do this sort of job much more readily'. Edward B. Irving, Jr, 'A Reading of *Andreas*: The Poem as Poem', *Anglo-Saxon England*, 12 (1983), 215–37, at 219.
3 The quotation comes from Bradley (trans.), *Anglo-Saxon Poetry*, p. 109. I gathered the information in the first paragraph from Bradley,

pp. 109–10; Brooks (ed.), *Andreas*, p. xi; Elaine Treharne (ed. and trans.), *Old and Middle English: An Anthology* (Oxford: Blackwell, 2000), p. 89.

4   Robert Boenig (trans.), *The Acts of Andrew in the Country of the Cannibals: Translations from the Greek, Latin, and Old English* (New York: Garland, 1991), p. ii.

5   Ibid., pp. viii–ix.

6   Ivan Herbison quotes Claes Schaar, who reached the conclusion about a lost Latin manuscript mostly based on *Praxeis* but resembling in some ways *Casanatensis*, in his *Critical Studies in the Cynewulf Group* (Lund: Gleerup, 1949), p. 23. See Ivan Herbison, 'Generic Adaptation in *Andreas*', in Jane Roberts and Janet Nelson (eds), *Essays in Anglo-Saxon and Related Themes in Memory of Lynne Grundy* (London: Centre for Late Antique and Medieval Studies, 2000), pp. 181–211, at 188 (n. 25).

7   Brooks (ed.), *Andreas*, p. xvi; Irving, 'A Reading', p. 215.

8   Brooks (ed.), *Andreas*, pp. xvii–xviii.

9   Both mentioned by Brooks (ed.), *Andreas*, pp. xxiv–xxv.

10 Anita R. Riedinger, 'The Formulaic Relationship Between *Beowulf* and *Andreas*', in Helen Damico and John Leyerle (eds), *Heroic Poetry in the Anglo-Saxon Period: Studies in Honor of Jess B. Bessinger, Jr.* (Kalamazoo: Medieval Institute, 1993), pp. 283–312, at 293, 301 (plundering), and 306 (haunting). Daniel Calder also invokes spoliation when he writes that 'the assumption instantly arose that the *Andreas* poet must have consciously used *Beowulf* as a quarry for the construction of his own work'. Daniel G. Calder, 'Figurative Language and its Contexts in *Andreas*: A Study in Medieval Expressionism', in Phyllis Rugg Brown et al. (eds), *Modes of Interpretation in Old English Literature: Essays in Honour of Stanley B. Greenfield* (Toronto: University of Toronto Press, 1986), pp. 115–36, at 116.

11 Irving, 'A Reading', p. 215. Brooks cautiously concludes his discussion of *Beowulf*'s influence on *Andreas* by quoting Dorothy Whitelock: 'one can make a case for the influence of *Beowulf* on *Andreas* … but it stops short of proof' (Brooks (ed.), *Andreas*, p. xxvi).

12 Calder, 'Figurative Language', p. 116. The authors here quoted are Rosemary Woolf, E. G. Stanley, Kenneth R. Brooks, and Edward B. Irving, Jr.

13 Aaron Hostetter, *Political Appetites: Food in Medieval English Romance* (Columbus: Ohio State University Press, 2017), p. 35.

14 Ibid., pp. 33 ('avant-garde'), 35 ('generic hybrid').

15 Dumitrescu, *The Experience of Education*, pp. 123–5.

16 Fabienne L. Michelet, *Creation, Migration, and Conquest: Imaginary Geography and Sense of Space in Old English Literature* (Oxford: Oxford University Press, 2006), p. 165. The other works she discusses are *Elene*, *Guthlac A*, and the *Fates of the Apostles*. According to her, the first two are *vitæ*, the second *passio*.

17 Michael Alexander, *A History of Old English Literature* (Peterborough, ON: Broadview Press, 2002), pp. 201–2.
18 Herbison, 'Generic Adaptation', p. 191.
19 Hostetter, *Political Appetites*, pp. 33–5.
20 In their new edition of the poem, Richard North and Michael D. J. Bintley offer about two and a half pages of proof for art-historical spoliation of marble pillars in early medieval England and on the Continent to contextualise the marble column episode. Richard North and Michael D. J. Bintley, *Andreas: An Edition* (Liverpool: Liverpool University Press, 2016), pp. 86–9. North and Bintley discuss only the pillar scene in terms of *spolia*; they cite my previously published article on *Andreas* ('*Spolia*-Inflected Poetics') in the note to the lines 1494–5 (p. 295).
21 Alexander, *A History of Old English Literature*, p. 201. Andrew worries about feeling culturally shocked in the land of Mermedonians. See the second note in this chapter.
22 Ibid., p. 199.
23 Penn R. Szittya, 'The Living Stone and the Patriarchs: Typological Imagery in *Andreas*, Lines 706–810', *Journal of English and Germanic Philology*, 72 (1973), 167–74, at 167.
24 I use Boenig's translation of *Praxeis* and *Casanatensis*. The original text of the latter comes from Blatt's edition (Franz Blatt (ed.), *Die lateinischen Bearbeitungen der Acta Andreæ et Matthiæ apud Anthropophagos* (Giessen: Alfred Töpelmann, 1930)). Boenig notes that sphinxes make sense because of the desert where Jesus encounters them in *Praxeis*, the locus with 'resonances of … the Exodus' ((Boenig (trans.), *The Acts of Andrew*, p. 8). The *Andreas* poet, usually quite enamoured of composite Otherness (he repeatedly, if indirectly, associates the Mermedonians with the Jews), misses this opportunity to take advantage of an Egyptian echo.
25 s.v. *awritan* in the *DOE*.
26 Seth Lerer and Christopher Fee focus on literary and literacy-related aspects of writing in *Andreas*, but not on the pictorial. Seth Lerer, *Literacy and Power in Anglo-Saxon Literature* (Lincoln: University of Nebraska Press, 1991), pp. 53–4; Christopher Fee, 'Productive Destruction: Torture, Text, and the Body in the Old English *Andreas*', *Essays in Medieval Studies*, 11 (1994), 51–62.
27 The Latin reads 'compositiones artifici manibus … similiter et as spingas in similitudinem cherubim, et seraphim, expressas sicuti sunt celo' (Blatt (ed.), *Die lateinischen Bearbeitungen*, p. 57).
28 'tu sculptilis … separa te de loco in qua stabis, et descende … et ut conprobes, et innotescas …' (ibid., 57–9).
29 Ramey, 'The Riddle of Beauty', pp. 477–81; Dumitrescu, *The Experience of Education*, p. 128.
30 Michelet makes a similar point (*Creation, Migration, and Conquest*, p. 191), but she sees the roadways not as pre-existent structures that

broaden the perspective and colour the text with some mystery, but rather as emerging proofs of a holy figure colonising by God-given power the marginal space, a theme she finds prominent in *Andreas* (p. 196).
31 The *Praxeis* author tinges the sphinx's adventures in the field of Mamre with some gentle humour. When it calls out to the tomb, twelve patriarchs come out, whereupon the statue has to specify that it needs only three and that the remainder of them can 'go and rest until the time of the resurrection' (Boenig (trans.), *The Acts of Andrew*, p. 10).
32 Constance B. Hieatt, 'The Harrowing of Mermedonia: The Typological Patterns in the Old English "Andreas"', *Neuphilologische Mitteilungen*, 77 (1976), 9–62, at 60.
33 Hermann, *Allegories of War*, p. 128.
34 Ibid.
35 Szittya, 'The Living Stone', pp. 174, 172. Szittya makes note of the fact that 'no mention is made of the fate of the *stan*' (168, n. 3) in *Andreas*, as opposed to the Greek text, but he goes no further.
36 Ruth Waterhouse, 'Self-Reflexivity and "Wraetlic word" in *Bleak House* and *Andreas*', *The Journal of Narrative Technique*, 18 (1988), 211–25, at 221.
37 Michael Chabon, *Maps and Legends: Reading and Writing Along the Borderlands* (San Francisco: McSweeney's Books, 2008), pp. 23–45, at 45.
38 '… the interruption must represent undiscovered generic territory for the poet: on available evidence, this is a unique "genre," wholly without a model or rules, and yet he carries on idiomatically and without apparent hesitation'. John M. Foley, 'The Poet's Self-Interruption in *Andreas*', in M. J. Toswell (ed.), *Prosody and Poetics in the Early Middle Ages: Essays in Honour of C. B. Hieatt* (Toronto: University of Toronto Press, 1995), pp. 42–59, at 55.
39 See A4, B, and C under *dæl* in the *DOE*.
40 '… capilli mei devellati sunt, per vicos aspersos, caro mea extirpata est, per plateas, sanguis meus aspersus … Tunc quando dicebas nobis, si me audieritis, et me secuti fueritis, nec minimus capillus capitis vestri peribit' (Blatt (ed.), *Die lateinischen Bearbeitungen*, p. 85).
41 'Vespere autem facto, tunc presides cum vidissent iam nimis defectus, retrudi eum in carcere dicentes, quia iam caro eius et capilli destructi sunt, forsitan in hac nocte morietur' (ibid., p. 87). Boenig makes the point that the man-eaters 'should, of course, lament the destruction of his flesh, which they want to eat' (Boenig (trans.), *The Acts of Andrew*, p. 51, n. 82).
42 Brooks (ed.), *Andreas*, pp. 106–7.
43 Michael D. J. Bintley claims that *Andreas* promotes Anglo-Saxon inhabitation of ruined Roman cities by portraying the transformed Mermedonia as 'a sanctified space appropriate for the habitation of

men in both literary and physical realms'. Michael D. J. Bintley, 'Demythologising Urban Landscapes in *Andreas*', *Leeds Studies in English*, 40 (2009), 105–18, at 117.
44 '... apparuerunt caro et capilli sui sicut arbores florentes et fructum afferentes' (Blatt (ed.), *Die lateinischen Bearbeitungen*, p. 87).
45 Brooks (ed.), *Andreas*, p. 113.
46 Foley mentions the possibility of the modesty *topos*, but he 'suspend[s] judgment' (p. 56) on this and many other fascinating issues at play in the excursus. See the last paragraph in 'The Poet's Self-Interruption', p. 57. He deems it sufficient that the self-interruption indicates the poet's desire for a better executed 'syncretic poetics', a matching of 'traditional oral register' to a written source text.
47 Christopher Fee writes that 'what is of interest is that Andreas, rather than practicing any kind of literacy at all, seems to be having "literacy" practiced *upon him*. Writing, broadly defined, is a central and unifying activity throughout *Andreas*: At the conclusion of his passion, Andreas has been "re-written" into the "Word" through the application of the text of torture upon the parchment of his flesh; the source texts, too, have been rewritten, in order to illustrate more fully this very same transformation' ('Productive Destruction', pp. 59–60 [his italics]).
48 Attention to distraction could be part of the design. Irina Dumitrescu argues for a productive failure intentionally orchestrated by the poet here and elsewhere. He teaches by both positive and negative examples. Dumitrescu, *The Experience of Education*, pp. 116–17.
49 Selections marked as AECHom I, 26 B1.1.28 1; LS 14 (MargaretCCCC 303) B3.3.14; and Exod B8.1.4.2 in the *Old English Corpus*.
50 AldV 1 (Goossens) C 31.1 2 in the *Old English Corpus*.
51 Brooks (ed.), *Andreas*, p. 113.
52 North and Bintley (eds), *Andreas*, p. 295. They make a comparison of the gaol cell's architecture to St Wystan's crypt in Repton, Derbyshire (pp. 89, 295).
53 Partially drawing on my '*Spolia*-Inflected Poetics', Dumitrescu incorporates the architectural and textual spoliation (from *Beowulf* but also Cynewulf's verse) in her analysis of *Andreas* (Dumitrescu, *The Experience of Education*, p. 118).
54 Boenig (trans.), *The Acts of Andrew*, p. 114.
55 Daniel Tiffany, 'Lyric Substance: On Riddles, Materialism, and Poetic Obscurity', *Critical Inquiry*, 28 (2001), 72–98, at 75.
56 Ibid., p. 83.
57 Ibid., p. 87.
58 Christopher Fee makes a similar point in 'Productive Destruction', but he focuses on writing on our protagonist's body.
59 Kenneth Gross, *The Dream of the Moving Statue* (Ithaca: Cornell University Press, 1992), p. 93.
60 James W. Earl, 'The Typological Structure of *Andreas*', in Niles (ed.), *Old English Literature in Context*, pp. 66–89, at 74.

61 'Et statim vidit columpnam marmoream erectam, et super ipsam columpnam stantem statuam marmoream' (Blatt (ed.), *Die lateinischen Bearbeitungen*, p. 87); 'statue parce, remitte et claude os tuum ...' (ibid., p. 89); Boenig explains the choice of the adjective 'small' thus: '*Parce* – the smallness of the statue and the greatness of the destruction that it has caused together emphasize the miraculous nature of the Flood' (Boenig (trans.), *The Acts of Andrew*, p. 52).
62 Irving, 'A Reading', p. 234.
63 Dumitrescu, *The Experience of Education*, p. 123. Also see her claim that this episode contains 'an embedded riddle with two solutions' suggested by three phrases borrowed from *Beowulf*: one, Beowulf; the other, Andrew (p. 125).
64 Tiffany, 'Lyric Substance', p. 75.
65 Irving, 'A Reading', p. 236.
66 Kate Koppelman, 'Fearing My Neighbor: The Intimate Other in *Beowulf* and the Old English *Judith*', *Comitatus*, 35 (2004), 1–21, at 21.
67 Earl, 'The Typological Structure', p. 86. On conversion as an ongoing process for Andrew or any Christian believer that ends only with his death, see Amity Reading, 'Baptism, Conversion, and Selfhood in the Old English *Andreas*', *Studies in Philology*, 112 (2015), 1–23, at 17.
68 Earl is rare among the contemporary critics in considering Cynewulf to be the author of *Andreas*.

4
Zooming out, cutting through: Resistance to incorporation in *Judith*

Introduction: The text as a *spolium*

The Old English poem of *Judith*, at first glance, seems fairly straightforward. Yet its seeming simplicity reveals a number of different plundered or about-to-be-plundered objects. They include the heroine's living body that her Assyrian adversary, Holofernes, wants to enslave and cut off from her people; the enemy's head which she expertly detaches and takes to the Israelites as a token of her previous and their imminent victories; and the complete bloody armour stripped from Holofernes, that the victorious Israelites offer to her after the battle with Assyrians. Most unexpectedly, the text itself has become a *spolium*, a detached bit of narrative that both encourages and resists complete readerly contextualisation, whether it happens by appealing to allegorical readings (exegetical or psychoanalytic) or by examining how the work fits with other poems in the miscellany in which it appears, MS Cotton Vitellius A. xv. I will begin by looking at attempts to contain the text at large before turning to individual instances of *spolia* within the narrative and attempts at their incorporation by characters into spaces. Two such spaces are the sleeping section of Holofernes's tent and the enclosure (*burh*) of Bethulia. My ultimate argument will be that the poem wants to have it both ways. It seeks to harness the energy of the incompletely digested, potentially dangerous detail by zooming in on it and presenting images of crowding and pressing – in short, of accumulation. Yet it also moves our attention away from it, by cutting through, speeding up the pace of the narration, and dramatically broadening the focus. In other words, it incorporates the strategies of both Exeter Riddles 40 and 66, as discussed in Chapter 1.

As it survives today, in fragmentary form, *Judith* has only 350 lines, making it shorter than either the Old English *Exodus* or

Andreas. Its storyline appears even simpler than that of its source, the relatively unadorned account from the Vulgate, now considered apocryphal, though deemed an integral part of the Bible in medieval Europe. The story's basic incident involves the heroine, a brave Bethulian woman, who by beheading the Assyrian oppressor saves her faithful people from the enemy. God shows his favour to the Israelites through her actions. The *Liber Judith* presents the reader with a number of characters from both camps: on the Jewish side, the protagonist, her servant, Ozias the prince, Joachim the high priest, and, on the Assyrian side, Holofernes the captain, his eunuch servant, Nebuchadnezzar their leader, and Achior, a Moabite who converts to Judaism. The Anglo-Saxon poetic version, however, cuts the cast down to four. Only two of the remaining characters are named, the heroine and the anti-hero, whilst the other two are their anonymous servants. Because of their isolation, the pair at the heart of the narrative gains importance: Holofernes is sole ruler, answering to no one, and Judith heads the Bethulians who seem to lack a prince. The omission of Nebuchadnezzar and Jerusalem removes any reference to the Temple and its vessels that the Israelites seek to protect from being despoiled in the biblical version.[1] Spoliation on behalf of Old English poetry of a biblical narrative in Latin, itself an appropriation of a Jewish narrative for Christian purposes, ironically leaves out some reference to literal plundering.

This 'polarisation and simplification of the narrative' leads easily to spiritual allegorisation.[2] Unattached to the larger geopolitical and historical forces present in the scriptural text, the struggle between Judith and Holofernes comes to represent a clash between good and evil: 'Her heroism is that of the daughter of faith; his evil that of the prince of darkness.'[3] Many scholars agree on the ultimate message of the Old English poem: 'faith in God ... and a sense of hope [for] a besieged people'; 'the theme of faith and salvation'; 'simple central themes of Judith's wisdom and faith and God's mercy and grace toward His faithful'.[4] Shorn of specifically Jewish references, the narrative more readily communicates a simple, powerful message to the Christian Anglo-Saxons; with the excision of Achior the convert, there is no longer a need to speak of his blessing of Judith 'by thy God in every tabernacle of Jacob' and of his circumcision.[5]

Complications quickly arise both at the macro- and micro-level, when readers step back from seemingly satisfactory religious interpretations to look at the poem in its most immediate surviving context, MS Cotton Vitellius A. xv. *Judith* is a fragment, missing some material in the beginning and at the end. A poem interested in cutting, of tyrants' heads and biblical material alike, has itself undergone some incisions. It follows the poem of *Beowulf* in the manuscript, and so might have been added afterwards, but the same scribe who transcribed *Beowulf* from the line 1939b to the end, copied it out, the so-called 'Hand B'. The question of how much of the poem is missing has not been settled. In general, the tendency has moved from postulating large portions of up to a thousand lines (making the poem in its original form resemble the biblical verse of MS Junius 11) to arguing that no more than a hundred to two hundred lines have been lost, or that the work in its present form is more or less complete.[6] The simplified and polarised handling of the Old Testament tale in what survives of the poem argues for the last view. The author would have had no good reason to introduce characters and provide political and historical background in the lost section of the text, only to ignore them altogether in the now extant portion. Foreshortened narrative can be assumed from the very beginning.

Another unresolved mystery deals with the relation of the fragment to the other poetry and prose in MS Cotton Vitellius A. xv and its ideological programme. Many critics follow Kenneth Sisam's earlier designation of the compilation as 'Liber de diversis monstris, anglice' [The book of various monsters, in English], though they modify it according to their own interpretations. Aside from *Beowulf* and *Judith*, the codex includes a saint's life, *The Passion of St. Christopher*, whose protagonist has a head of a dog[7] and two equally fictional accounts of Alexander the Great's exploits with marvels and monsters in the exotic East, *The Wonders of the East*, written in the third person, and *The Letter of Alexander to Aristotle*, in the first person.[8] Grendel, his mother, and the dragon in *Beowulf*, along with the hero who has the strength of thirty men, are obvious candidates for inclusion in a book of monsters. But *Judith* only has Holofernes, a man not literally monstrous, although called 'a heathen dog',[9] who either roars like an animal or is silent and unconscious.[10] Another solution would be to consider the title heroine as 'wondrous and strange as a dragon slayer, a one-legged man, and a king who campaigned to India [St Christopher]'. To do more justice to the sheer colourful strangeness of the compilation, we could add the Corsiæ (horned, pepper-hoarding snakes), the Donestre (gigantic, multilingual cannibals who weep over their victims' heads), and the long-haired giantesses composed of human, porcine, dromedary, asinine, and bovine parts.[11] Neither Judith nor Holofernes fit well into this extraordinary company.

Andy Orchard extends the notion of the miscellany as a book of monsters by identifying the organising principle as the 'twin interest in the outlandish and in the activities of overweening pagan warriors from a distant and heroic past: pride and prodigies'.[12] Kathryn Powell offers a theme with a political twist, whereby all the texts in Cotton Vitellius A. xv exhibit 'an interest in rulers and rulership, particularly in the ethical conflicts that arise in their interactions with foreign peoples as those rulers defend and expand their kingdoms'. This would accord with the probable time of the manuscript's compilation, late tenth or early eleventh century, the period of Viking invasions.[13] Powell's solution would marry the spiritual and the political. More carnal visions also centre on disintegration. Heather Blurton argues that the emphasis lies on cannibalism, since the two Alexander narratives and *Beowulf* feature ferocious man-eaters.[14] Mary Godfrey remarks that *Beowulf* and *Judith* alike draw attention to 'scenes in which [decapitated] heads [of Grendel and Holofernes] ... become foci of signification, reiterative of the intellectual functions they symbolize, of the employment of those functions by the poem's characters, and the making of poetry itself'.[15] With some imagination, keeping in mind the remarkable heads of the composite creatures in *The Wonders of the East*, and St Christopher's case of cynocephaly, we could call Cotton Vitellius A. xv a book of the head. These interpretations foreground the question of a detached – literally removed or radically distinct – head's relationship to the body and the ability of a part to suggest the whole. Holofernes's decapitated head that powerfully betokens Judith's accomplishment forms the extent of her plunder.

Another approach to discussing *Judith*'s place in the miscellany highlights its difference from the other texts. According to Nicholas Howe, Cotton Vitellius A. xv is a 'book of elsewhere', a 'site ... where the past can be held in its complexities, even in its contradictions', with diverse notions of place appearing one alongside another in whichever order the reader prefers. In such an assemblage, *Judith* signals a return to Christian time, in contrast to the heathen, exotic elsewhere of *Alexander's Letter to Aristotle* and *Beowulf*.[16] Presumably, the story of Judith would comfort readers skilled in exegesis when they reach the end of the compilation. The heroine has a clear place in the scriptural trajectory; she even prays to the Trinity in the Old English poem, 'Ic ðe, frymða god, ond frofre gæst, / bearn alwaldan, biddan wylle' [I wish to beseech you, God of creation, and the spirit of comfort, almighty son] (83–4). 'Elsewhere', the Bethulia of *Judith*, comes home to England with force.[17]

For ultimate comfort this act of translation appears to have required yet another excision, that of most references to the female protagonist's seductiveness. We know from previous chapters that expanding scriptural matter was not unusual, but Anglo-Saxon literary corpus at large avoids eroticism (except for the riddles).[18] Unlike its biblical source, the Old English poem omits Holofernes's invitation to Judith, 'her acceptance, her dressing, her entrance, his desire for her, their conversation, her eating and drinking, and the cause of his excessive drinking'. In the vernacular version, the party has already ended, and the Assyrian general is too drunk to defend himself, let alone to defile the chaste widow with his hands or eyes.[19] Mark Griffith explains that the changes stem from the general sense of Anglo-Saxon Christian propriety. The Vulgate, on the contrary, paints a scene of anticipation with a celebratory summary of Judith's body and accessories. It starts off with a wardrobe change. She is, in Samantha Zacher's words, 'dressed to kill':[20]

> For she put off her garments of widowhood, and put on her garments of joy, to give joy to the children of Israel. / She anointed her face with ointment, and bound up her locks with a crown, she took a new robe to deceive him. / Her sandals ravished his eyes, her beauty made his soul her captive, with a sword she cut off his head. (16:9–11)[21]

The suppression of most of the potentially distracting, erotic detail belongs to the same arsenal of narrative transformation as the reduction of characters and removal of larger sociopolitical context and specific Jewish customs. Naomi Schor has written on the danger of detail and its association with the feminine in the nineteenth-century novel and beyond. Some of her comments could apply to the Old English *Judith*. Schor finds feminine detail, 'the bad detail ... which ... [became] an end in itself, a detail for detail's sake', to be distinct from the epic detail as theorised by Georg Wilhelm Friedrich Hegel in his *Aesthetics*.[22] Hegel argues that the epic detail slows down the narrative tempo, enabling the reader to enjoy the text without taking away from its overall vision because 'this detailed attention is the very spirit of the men and situations described'.[23] While Hegel has Homeric epics foremost in his mind, we could apply this characterisation to the many scenes in *Beowulf*, in which various details – sartorial, armorial, funerary, corporeal – invite the audience to gaze and wonder. We would also have to acknowledge that many of them seem menacing, that they should not be allowed to capture the reader, and that they are ultimately burned, buried, or both. The protagonist's gender might have led the author of *Judith* to schematise his source and strip both the woman and the text of their ornamentation to a large degree, but not completely. Judith is famously only the third heroine in the extant corpus of Anglo-Saxon poetry to have a poem dedicated to her.[24] She is furthermore the only woman to brandish a weapon, unless we count Grendel's mother who attacks Beowulf with a short dagger. The epic detail in this case would have been the feminine detail.

Despite his simplifying and polarising tendencies, which result in the removal of many sensuous specifics, the poet of *Judith* brings to the fore other vivid, possibly disturbing, details. Then he briskly moves the narrative forwards and outwards. A sustained close focus on *spolia*-like objects and individuals is combined throughout the text with a series of ever-decreasing cramped spaces, which signify death and oppression. A more positive arrangement of artefacts, humans, and enclosures emerges alongside images of breaking or cutting through. The poem in one moment creates the discomfort of implicit sexuality and explicit violence, which involves literal plundering of bodies and body-armour, a rich field of study for psychoanalytic critics. In the next, it suggests the comfort of cross-temporal, spiritual integration of radiant *spolia* upholding the overarching Christian message, which fits well into exegetical interpretations of *Judith*.

When a possessor becomes possessed

Judith, or her body, appears as the first instance of plunder in the poem. We have already encountered the phenomenon of women as a focus of spoliation – as treasure seized in war and a site for its display – in the 'Afrisc meowle' [African woman] passage of *Exodus* and the wife's confrontation with the sword/phallus in Exeter Riddle 20. Holofernes intends to possess Judith by having her move through increasingly smaller enclosures. She steps into action at nightfall. After the mention of her name comes a resplendent detail, her designation as 'ides ælfscinu' [an elf-radiant woman] (14), on which the author spends no time. Patricia Belanoff writes that the connotations of the compound are 'far more complex than ordinary beauty [...] suggestive of beauty deceptively manipulated. The word becomes both Christian and pagan'.[25] The author leaves an indication of Judith's seductive power for the readers to trip on. In a highly reduced account, such a small but significant detail stands out more. At this crucial point in the narrative, enclosures appear along with treasure that they are supposed to contain. Here, too, a sense of urgency pervades the text. The Assyrian leader commands that the heroine be 'ofstum fetigan / to his bedreste, beagum gehlæste, / hringum gehrodene' [fetched hastily to his bed, laden with necklaces, adorned with rings] (35–7). The servants do as the 'byrnwigena brego' [chief of the byrnie-warriors] asks (39). Judith's accessories and her body function ironically: while Holofernes considers both fuel for a sexual encounter, they ultimately bring down ruin on the enemy inadequately protected by his own armour. Her treasure will counter his. After she triumphs over him, her city will clash against his tent; her *burh*, an image of stability, will vanquish his temporary structure. And, finally, his byrnies will become hers.

The poem emphasises that it is Holofernes and his followers – not Judith – who are held down by his objects and enclosure. In its beginning, the Assyrians join their leader at a feast. Increasingly claustrophobic spaces signal more intense containment for a number of characters. Downward movement followed by stasis works the same way. Once again, enclosures, people, and treasures – all aspects intrinsically linked with spoliation – emerge simultaneously. All Holofernes's 'weagesiðas, / bealde byrnwiggende' [comrades in woe, bold warriors in byrnies] arrive at his celebration to *sittan*, 'sit' (15–17). Ciaran Arthur observes that the poem never shows the Assyrian ruler standing up. He and his followers are consistently 'lowered in posture': first they sit, then they lie down, drunken or dead.[26] We soon learn that 'bollan steape/... swylce eac bunan ond orcas' [deep bowls ... and also cups and pitchers] were brought to the *fletsittendum* [those sitting in the hall] (17–19). Two of the three words for the drinking containers, 'bunan ond orcas', have a mysterious, more menacing sound,[27] so much so that the guests seem weighted down by the objects.

Finally, *flett* [hall] can also mean 'floor, ground'. The *Dictionary of Old English* remarks that '[s]ense two ["dwelling, house, hall"] is not always to be distinguished from sense one, perhaps by synecdoche (in poetry)'. The *Judith* author implies that the warriors – participants in the courtly civilisation familiar to us from other Anglo-Saxon poems – are brought low through the very trappings of that civilisation. Held down by their byrnies, ready to embark on a journey of sorrow with their leader, they already, paradoxically, sit unmoving on the ground. The next two half-lines provide more evidence for this supposition: 'hie þæt fæge þegon, / rofe rond-wiggende ...' [They served those doomed ones, the courageous shield warriors] (19–20). *Hie* could refer to the invisible attendants, those who carry the bowls, cups, and pitchers to the guests. Yet the pronoun could also modify the containers. In that case the image would inextricably connect the men, the objects they wear and touch to their mouths, their vertical and horizontal surroundings (both contained in the word *flett*), and their destiny of doom. Rather than pushing the narrative along, these terms suggest a dangerous, seductive charge of pagan material culture. It is not only the posture of the enemy[28] that communicates their literal drunkenness and spiritual iniquity, but also their vessels.

To contain the woman ornamented and, as they wrongly suppose, restrained by metal, the Assyrians lead her surprisingly quickly into an elaborate structure. It resembles Chinese boxes, enclosures nestled within other enclosures:

> bearhtme stopon
> to ðam gysterne, þær hie Iudithðe
> fundon ferhðgleawe, ond ða fromlice
> lindwiggende   lædan ongunnon
> þa torhtan mægð   to træfe þam hean,
> þær se rica hyne reste on symbel
> nihtes inne, nergende lað,
> Holofernus.   Þær wæs eallgylden
> fleohnet fæger   ond ymbe þæs folctogan
> bed ahongen ...
> ... Hie ða on reste gebrohton
> snude ða snoteran idese ...
> (39–48; 54–55)
> [They stepped instantly into the guest-chamber (or: into the tumult of the guest-chamber), where they found the wise Judith, and then quickly the shield-warriors began to lead the bright maiden to the lofty tent, where the ruler, Holofernes hateful to the Saviour, rested always at night. There was a beautiful fly-net, all in gold, hung around the folk-leader's bed ... They brought her swiftly to the bed, that sagacious woman.]

Judith is moved from the larger feasting area to Holofernes's sleeping quarters. Then she goes through the two-way mirror-like gilded netting (an addition of our poet, not present in the Vulgate) to Holofernes's bed. The heroine journeys from the greater tumult, the world of noisy revels, into a more intimate but more dangerous frame. The leader of the warriors wishes to wrap and thus subsume her brightness in the *fleohnet*, but her brightness exceeds the all-golden beauty of the contraption even semantically, since *torht* is often translated as 'illustrious'. The sense of urgency continues, indicated the adverbs *bearhtme* [instantly], *fromlice* [quickly], and *snude* [swiftly]. As Thomas Bredehoft has remarked, the narrative unrolls with remarkable speed in the first 120 lines before Judith dispatches Holofernes.[29] The text might rush to the moment of the tyrant's gruesome death to increase the audience's excitement. It might additionally communicate its unease with the heroine's role as a murderous seductress. Holofernes and his attendants wish to contain their human *spolium*; the poem does, too.

After the report that the servants fetched Judith, we immediately learn of Holofernes's intentions. Having heard that Judith was brought to 'his burgetelde' [his private tent], the 'burga ealdor' [lord of cities] rejoices (57–8). By naming him thus, the poet draws our attention to the character's presumed mastery over smaller and larger spaces alike. We recall that the heathen's planned subjugation of the heroine has direct links with his desire to crush her homeland of Bethulia. The master of enclosures 'þohte ða beorhtan idese / mid widle ond mid womme besmitan' [intended to defile the bright woman with corruption and sin] (58–9). Karma Lochrie observes that these lines reveal that '[w]arfare is ... conducted through the inscription of bodies toward the end of inscribing cultures, property, and possessions with the proprietorship of the victor.'[30] Lochrie's words bring to mind the body-as-text metaphor, to which she, in fact, explicitly refers. Judith's decapitation of her adversary 'renders Holofernes's body into a text'.[31] I would like to suggest that in addition to textual, these acts of 'inscribing cultures, property, and possessions with the proprietorship of the victor' can take a visual-artistic turn. The adorned woman taken away from her people and separated from the revelers in the hall becomes a resplendent fragment, a *spolium*, whose incorporation into the culture imagined as dominant requires careful and rapid staging.

The irony culminates when Judith deploys the identical tactic against her enemy. This tactic of possession is reversible, as shown also in Riddle 20, where the sword and the woman could belong to any side in a conflict. In *Judith*, Holofernes's body becomes fragmented. The head of the chief – and the pun is pervasive in the Old English[32] – placed in a bag arrives with the heroine in Bethulia, where it has no clear status and needs to be contained. Even before the actual beheading begins, the poet shows Holofernes's restriction in spatial terms. He reports, ironically in sprawling, hypermetric lines, that the horrible man reached his end on earth, 'swylcne he ær æfter worhte, / þearlmod ðeoden gumena, þenden he on ðysse worulde / wunode under wolcna hrofe' [such as he, the resolute lord of men, had striven for before when he had lived in this world under the roof of the clouds] (65–7). Hypermetric lines in *Judith* slow the pace of the text, forcing the readers to turn their attention to the passage at hand.[33] Megan E. Hartman argues that the poet purposefully reworks 'traditional styles of hypermetric composition' to craft a special, uplifting tone to underline his crucial themes: 'moral contrast,' 'reversal of fortunes', and God's ultimate control.[34] In a further ironic move, the theme of restriction, cutting off, manifests itself in expansive, flowing lines.

While some things become shorter, others lengthen in the poet's signature back-and-forth style. The phrase 'þearlmod ðeoden gumena' refers to God later (line 91), when Judith entreats the Lord to grant her salvation. Mark Griffith has noted that, in the first instance, the poet mocks Holofernes who 'like Satan and his king [Nebuchadnezzar, absent in the poem], tried to set himself up in rivalry to God'.[35] Unlike God, with whom he shares the epithet, the Assyrian only lives – does not even rule – on earth, in such a way that he has no access to what lies beyond the clouds. From the world that holds him in, the villain will quickly proceed to more cramped spaces. Once in his chamber, Holofernes falls 'on his reste middan' [in the middle of his bed], and he 'nyste ræda nanne / on gewitlocan' [he has no sense in his mind-locker (i.e., mind)] (68–9). Immediately after the attendants transport Judith from the guest-hall to Holofernes's tent and through the net to his bed, the poet moves the antagonist from the larger terrestrial sphere to the middle of his bed. He finally focuses, for a split second, on a more diminutive enclosure, the one holding the Assyrian's thoughts and feelings, his 'mind-locker'. Mental restriction parallels corporeal restriction in Holofernes's case. As far as Judith is concerned, Holofernes's attempt to constrain her fails because her spiritual expansion counters it.

Notions of physical posture, heroism, and moral uprightness intertwine in these depictions.[36] While the doomed revellers sit on the ground or in the hall in the beginning of the poem, their cursed lord falls on the bed before continuing his downward movement to hell. Unlike God who controls everything, Holofernes is unable to possess either his body or mind, let alone the beautiful Hebrew woman or the area under the celestial roof. Judith invokes the guardian of heaven ('swegles weard') by name, the saviour of all the world-dwellers ('nergend ealra / woruldbuendra') (80–2), to help her in her mighty endeavour. Judith's epithets emphasise how far the Lord's reach extends. It stretches from the firmament to each inhabitant of the earth. Following Judith's hypermetric prayer to the Trinity,[37] the poet assures his audience that just as the Lord gives support to the protagonist, so, too, does he provide for 'anra gehwylcne / herbuendra' [each of those who dwell here] who seek his aid with sensibility and true belief (95–6). Broadening of focus becomes absolutely necessary now, when the sagacious woman faces up-close her enemy reduced to his empty *gewitloca* [mind-locker]. *Her* [here] in this passage covers the entire planet. In contrast to Holofernes's very specific suffering, the succour from the divine combines the specific with the general. After this statement of assurance, we hear that 'wearð hyre rume on mode' [lit., it became spacious in her (Judith's) mind/heart/spirit] (97), meaning that she felt relief. B. J. Timmer gives, alongside 'spaciously', another rather beautiful gloss for *rume*: 'wide and light'.[38] The heroine's mental expansion enables her to restrain the unconscious body lying next to her.[39] She out-Holoferneses Holofernes by doing what he has failed to do, carefully staging the performance of rendering an adversary into a portable artefact of triumph. Her status changes from that of an object to be possessed to that of a possessor.[40]

While the poet never depicts Judith explicitly as a warrior,[41] he describes her struggle against the unconscious brute with sustained attention to its physicality. *Spolia* embody a certain materiality at the same time as they refuse to be fixed. Compare the account of the battle in the Vulgate ('and she struck twice upon his neck, and cut off his head, and took off his canopy from the pillars, and rolled away his headless body' [13:10])[42] to the following passage:

> Genam ða þone hæðenan mannan
> fæste be feaxe sinum; teah hyne folmum wið hyre weard
> bysmerlice,   ond þone bealofullan
> listum alede,   laðne mannan,
> swa heo ðæs unlædan   eaðost mihte
> wel gewealdan.   Sloh ða wundenlocc
> þone feondsceaðan   fagum mece,
> heteþoncolne,   þæt heo healfne forcearf
> þone sweoran him,   þæt he on swiman læg,
> druncen ond dolhwund.   Næs ða dead þa gyt,
> ealles orsawle. Sloh ða eornoste
> ides ellenrof   oðre siðe
> þone hæðenan hund, þæt him þæt heafod wand
> forð on ða flore. (98–111)

[Then she seized the heathen firmly by his hair. She pulled him with her hands towards herself ignominiously[43] and positioned the evil, hateful man skilfully, in such a way that she could well manage/possess the wicked one the most easily. The curly-haired woman struck that bitter enemy, the hostile-minded man, with the decorated/shining sword so that she cut through a half of his neck, so that he lay in a swoon, drunk and wounded. He was not dead yet, (not) entirely lifeless. The courageous woman struck fiercely the heathen dog for the second time, so that his head rolled down to the floor.]

The author, who earlier excises distracting, seductive details of Judith's appearance, provides ten lines, some of them hypermetric, of overt violence and covert eroticism to translate a single, matter-of-fact biblical sentence. This is an unusual episode for a literary tradition that typically avoids showing a man and a woman close together in bed. The ten lines have generated lively critical readings and disagreements. Alexandra Olsen identifies in the scene 'an ironic inversion of that realistic situation in which men reduce women to objects to be abused'. She further argues that 'the decapitation of Holofernes is presented as the symbolic rape of a man by a woman'.[44] Susan Kim goes further by claiming that the passage implies multiple, sexually charged actions: castration, circumcision, intercourse, and even 'a perverse sort of impregnation'.[45] On the contrary, Samantha Zacher dismisses psychoanalytic readings because the Old English poet removes references to actual circumcision (of Achior the convert) or a castrated character (Holofernes's eunuch Vagao).[46] Zacher's argument illuminates the situation from a different angle. As we have seen above, the poet tends to remove certain details in order to present others in another place, sometimes cutting, sometimes extending. The sheer concentration of critical readings on this scene testifies to its textual power.

While I acknowledge the more corporeal connotations at play here, I also wish to recognise the artistic reverberations of the heroine's actions. Incorporation of plunder once again brings to mind the creative process. Rather than emphasising her weakness,[47] the poet draws attention to Judith's expert manipulation. Judith rules Holofernes, controls him, has power over him, but also wields him as one would a weapon: 'in order to defeat the enemy and become the hero … [she] must come to have, to possess, to hold part of the enemy securely in [her] hands'.[48] Moreover, the heroine makes sure she carries out her job *wel*. We hear about her hair, either naturally curly or braided,[49] as well as a *fah* sword, a 'patterned or gleaming' implement that she apparently finds hanging by the enemy's bed in line 78. Hair, fashioned either by woman or by God, recalls the texture and radiance of the wrought object much described and appropriated in heroic verse. Artifice signifies power. The poem not only 'effectively constructs femininity as coextensive with divine love and martial success',[50] but also characterises creativity in the same manner, even paradoxically through the act of bodily disintegration. Like the narrative, Holofernes had tried to cut Judith down, but she emerges, more extended and triumphant than ever.

Judith's heroic and ironic act of plundering her enemy establishes a connection between the poem and its nearest neighbour in the compilation. The image of a creature lying in an enclosed space near an especially charged artefact or a group of them reverberates through Cotton Vitellius A. xv. Fabienne Michelet shows that Heorot, Grendel's cave, and the dragon's lair in *Beowulf* are all connected with examples of this particular 'cluster of images': Beowulf sleeps in his armour, Grendel's corpse lies near the famous rune-inscribed sword, and the dragon is coiled atop a heap of valuables. Michelet brings in the decapitation passage in *Judith* to make a further point: '[t]hese various episodes [in both poems] depict places where extraordinary events happen which ... all involve a specific body part: the head.'[51] She lists the situations in *Beowulf* that carry associations similar to the decapitation scene in *Judith*: the cup that the unfortunate slave takes lies by the dragon's head; the Geats in Hrothgar's hall put their shields by their heads before going to sleep; Scyld's followers place a golden standard over this head in preparation for the ship-burial. 'All these scenes', she concludes, 'are built on a cluster of images including a reclining figure, weapons, and precious objects, and something happening to the head.'[52] Remembering Lochrie's characterisation of Judith's act of decapitation as a corporeal-textual intervention, a victorious possession of him who would victoriously possess her, we can look for traces of the poet's awareness of his project of translation, a re-inscribing of a biblical story. We could then argue that the cluster of images identified by Michelet, along with the proximity of Judith's *wundenlocc* to her *mece* [sword], reveals the poet as a self-conscious spoliator. To do this, we need to follow Holofernes's head and the effect it has on its surroundings.

Losing his head

Judith's second strike sends Holofernes's head rolling 'forð on ða flore' (111). Downward movement continues. While his head lies on the floor and his body remains on the bed, his spirit departs elsewhere 'under neowelne næs' [under a steep cliff] (113), where he is quadruply restrained: 'susle gesæled ... / wyrmum bewunden, witum gebunden / hearde gehæfted in helle bryne' [fettered with torments ... wound about with serpents, bound with sorrows, imprisoned hard in the fire of hell] (114–16). He will forever stay in *wyrmsele* [snake-hall], a 'heolstran ham' [dark home] (119, 121). Donald Fry has identified this description as an instance of 'The Cliff of Death', an Anglo-Saxon formulaic theme featuring cliffs, serpents, darkness, and deprivation, which does not occur in the Vulgate.[53] As we have already seen in the winter-weather interlude in *Andreas* and the city of the sea in *Exodus* (as well as in the decapitation scene in *Judith*), Old English poets often elaborate on or expand their sources when treating spaces, artefacts, and artefact-marked spaces. Lori Ann Garner indicates that the scene of Holofernes's descent to hell employs certain details from the end of the Book of Judith, in which the heroine sings of the punishment that the Lord will inflict on the enemies of Israel. Garner writes that '[t]he movement of this idea from the end of the *Liber Judith* to its location in the Anglo-Saxon text corresponds well with [Alain] Renoir's observation that the poet far preferred specific, vivid imagery to general abstractions.'[54]

But the 'specific, vivid imagery' introduced here functions not to enchant and captivate the readers but precisely to push them into a 'general' abstraction, the idea of the heathen's ultimate doom. Not only does the poet transform a portion of the Old Testament, the story of Judith so powerfully marked by a bleeding fragment, into Old English verse, but he also populates his poem with self-contained spaces, such as the bed covered with the fly-net or 'The Cliff of Death' inferno. They stand out from the well-known story, upholding it while taking the readers out of it. These *loci* that restrain and frame the antagonist cannot imprison the protagonist, and they paradoxically liberate the audience.

While Holofernes's body is tied up in hell, his head comes into one final container, Judith's *fætels* [meal-bag] (127).[55] Everything opens up as the heroine walks towards Bethullia with it in her hand and a maidservant by her side. We follow the pair and stop to look on with them at the moment when the vista of their home town emerges before them. Judith and her servant 'sweotollice geseon mihten / þære wlitegan byrig weallas blican, / Bethuliam' [can see clearly the beautiful city walls of Bethulia shine] (136–8). They hurry onward, *beahhrodene* [laden with rings] (138), to the *wealgate*

[gate in the wall] (141). Another cluster of bright and concrete images surfaces here. The joy of the two women escaping with a precious prize from the Assyrian camp reflects on the outer walls of Bethulia. Everything shines – the protective walls, then, presumably, the jewellery on the pair – as the alliteration follows the movement of radiance: 'byrig ... blican ... Bethuliam ... beahhrodene'. Whereas before Judith's armour clashed against that of her enemy, now her city's adornments fuse with hers. Stacy Klein describes this phenomenon and its effect memorably: 'The poet's glowing praise for Judith's bright appearance, shining jewels, and gleaming weapons works to conflate the bright *ides* [woman] and her bright accessories – to the point where the two begin to merge and to become virtually indistinguishable from one another.'[56] Rather than becoming Holofernes's prize, another piece in his collection of plunder, Judith spills out of herself and her treasure into Bethulia and Bethulians, and, metaphorically, into the Christian community of the poem's readership. Connection triumphs over isolation, expansion over restriction. This type of dissolution would begin to neutralise any dangerous charge still hanging on the protagonist. The *spolium* would merge seamlessly into her new/old context.

When we first glimpse the Bethulians, they are keeping watch at the gate. Three elements closely associated with spoliation, the people, the treasure, and the architecture are all mentioned in succession prior to a promise of an opening through the *wealgate*. For Paul Zumthor, the gate, even more than the walls, is the perfect emblem of a city. It is:

> a two-faced place, the entrance and the exit for people and goods, absorbing raw material to yield crafted objects; a weak point of the fortification, and therefore the most ardently defended; but, also, in the times of peace, a place where one waits, chats, drinks, eats, and trades, where jongleurs stand around.[57]

As a liminal place of commerce and exchange, the *wealgate* corresponds nicely with the larger vision of the poem, the Janus-faced or 'double perspective' that looks back to the Vulgate and forwards to the contemporary audience,[58] or the back and forth between restriction and release, cutting down and extension.

The Bethulians sit as did the Assyrians when the poet first introduced them ('[w]iggend sæton' [the warriors were sitting]) (141), but, unlike the Assyrians, they will soon stand. Three lines down, the author refers to the city as a *fæsten* [stronghold]. Judith asks 'gumena sumne / of ðære ginnan byrig' [one of the men from that spacious city] (148–9) to come and let her in through the gates. *Ginn*, the adjective here modifying *burh*, occurs in the Old English *Exodus* in the phrase 'ginfæsten god' [wide, steadfast good] (525) that the guardian of the soul unlocks, as well as in the expression 'garsecges gin' [the ocean's wide abyss] that cannot hold in God's glory (431). Bethulia's expansion, like the sudden brightness of its walls at night, reflects its metamorphosis. Judith's home town experiences the same widening that the heroine felt when 'it became spacious in her heart/mind/spirit'. That stretching of space enabled the gradual containment of Holofernes who had fancied himself a ruler underneath 'the roof of the heavens'. Once again, a single fact takes in incredible largeness. The protagonist calls what she is soon to reveal to her people a 'þoncwyrðe þing' [thanksworthy affair/ deed/thing] (153). Her plans and actions indeed result in an object; the entire affair of Bethulian liberation from the Assyrians revolves around a thing.

Still, the resonances of that one event are cosmic, as Judith promptly explains. Because of the Lord's favour, it is revealed 'geond woruld wide' [throughout the wide world] that the citizens will receive a great reward for their long suffering (156). Despite Alain Renoir's assertion that *Judith*, unlike other religious poems and even *Beowulf*,[59] does not pause for an elaborate presentation of a larger spiritual message, focusing instead on the action of the Old Testament narrative, we have seen that the text does, in fact, provide moments that allow for a transhistorical zooming out 'geond woruld wide'.[60] The heroine's rousing speech at this moment is sufficiently vague for the readers to extend it to any situation in which they find themselves as God's people.

The power of Judith's speech moves the *burhsittende* emotionally and physically. The compound meaning 'city-dwellers' (literally 'those sitting in the city') underlines their similarity to and difference from the Assyrians. There are quick references to an unspecified number of warriors, and then to one of the inhabitants of the spacious *burh*, whom Judith asks to open the gate. Suddenly, we learn of an enormous number of Bethulians, 'weras wif somod, wornum ond heapum, / ðreatum ond ðrymmum ... þusendmælum, / ealde ge geonge' [men along with women, in crowds and throngs, in groups and hosts ... in thousands, old and young] (163–6). They all move in anticipation 'wið þæs fæstengeates' [towards the gate of the stronghold] (162). Before Holofernes's retainers had led the heroine away from the tumult into a bed covered by a fly-net within the tent. Now the brave woman goes from being almost alone – she has her trusty servant with her – to an impending incorporation into a tumultuous mass of humans.[61] Intensity subsumes details that glitter only for a short time. Griffith claims that no other Anglo-Saxon poet can 'evoke scenes so powerfully and realistically as the *Judith* poet', but he emphasises that it is style rather than content that distinguishes our author. Griffith continues, 'He is as little interested in the detailed description of people, places, and objects as the other poets.'[62] In the scene of Judith's homecoming, a detailed description would go against the idea that the multitude within the Bethulian walls cannot be contained by an object or a text.

Judith's presence generates a sense of urgency. Just as Holofernes's servants had rushed to bring the heroine into their leader's quarters, to rein her in, so the Bethulians, 'men on ðære medobyrig' [men in that mead-city], let her in with haste ('ofostlice ... in forleton') (167–70). On the one hand, the touch of the monstrous with which the protagonist grappled makes the guardians of the city hesitate before opening the gates for her. She has to wait 'for ten anxiety-provoking lines'.[63] On the other hand, it could just as well be that they are eager to consume her, to incorporate her successful attempt at beheading within the narrative of war against the enemy.[64] In both cases, the protagonist would appear as a fragment that requires containment, either by being distanced from or subsumed within the city. *Medoburh* recalls various other compounds with mead that refer to the Assyrians, *medugal* [drunk with mead] (26) and *medowerig* [weary from mead, i.e., drunk; hung over] (229, 245), and, as such, it connects the world that Judith left to the world to which she returns.[65] She successfully leaves one heroic or anti-heroic feast, but what will happen to her when she encounters another?

Once admitted back to the *medoburh*, the wise woman adorned with gold ('golde gefrætewod') orders her maid to display the bloody head to the citizens (171). Here, once more, the three components of the image cluster come up at once: the treasure (on Judith), the fragment (Holofernes's head), and the stronghold that encloses them both (with the townspeople as the audience). Judith's following speech meant to rouse the Bethulians to war, features identical elements, but in a different order. The heroine's inspiring discourse also brings in God and light. She asks the people to 'fysan to feohte, syððan frymða god, / arfæst cyning, eastan sende / leohtne leoman' [hasten to battle, after God of creation, the gracious king, sends forth a shining light from the east] (189–91). That light spills over the equipment that the speech enjoins Israelites to carry, 'linde ... bord

... ond byrnhomas, / scire helmas' [shields ... and byrnies, gleaming helmets] (191–3). In short, they should kill 'fagum sweordum, / fæge frumgaras' [doomed chieftains with patterned swords] (194–5). The compound for 'chieftains', apparently modelled after the Latin *primi-pilus*, contains two parts, *fruma* [origin] and *gar* [spear], fusing the people with their armour. Judith urges the Israelites to take up their arms to clash with another set of arms. God's light and creation will help them counteract the flash of origin-spears.

Her final addition to the creation-light-treasure cluster testifies further to the presence of divine strength. Perhaps gesturing towards the decapitated head, the heroine exclaims, 'swa eow getacnod hafað / mihtig dryhten þurh mine hand' [so has the mighty God betokened to you by means of my hand] (197–8). Griffith notes that a key moment in the Old English *Exodus*, in which Moses narrates the raising of the waves (line 262), is 'lexically identical' with the lines just quoted. Both Old Testament heroes 'make clear to their followers that divine power operates through their hands (an emphasis which derives from the source)'.[66] One could add that the hand for both poets is also an emblem of creation. Both Moses and Judith point to their hands when the Israelites witness a miracle resulting from God's powerful creation of an artefact. It is the temporary city constructed from the waves of the Red Sea in *Exodus*, and the enemy's detached head in *Judith*.

Like other *spolia*, Holofernes's head marks an occasion for metatextual reflection in *Judith*. Scholars like Heide Estes and Fabienne Michelet have written about this phenomenon variously. The debate centres on the issue of 'indigestion' or 'integration', stasis or dynamism, regarding the role of Holofernes's corporeal fragment in Bethulia and the work.[67] While the head does not undergo much change, the text of the poem and the character of the heroine do with each new reading. The lack of explicit allegorisation seems to indicate that the poet does not wish to circumscribe the meaning of his work despite frequent simplification and polarisation. Expansion exists at the core of tightest compression, which is one of the most exciting effects of *spolia*. Perhaps the author (or his patron) picked the story exactly because it resists a complete levelling of distracting detail, a voiding of undigested material. It is still correct that Holofernes's head in Bethulia does not receive nearly as much attention as Grendel's does in Heorot. If we envision the body part as a token of objects to come, the first *spolium* in a series of many, then we could begin to move away from the feeling of stagnancy or poetic indigestion. At the same time, we should recognise that some fragments do not allow a smooth incorporation into a new society.

Cutting through, *spolia* to come

On the morning following Judith's escape, one of the Assyrian warriors discovers the beheaded corpse after the somewhat humorous attempts of the rest to awaken the lord who, they assume, is still resting from the night before. The meaning of the act becomes immediately clear to him. He re-enacts spatially the downfall of his king: '[h]e þa lungre gefeoll / freorig to foldan' [he fell at once, shivering, to the ground] (280–1).[68] He exclaims then that their imminent destruction is revealed and signified ('geswutelod ... getacnod'), and that time is pressing upon them with sorrows ('tide ys / mid niðum neah geðrungen') (285–7). His comrades throw down their weapons, 'wurpon hyra wæpen ofdune' – more downward movement – and flee (290). Revelation, signification, and crowding appear together, linked by the successive participles in 'geswutelod ... getacnod ... geðrungen', carrying a promise of doom. The image of time acting as a throng of malevolent people recalls earlier moments of groups of humans in physical motion. They include the tumult in the Assyrian hall, which could not affect the heroine; the movement of the Bethulian masses, who rush forward to take in Judith and her prize; and the final retreat of the panicked Assyrians, who, upon hearing of the advance of the Israelites, 'burgeteldes/... hwearfum þringan / Holofernus' [press forward to Holofernes's tent] (248–50). The Chosen People make their attack:

Hi ða fromlice   fagum swyrdum,
hæleð higerofe,   herpað worhton
þurh laðra gemong,   linde heowon,
scildburh scæron. [...] (301–4)
          Þær on greot gefeoll
se hyhsta dæl   heafodgerimes
Assiria   ealdorduguðe,
laðan cynnes. (307–10)
[Then the brave-hearted men promptly made a warpath with patterned swords through the crowd of the hateful ones; they cut through their shields, they pierced their shield-formations ... The largest portion of the head-count of the Assyrian leaders, of that hateful race, fell there in the dust / on the ground.]

The adverb *fromlice* fortifies the narrative's fast tempo. While before the jubilant crowd of Bethulians yearned to come together with the heroine and her spoils of war, now the mass of Assyrians is violently broken through, and their battle-gear scattered. The Israelites appear to be opening up space: their men on the warpath cut through a *burh* made out of shields. The *Judith* poet presents us with yet another instance of downward movement when the enemy troop falls on the ground like their leader before them. In removing an essential part, a portion of the *heafodgerim* [head-count/total number] of the Assyrians, Judith's compatriots metaphorically repeat her act of decapitation.

Soon a heap of bodies and armour forms in front of the victors, who plunder it. 'Rum wæs to nimanne … heolfrig herereaf, hyrsta scyne, / bord and bradswyrd, brune helmas, / dyre madmas' [There was an opportunity to take bloody plunder, bright trappings, shields and broad swords, burnished helmets, precious treasures] (313, 316–18). *Rum*, which means 'an opportunity' here, elsewhere in Old English also signifies 'space, room'. It is related to the adjective *rum* [spacious] from which the adverb *rume* [spaciously (or, in Timmer's translation, 'wide and light')] derives. *Rume* describes Judith's feeling upon receiving God's favour to behead Holofernes: 'wearð hyre rume on mode' [it became spacious in her mind/heart/spirit] (97).[69] A space must be cleared to claim a pile of objects, some of them called *brad* [broad], still attached to the humans who wore them.

In the following lines, however, the 'width and lightness' permeating the scene become somewhat qualified. It takes no less than a month and the entirety of the Bethulian army to transport the *spolia* taken from the enemy. The poet enumerates the plunder again, in more explicit terms: helmets and hip-daggers, grey byrnies, and battle-armour adorned with gold (327–8). More detail appears with some indication of length with *hupseax* [hip-dagger, short sword]; of colour with *har* [grey]; and of material with gold. But the author does not let us meditate on the plunder for too long. He acknowledges his inability to describe the treasure and endows it with metaphorical force not unlike that of the Egyptian treasures at the end of the Old English *Exodus*. Here, he narrates, were 'mare madma þonne mon ænig / asecgan mæge searoþoncelra' [more treasures than any men from among the discerning could say] (329–30).

The same movement occurs, with even more triumphalism, in long, rolling, hypermetric lines at the very end of the poem. In the Vulgate, Judith celebrates her own seductiveness, which enabled her to trap Holofernes and behead him. In the Old English poem, here as elsewhere, there is no trace of ointment on her face, of a crown on her head, or of a new robe and sandals that would have enticed the tyrant.[70] Instead of the physical details of the heroine's beauty, the Anglo-Saxon poet adds her acceptance of the plunder that once belonged to her enemy, that is, the objects still bearing a trace of his body. Judith of the scriptural account rejects the goods in no uncertain terms: she 'offered for an anathema of oblivion all the arms of Holofernes, which the people gave her' (16:23).[71] This crucial change from the Vulgate can be interpreted more menacingly than a mere heroic-epic flourish. Ælfric and Aldhelm, for example, use the story of Judith and Holofernes as an exemplum warning against sexual lust and the desire for material objects or goods.[72] Our poet takes out one danger and replaces it with another. But, as usual, it is not long before he provides escape routes.

The text lingers on what was brought to Judith as a reward from the Israelite military expedition ('to mede hyre / of ðam siðfate') (334–5). Her reward consists of more than the expected items, the enemy's 'sweord ond swatigne helm, swylce eac side byrnan / gerenode readum golde' [sword and bloody helmet, as well as his wide byrnie, adorned with red gold] (337–8). She receives 'eal þæt se rinca baldor / swiðmod sinces ahte oððe sundoryrfes' [all that the resolute leader of warriors owned in terms of treasure or personal belongings] (338–9). The entirety of the Assyrian ruler's material culture flows to his attacker. Spaciousness seems to reside in one item, Holofernes's mail-coat, linking the imagery to the previous instances of *rum* and those soon to come. Judith herself is finally associated with treasure in one symmetrical statement. The poet reports that all of the bright treasure ('beorhtra maðma') was given to the bright woman ('beorhtan idese') (340). It is as if the author were creating little openings in the staggering heap of objects and stretching the hoard to enable it to contain a larger narrative. Erin Mullally argues that the poet means to invoke the logic of the heroic gift-giving at this important juncture. As Judith gave the head of Holofernes to her people before, so now they present her with a material reward, a gesture that suggests that it is again her turn to obtain more presents for them. 'Having given Judith armor, the Bethulians acknowledge that they expect a particular type of reciprocation – martial prowess.'[73] This exchange might well serve as an opening of the narrative, now incomplete, into another adventure or as an encouragement for the readers to imagine what happens next. Holofernes's head, likewise, disappears.

The *Judith* poet seizes on the idea of 'reward',[74] and links this material reward on earth with that in heaven. The heroine thanks the Lord for the honour she gained in this world and 'swylce eac mede on heofonum' [also for a reward in heaven] (343). One final zooming out occurs in the blessing in which the poet's and Judith's voices come together:

> Þæs sy ðam leofan dryhtne
> wuldor to widan aldre,   þe gesceop wind ond lyfte,
> roderas ond rume grundas,   swylce eac reðe streamas
> ond swegles dreamas   þurh his sylfes miltse. (346–9)
> [For that let there be glory to the dear Lord for ever, who created the wind and the sky, heavens and spacious earth, as well as raging seas and heavenly joys through his own mercy.]

At the end, everything is washed in spaciousness. *Wid* invoked in the context of time and *rum* of space tear through time and space. The four elements close this poem (as it now stands), as they do the Old English *Exodus*. First, the air occurs in its form as the wind and the sky, and then in plural form as 'heavens'. Then follows the earth, invoked by the term *grund*, so crucial for the beginning of the poem, but now pluralised and liberating. The water finally appears, energised, flowing, and multiplied, alongside the fire, latent in the 'swegles dreamas', because *swegl* can mean 'the sun' as well as 'the sky'.[75] After all that cosmic uproar, *Judith* ends on a note of particularity, invoking God's 'sylfes miltse' [his own mercy], a very individual quality that can break through the enclosures of a body, a mind, a room, and a coat of armour to redeem a plundered fragment and to encompass all creation.

Notes

1 Samantha Zacher, *Rewriting the Old Testament in Anglo-Saxon Verse: Becoming the Chosen People* (New York: Bloomsbury, 2013), pp. 127–8, 147.
2 The phrase comes from Andy Orchard, *Pride and Prodigies: Studies in the Monsters of the* Beowulf-*Manuscript* (Toronto: University of Toronto Press, 1995), p. 7. There he presents two boxes with the characters from the Vulgate and Old English poetic versions of the Judith story.
3 Bernard F. Huppé, *The Web of Words: Structural Analyses of the Old English Poems* Vainglory, The Wonder of Creation, The Dream of the Rood, *and* Judith (Albany: State University of New York Press, 1970), p. 187. On geopolitical implications, see Haruko Momma, 'Epanalepsis:

A Retelling of the Judith Story in the Anglo-Saxon Poetic Language', *Studies in the Literary Imagination*, 36 (2003), 59–73. 'By eliminating most of the Assyrian and Hebrew characters ... the poet alters the social structure of these two communities. Without Nebuchadnezzar, Assyria is no longer a centralized kingdom that dispatches a general and his soldiers to punish the disobedience of satellite countries [in this case, Israel]' (p. 60).

4 Paul de Lacy, 'Aspects of Christianisation and Cultural Adaptation in the Old English "Judith"', *Neuphilologische Mitteilungen*, 97 (1996), 393–410, at 410; Momma, 'Epanalepsis', p. 71; Howell Chickering, 'Poetic Exuberance in the Old English *Judith*', *Studies in Philology*, 106 (2009), 119–36, at 136.

5 Mark Griffith (ed.), *Judith* (Exeter: University of Exeter Press, 1997), pp. 58–9. De Lacy argues that 'Christianisation meant deleting large non-Christian portions of the original text' ('Aspects of Christianisation', p. 400).

6 See for a quick exposition of the problem, footnote 33, pages 265–6, in Erin Mullally, 'The Cross-Gendered Gift: Weaponry in the Old English *Judith*', *Exemplaria*, 17 (2005), 255–84. I agree with Mullally (and others) that 'to hypothesize about what isn't present in the poem is less fruitful than analyzing what is present' (n. 67, p. 280).

7 That part of the story, unfortunately, no longer survives in Cotton Vitellius A. xv.

8 Orchard has published his edition and Modern English translation of the Alexander texts in *Pride and Prodigies*. For all five texts, newly edited and translated, see R. D. Fulk, *The Beowulf Manuscript: Complete Texts and The Fight at Finnsburgh* (Cambridge, MA: Harvard University Press, 2010). Fulk dedicates only one sentence to the possible logic behind the compilation: 'Why these particular texts were collected in one book is not plain, but one influential explanation that has been offered is that the manuscript is devoted to narratives about monsters' (p. x).

9 When he narrates how the heroine struck 'þone hæðenan hund' (110). All quotations from the Old English *Judith* come from Mark Griffith's edition, cited above.

10 Ciaran Arthur, 'Postural Representations of Holofernes in the Old English *Judith*: The Lord who was Laid Low', *English Studies*, 94 (2013), 872–82, at 877.

11 The quotation comes from Momma, 'Epanalepsis', p. 59. In *Pride and Prodigies*, Orchard lists the wonders from *The Wonders of the East* on pages 18, 19, and 20, from which I took the Cosiæ, the Donestre, and the giantesses.

12 Ibid., p. 27.

13 Kathryn Powell, 'Meditating on Men and Monsters: A Reconsideration of the Thematic Unity of the *Beowulf* Manuscript', *The Review of English Studies*, 57 (2006), 1–15, at 10.

14 Heather Blurton, *Cannibalism in High Medieval English Literature* (New York: Palgrave, 2007), pp. 35–58.
15 Mary F. Godfrey, '*Beowulf* and *Judith*: Thematizing Decapitation in Old English Poetry', *Texas Studies in Literature and Language*, 35 (1993), 1–43, at 30. She adds that *The Passion of St. Christopher* showcases a common hagiographic motif, a head that continues speaking after its removal from the body.
16 Howe, *Writing the Map*, p. 193.
17 Ibid.
18 See, for instance, Hugh Magennis, 'No Sex, Please, We're Anglo-Saxons?', *Leeds Studies in English*, 26 (1995), 1–27.
19 Griffith (ed.), *Judith*, pp. 56–7.
20 Zacher, *Rewriting the Old Testament*, p. 126.
21 'exuit enim se vesitmenta viduitatis et induit se vestimenta lætitiæ in exultatione filiorum Israhel/ unxit faciem suam unguento conligavit cincinnos suos mitra ad decipiendum illum/ sandalia eius rapuerunt oculos eius pulchritudo eius captivam fecit animam eius amputavit pugione cervicem eius.' I quote the Bible from the Vulgate and its English translation (Douay Rheims).
22 Naomi Schor, *Reading in Detail: Aesthetics and the Feminine* (New York: Methuen, 1987), p. 50.
23 Quoted in Schor, *Reading in Detail*, p. 31.
24 The other two are Constantine's mother Helen and St Juliana.
25 Patricia Belanoff, '*Judith*: Sacred and Secular Heroine', in Helen Damico and John Leyerle (eds), *Heroic Poetry in the Anglo-Saxon Period: Studies in Honor of Jess B. Bessinger, Jr.* (Kalamazoo: Medieval Institute Publications, 1993), pp. 247–64, at 251.
26 Arthur, 'Postural Representations', p. 880ff.
27 Roberta Frank, 'Three Cups and a Funeral in *Beowulf*', in Katherine O'Brien O'Keeffe and Andy Orchard (eds), *Latin Learning and English Lore: Studies in Anglo-Saxon Literature for Michael Lapidge*, I (Toronto: University of Toronto Press, 2005), 407–20, at 410–11.
28 Arthur, 'Postural Representations', p. 875.
29 Thomas Bredehoft, *Early English Metre* (Toronto: University of Toronto Press, 2005), p. 64.
30 Karma Lochrie, 'Gender, Sexual Violence, and the Politics of War in the Old English *Judith*', in Britton J. Harwood and Gillian R. Overing (eds), *Class and Gender in Early English Literature: Intersections* (Bloomington: Indiana University Press, 1994), pp. 1–20, at 10.
31 Ibid., p. 12.
32 The poet calls the troops of the decapitated leader, who are yet unaware of his condition, *heofodweardas* [head-guards] in line 239. Chickering says that even though sometimes we wish to state that 'a head is only a head … in point of fact, we cannot easily limit its meaning as a sign when in the poem itself the word "heafod" is a deliberate and playful pun' ('Poetic Exuberance', p. 121). Mullally uses the same construction

in the expected way: 'Perhaps, of this instance [reading Judith's decapitation of Holofernes as a castration], we might say that sometimes a decapitation is just a decapitation' ('The Cross-Gendered Gift', n. 49, p. 272).
33 Bredehoft, *Early English Metre*, p. 64. Jackson Campbell writes, 'Remarkably little detail – only a few standard items like the cupbearers – creates in extremely short space an effect of chaotic frenzy'. Jackson Campbell, 'Schematic Technique in *Judith*', *English Literary History*, 38 (1971), 155–72, at 167.
34 Megan E. Hartman, 'A Drawn-Out Beheading: Style, Theme, and Hypermetricity in the Old English *Judith*', *Journal of English and Germanic Philology*, 110 (2011), 421–40, at 423 (styles) and 432–3 (themes listed).
35 Griffith (ed.), *Judith*, p. 77.
36 Arthur, 'Postural Representations', p. 875.
37 Hartman, 'A Drawn-Out Beheading', p. 433. Hypermetric lines, according to Hartman, seem to be a particularly apt choice for reported speech in *Judith*.
38 Timmer (ed.), *Judith* (London: Methuen, 1952), p. 49.
39 R. E. Kaske understands the expression as 'an allusive development of the wisdom mentioned in the preceding half-line'. In support of this assertion he quotes Ambrose's commentary on verse 32 of Psalm 118 ('Viam mandatorum tuorum cucurri, cum dilatasti cor meum' ['I have run the way of your commandments, when you have widened my heart']) and the lines from the Old English *Genesis*, *Beowulf*, and *Elene*, in which wisdom or knowledge widens minds conceptualised as containers like breasts and coffers. R. E. Kaske, '*Sapientia et Fortitudo* in the Old English *Judith*', in Larry D. Benson and Siegfried Wenzel (eds), *The Wisdom of Poetry: Essays in Early English Literature in Honor of Morton W. Bloomfield* (Kalamazoo: Medieval Institute Publications, 1982), pp. 13–30, at 23–4.
40 Mullally, 'The Cross-Gendered Gift', p. 257.
41 Griffith (ed.), *Judith*, p. 67.
42 '[E]t percussit bis in cervicem eius, et abscidit caput eius, et abstulit canopoeum eius a columnis, et evolvit corpus eius truncum.'
43 I follow Griffith's suggestion to translate *bysmerlice* here as 'ignominiously' rather than 'shamefully' because 'the shame is Holofernes', not Judith's' (*Judith*, p. 123). Mullally follows Mary Godfrey by preferring 'mockingly' or 'disgracefully', but states that it is not possible to determine to whom the word refers, whether Judith or Holofernes, before concluding that '[t]he multiple nuances of *bysmerlice* suggest ultimately that Judith has abandoned her previously passive role' ('The Cross-Gendered Gift', p. 271).
44 Alexandra Olsen, 'Inversion and Political Purpose in the Old English *Judith*', *English Studies*, 63 (1982), 289–93, at 291. She gives a historicist reading, in which *Judith* functions as a call to arms for the English

noblemen whose honour and women have been threatened by the marauding Vikings.
45 Susan Kim, 'Bloody Signs: Circumcision and Pregnancy in the Old English *Judith*', *Exemplaria*, 11 (1999), 285–307, at 300. She finds a suggestion of pregnancy in Judith's storing of her enemy's head in a bag, which she later delivers and presents to the Bethulians.
46 Zacher, *Rewriting the Old Testament*, p. 130.
47 This is a common scholarly claim. For example, Peter Lucas says that being 'no wonderwoman with bionic powers … Judith's practical difficulties … in arranging Holofernes's sleeping body … are almost pedantically spelt out' (p. 21). Peter Lucas, '"Judith" and the Woman Hero', *The Yearbook of English Studies*, 22 (1992), 17–27.
48 All the verbs are definitions of *gewealdan* in Bosworth and Toller, *Anglo-Saxon Dictionary*. The quotation in the second sentence comes from Koppelman, 'Fearing My Neighbor', p. 20.
49 Griffith translates *wundenlocc* as 'with braided locks', following the brief mention of Judith's hair in the Vulgate. He remarks that the compound occurs in the Old English poem in reference to Judith and, later (line 325), to her people, in which case it has to mean 'curly-haired'. The only other place where the compound appears in the Old English corpus is in Riddle 25 to describe a churl's daughter who deprives an onion, or a penis, of its head (Griffith (ed.), *Judith*, p. 120). John Hermann and Susan Kim employ this intertextual echo to fortify their psychoanalytic readings; for both, see Kim, 'Bloody Signs', p. 299. For a reaction against using the compound in one context to explain its implications in another, see Chickering, 'Poetic Exuberance', p. 120 (n. 3).
50 Stacy Klein, 'Gender', in Jacqueline Stodnick and Renée R. Trilling (eds), *A Handbook of Anglo-Saxon Studies* (Oxford: Wiley-Blackwell, 2012), pp. 39–54, at 51.
51 Michelet, *Creation, Migration, and Conquest*, p. 90.
52 Ibid.
53 Fry, 'The Cliff of Death in Old English Poetry', in John Miles Foley (ed.), *Comparative Research on Oral Traditions: A Memorial for Milman Parry* (Columbus, OH: Slavica, 1987), pp. 213–33, at 215–16.
54 Lori Ann Garner, 'The Art of Translation in the Old English *Judith*', *Studia Neophilologica*, 73 (2001), 171–83, at 178.
55 The maidservant had brought the bag with provisions for both of them (lines 127–9), so that they would have something kosher to eat even among the Assyrians.
56 Klein, 'Gender', p. 47.
57 My translation. In the original it reads: 'Lieu biface, entrée et sortie d'hommes et de biens; absorbant la matière première pour livrer des objets façonnés; point faible de la fortification, d'autant plus ardemment défendu; mais aussi, en temps de paix, endroit où l'on attend, bavarde, boit, mange, marchande, où stationnent les jongleurs.' Paul Zumthor,

La Mesure du Monde: Représentation de l'Espace au Moyen Age (Paris: Seuil, 1993), p. 129.
58 Zacher, *Rewriting the Old Testament*, p. 149.
59 Renoir quotes George Anderson's positive appraisal of *Judith* as 'a narrative poem of great energy and fiery story-telling... devoid of the superfluity of homiletic elements which so often mar its companion *Beowulf*'. Alain Renoir, '*Judith* and the Limits of Poetry', *English Studies*, 43 (1962), 145–55, at 146.
60 My 'view-from-above' language draws inspiration from the same article by Renoir, in which he states that 'the method whereby the [*Judith*] poet moves through space and time, and shifts the point of view of his narrative, is one that can best be understood through the analogy of the cinematograph' (ibid., p. 150).
61 Arthur Brodeur has noted that this passage features particularisation within accumulation, a vigorous movement of nouns and verbs, that contributes to 'the vividness and force of a moment of intense feeling or action'. Arthur Brodeur, 'A Study of Diction and Style in Three Anglo-Saxon Narrative Poems', in Allan H. Orrick (ed.), *Nordica et Anglica: Studies in Honor of Stefán Einarsson* (The Hague: Mouton, 1968), pp. 97–114, at 107–8.
62 Griffith (ed.), *Judith*, p. 85.
63 I refer to Koppelman's argument; the quote is on page 13 of her article, 'Fearing My Neighbor'.
64 They may even seek to end the 'moment of female community' between the heroine and her maid. Mary Dockray-Miller argues that in the space between the Assyrian camp and Bethulia, the pair formed by Judith and her female servant signifies a transcendence of 'the paradigm of two lovers ... to encompass different ... generations and a multiplicity of bonds, with men, with women, with mothers, with children, whether or not related by blood'. The relationship forms an opposition, however brief, to 'aggression and domination' characteristic of male-controlled enclosures. Mary Dockray-Miller, 'Female Community in the Old English *Judith*', *Studia Neophilologica*, 70 (1998), 165–72, at 165 ('aggression and domination') and 171 (transcendence).
65 Griffith wishes for 'the disassociation of the word and the drink in this type of c[om]p[oun]d [*medoburh*]' (Griffith (ed.), *Judith*, p. 128).
66 Ibid., p. 130.
67 Estes sees the bloody *heafod* as a symbol of the textual failure to 'transform the biblical figure of Judith into a fully acceptable Anglo-Saxon Christian heroine'. She argues against Susan Kim's reading of the scene of the revelation of the head as 'a metaphorical pregnancy and birth'. Pregnancy in Estes's opinion implies development and progress, whereas the disembodied body part taken out of a meal-bag resembles nothing other than 'a meal that cannot be digested'. Heide Estes, 'Feasting with Holofernes: Digesting Judith in Anglo-Saxon England', *Exemplaria*, 15 (2003), 325–50, at 350. Michelet offers a

contrasting interpretation. While not addressing metatextual concerns, she declares that the public display of the corporeal fragment 'signals its integration within the home society and the circumventing of its disruptive potential'. *Creation, Migration, and Conquest*, p. 106.
68 Arthur, 'Postural Representations', p. 880.
69 See the discussion of this expression regarding Judith's mind above.
70 Griffith (ed.), *Judith*, pp. 56–7.
71 'universa vasa bellica Holofernis, quæ dedit illi populus ... obtulit in anathema oblivionis.'
72 Mullally, 'The Cross-Gendered Gift', p. 265.
73 Ibid., pp. 283–4.
74 Zacher, *Rewriting the Old Testament*, p. 137.
75 *Swegl* may have connections to *segel* (see Bosworth and Toller, *Anglo-Saxon Dictionary*, *swegl* III). For Tolkien's definitions of *siegel* and its relevance to the Old English *Exodus*, see Chapter 2.

5
A hoard full of plunder: Paradoxical materiality of loss in *Beowulf*

Introduction: A high concentration of hoards

Unlike most of the texts discussed so far, *Beowulf* not only features crucial artefacts that are spoliated or behave like *spolia*, but it also dramatises their accumulation, at once exciting and disturbing. The orthodox consolation that the readers can appeal to in the Creation riddles or the biblical verse does not apply in the unquestionably pagan universe of the most famous Old English epic. In the last part of the poem especially, the paradox of inconstancy of human life and material weight of the past is embodied in the image of the hoard. Fifty years pass imperceptibly in one line (2208) between Beowulf's assumption of the Geatish throne and his next appearance, as an old, venerated ruler of his people facing a dragon problem. The events leading to his death centre on a hoard full of plunder; his funeral concludes with his incorporation in it. The compilation of treasure in *Beowulf* brings up the question of proper use of material culture – and, by extension, its own narrative – that is never resolved. It is clear that the warrior world of the hero depends on circulation of precious weapons and armour that produce, maintain, and contain stories. Still, the poet cannot praise this project without revealing its darker sides.

A veil of mystery hovers over the provenance of the hoard as it does over other key funerals in *Beowulf*. A mysterious Last Survivor, who belonged to an ancient race that became extinct, buried their treasure in a barrow while lamenting their end. The accumulation is associated with more than loss. It results from near extermination. Somebody has cursed the collection of valuables, though the poet does not make it clear who. This hoard is found by a dragon who guards it for three hundred years, until a pitiful, nameless character chances upon the hoard. The man enters it, and takes a single goblet from it in hopes of making up with his master. His act unleashes a series of events that lead to Beowulf's death and beginning of his memorialisation that culminates for us in the text of the poem.[1] In this chapter, I argue that Beowulf's barrow, rather different in its composition from historical Anglo-Saxon treasure-troves, is a metatextual rather than an archaeological phenomenon. Further, I suggest that analyses of modern hoarding offer useful insights that help us identify one of the poem's main concerns: the question of normative and non-normative use of material culture. For all their differences, recoverable early medieval hoards like the Staffordshire Hoard, the Lone Survivor/dragon/Beowulf's barrow, and massive modern compilations of 'stuff' have something important in common. They transcend the binaries of material/immaterial, memory/forgetting, destruction/security, and person/thing to communicate both ambivalence and hope about human creative endeavours. Filled with recycled fragments, hoards maximise the power of *spolia* and *spolia*-like objects to extend themselves, spatially and temporally, into the world.

Our hoarding and their hoarding

Material culture from any period, especially if it involves precious metals and jewels, rarely fails to excite large audiences. The recently discoved Staffordshire Hoard[2] and the perennially fascinating Sutton Hoo have a place in popular and academic imaginations matched only by some of the more bombastic adaptations of *Beowulf* for the big screen. An uncovered collection of objects deemed valuable appears to us as a startling message from the past, more so because a hoard does not need a translator to communicate. Our ideas of splendour do not differ significantly from those of aristocratic classes of a thousand years ago, and we easily recognise the preciousness of metal or intricacy of craft expended to make these artefacts. The centrality of hoards in scholarship and beyond results partly from the fact that, in addition to graves, they provide considerable evidence of material culture surviving from the pre-Conquest period. Lavish furnishing of graves ceases after the triumph of Christianity in England in the later seventh century,[3] but hoards continue at a pace sufficient for scholars to construct a narrative: precious metal in form of coins and objects survives in ninth-century hoards; those from the first half of the tenth century tend to focus on silver, but 'on a smaller scale' than before, and so on.[4] Whatever their romantic appeal for us today and for the readers of *Beowulf* back then, they also played a practical role. They were like a hidden bank account, created to keep silver (useful to 'make payments and give as rewards') away from potential plunderers for later recovery and circulation within 'a bullion economy'.[5] A strong connection between hoards and looting therefore exists because they are created to prevent spoliation or to avoid losing one's plunder to someone else. Hoards are also constantly changing, so that even a single one obtains a plural identity.[6]

We can see even from this brief foray into historicisation that *Beowulf* does not consistently reflect the archaeological record from whatever time, and, when it does, it does very selectively. We know that the common practice of superimposing the images from a specific archaeological site like the seventh-century Sutton Hoo distorts our perception of the text attested only in the late tenth century.[7] More general drawing of parallels presents problems, as well. While silver and coins play a crucial role in real hoards, *Beowulf* is interested only in gold, the metal of distinction par excellence, and makes no reference to coinage.[8] The physical traits of this heathen gold can perplex a literary critic who implies that the dragon's hoard must have contained artefacts created from other metals because pure gold does not rust.[9]

This chapter examines the dragon's barrow in *Beowulf* in light of the poem's complex characterisation of treasure, especially treasure as booty. The intertwining of gold and plunder may be so pervasive that scholars could even maintain that most, if not all, treasure in the world of *Beowulf* comes from looting during war.[10] We can acknowledge the ambivalence of the valuables in the text without trying to resolve whether the poet ultimately condemns or praises the heroic pursuit of material culture and its subsequent display. The poem of *Beowulf* imagines itself as a hoard filled with plunder, with its attendant overflow of ambivalent energy, a melding of a loving backwards glance and the horror at what might receive that glance. Through this act of metatextual envisioning, the author brings forth a wealth of questions, including 'What is valuable?', 'How much do we keep?', and 'How do we decide?'.[11] The poet of *Beowulf*, characteristically, does not offer a response to these enquiries regarding what should be memorialised and how, and what should be sent off into the oblivion.

As Andy Orchard says concerning another question ('Is *Beowulf*, then, in any sense beyond criticism?'), 'it may be that the answer is that there is no final answer: it depends on the audience-perspective. One is left in sheer admiration of this deeply layered and textured work, the resonances of which remain long after it is read or heard read'.[12] Layering and texturing fit well within a hoard. *Spolia*, whether items of literal loot or repurposed architectural features, add both qualities to their new context. Finally, the chapter will extend the characterisation of the author as a historian[13] or at least someone with a sharp sense of history,[14] and mark him as a self-conscious hoarder, an artist who dramatises the interplay of two paradoxical powers in his work: the sense of irrevocable loss and the excessive materiality of the past.

We may begin by wondering whether an apparent anachronism can help us gain a helpful entry-point into *Beowulf*. Hoarding nowadays has a rather different sense from a thousand or even seventy years ago. The crucial difference is the social agreement on the value of objects contained in their hoards in opposition to ours. Scott Herring identifies the moment when one definition gave way to another. It happened after the report from the *New York Times* dated 22 March 1947, about two bachelor brothers, Homer and Langley Collyer, whose corpses were recovered in their Harlem home within an extravagant and varied accumulation of belongings, all together 'over one hundred tons of material', a hoard in our sense of the word. 'Prior to fallout from the Collyer mansion', writes Herring, 'hoarding referred primarily to the accumulation of wealth – not to trash.'[15] Sylvia Lavin likewise argues that excessive collecting of 'worthless' stuff has only recently attained the status of a defined psychological problem. She, too, refers to the death of the Collyers, before concluding that 'Every age has its favorite neurosis', ours being hoarding. Lavin finds the proof for her claim in popular reality TV shows such as *Hoarders* (on the channel A&E) and in the *Diagnostic and Statistical Manual of Mental Disorders* (*DSM*). The manual, with its three hundred categories of mental disorders on nearly a thousand pages, displays the psychiatry profession's own 'hoarding problem'.[16] The twenty-first-century technologies, seemingly virtual but dependent on maintenance of physical parts, only enable our hoarding tendencies. Jane Bennett lists such examples of our persistent drive to accumulate as the National Security Agency collecting extensive information on the United States (and other) citizens from their cell phone and Internet usage; individuals backing their data up on 'disks and drives and clouds'; and the wide expanses of the Internet itself.[17] If hoarding surfaces whenever we turn to postmodern culture or premodern literature, its omnipresence might indicate that it is 'a postmodern, premodern, precondition for making sense of the material world'.[18]

The dragon is not as a hoarder absolutely comparable to the Collyer brothers, the subjects of *Hoarders*, or contemporary Big Data addicts. For one, he did not collect the objects himself, but rather found the hoard left behind by the Lone Survivor: 'Hordwynne fond / eald uhtsceaða' [an old night-enemy found the hoard-joy] (2270–1). Yet, as Mary Kate Hurley reminds us in her analysis of these lines, *findan* possesses a wider semantic range than its Modern English descendant, including 'to invent ... order, dispose, arrange, or determine'. Though not exhibiting human intentionality, the dragon still manifests 'some kind of volition ... an active searching which leads [it] to find the hoard'.[19] Remembering that the distinction between old hoarders and new hoarders lies in the perceived worth of the accumulated items, we might note that the state of the dragon's treasure brings up the very question of value. Do not precious things decay after centuries of neglect? Cursed or not, do they not depreciate? The narrator gives the following comment as Wiglaf glimpses the hoard:

> ... orcas stondan,
> fyrnmanna fatu,   feormendlease,
> hyrstum behrorene;   þær wæs helm monig
> eald ond omig,   earmbeaga fela
> searwum gesæled.   Sinc eaðe mæg
> gold on grunde,   gumcynnes gehwone
> oferhigian,   hyde se ðe wylle. (2760–6)
> [... there stood heathen chalices, vessels of ancients (left) without a polisher, deprived of ornamentation. There was many a helmet, old and rusty, and numerous arm-bands crafted with skill. Treasure, gold in the ground, may easily overtake (or: pass away from) any (member) of the humankind, however much he tries to hide (or: keep) it.]

I translate *orcas* as 'heathen chalices', keeping in mind Roberta Frank's observation that the poet reserves this term only for these objects. *Orcas* do not appear in any textual or archaeological record from Anglo-Saxon England.[20] It is hard nowadays to find a sufficiently menacing and mysterious word for 'cup'. Aside from this particular charge, the artefacts that Wiglaf sees lack polish and decoration due to centuries of neglect. In their name and appearance they display 'a discontinuity, a rupture, a yawning gap between worlds long past'.[21] 'Gold on grunde' indicates that the gold has been lying in humid conditions, and the proximity of a winged reptilian body could have had further deleterious effect. Decayed, broken, unpolished objects, which have moved on past their utility, still hold appeal for the fire-breathing enemy of *Beowulf* and the 'pack rats' of our time. The dragon's hoard that mingles socially desirable and stigmatised, possibly dangerous objects, recalls modern hoards that preserve items of universally recognised worth buried among or interspersed with those only their owners could love. One famous example is Andy Warhol's massive, eclectic collection that caused a scandal when it came up for auction after the artist's death. It incorporated kitschy keepsakes like biscuit barrels of varying sizes and shapes, and Muppet- and Superman-themed paraphernalia alongside undisputable artworks by Picasso and others.[22] A more ordinary hoarder can chance upon a cashpoint envelope with a hundred dollars in an old copy of the Sunday *New York Times*.[23]

Finally, the last three lines of the passage contain a message or a warning about the power of material goods. They do present some difficulties, and I translate them according to the new Klaeber threesome's notes. The editors read *oferhigian* as 'pass away from', while allowing for the possibility of the sense 'overtake', suggested by Klaeber himself.[24] In either case – be it overwhelming or merely inconstant – treasure refuses to remain in any person's possession. Yet, the poem acknowledges, it is universally sought, by 'gumcynnes gehwone' [any (member) of the humankind]. Anyone can become a hoarder if they are not careful. Wiglaf realises the danger of the hoard when he orders it to be reburied at the end of *Beowulf*.

More similarities emerge after more consideration. The dragon knows where each component of his treasure-trove lies, since he reacts or over-reacts to the loss of a single goblet. His protectiveness of even the smallest of his possessions is found among present-day hoarders. Immediately after noticing the *fotlast* [footprint] (2289), a sign of breaking and entering, the reptile goes searching for his *sincfæt* [precious cup] (2300). The dragon, like his modern counterparts,[25] does not use his possessions 'properly', thus providing a negative example of societal expectations concerning objects. Scott Herring speaks of the need to combine material culture studies and queer theory to investigate 'how object pathology and deviant object conduct such as hoarding can upset normative social boundaries [...] how they defamiliarize the material relations that make up any world of goods'.[26] In the world of *Beowulf*, treasure circulates, cementing the social bonds, for instance between a warrior who takes it from his enemy's corpse and gives it to his king, and the king who in turn rewards his thane. The heroes who obtain it, display it, demonstrating their own value within the group. According to this scholarly trope, the dragon is anti-social, the opposite of a properly socialised aristocratic warrior (the focus of *Beowulf* for the most part). The monster 'locks up the wealth that holds society together'.[27] The purloined cup in particular is no accident, because the artefact stands for the back and forth of the heroic community, the passing of the drinking vessel that signifies conviviality.[28] We may assume that the creature does not use the goblet appropriately, not only because he has no thanes and holds no beer-gatherings, but also because dragons do not drink from such objects. The cup cannot lose its association with its previous owner; a piece of plunder seized by the servant to reintegrate himself into the society cannot itself be reintegrated. Indirectly, it causes havoc.[29]

Yet the dragon's relationship to the hoard is unsurprising, perfectly natural judging from the much-quoted Anglo-Saxon maxim: 'Draca sceal on hlæwe, / frod, frætwum wlanc' [A dragon should be in a barrow, old (or wise), proud in (his) treasure] (26–7).[30] Extreme old age happens to characterise dragons. The one in the poem is at least three hundred years old (2278), which is another possible link to modern hoarding.[31] The reptile's existence in the text impedes full allegorisation; he has a physical presence: 'se wæs fiftiges fotgemearces / lang on legere' [he was fifty feet long prone] (3042–3). He gets a precise measurement in a poem usually unconcerned with exact description of characters (all we know about the hero's appearance is that he is tall and has the strength of thirty men). The dragon is not a person, not even humanoid like the Cain-descended Grendelkin of the first two-thirds of *Beowulf*. By his nature, he does not follow the rules of human society, but the poet reserves one last elegiac glance for him, as he is disposed of unceremoniously by Beowulf's men: '… dracan ec scufun, / wyrm ofer weallclif, leton weg niman, / flod fæðmian frætwa hyrde' [they also pushed the dragon, the serpent over the wall-cliff, they let the waves take, the sea enfold the guardian of the treasure] (3131–3). Although the narrator claims that the possessions did their monstrous owner no good ('ne byð him wihte ðy sel') (2277), his attachment to the *sincfæt* indicates otherwise.[32] He appreciates it in some mysterious reptilian way, just as hoarders of today have relationships to their possessions that more normative users cannot fathom.[33]

The power of the image of gold kept out of circulation makes clear the political and economic impact of the precious metal on the society, but also 'its value as cultural currency and its meaning as a storehouse of cultural memory'.[34] The poem stores a hoard, which stores treasure, which stores memory, all in hopes of later display and circulation. In this way, the hoarding in *Beowulf* looks different to today's very individualised practice. Modern hoarders sometimes preserve their own memories, not that of their culture, and in most cases do not desire to display, let alone circulate, their keepsakes. The poem would have different motivations from the dragon, and the reptile again bears a resemblance to non-normative users of material culture now. The text lies in wait, expecting to be activated. Objects underground, guarded by the cold, sleeping body of a winged reptile, cannot inspire any poetic flights of fancy – suggests the poem of *Beowulf*, which did just that. Live or dead, dragons tell no tales, whilst, even dying, Beowulf has the time for lengthy speeches. But the reclaimed treasure is buried again before the text concludes. Maybe its association with the 'irreplaceable' protagonist is so strong that the objects cannot belong to anyone else:[35] touched by the hoard and dead by the hoard, the Geat becomes a part of it at the end. Roberta Frank interprets Wiglaf's reburial of the hoard as the *Beowulf* poet's turning away from the past at this crucial point and plunging into the future.[36] If we agree with Herring's argument that modern hoarding is an example of non-normative engagement with material goods that exposes and resists larger cultural injunctions, could we conclude that *Beowulf* vindicates the dragon's use, or non-use, of the valuables in opposition to the model of circulation of wealth in the ancient Germanic society of the poem? Weighty, dusty, rusted past ought to have stayed in the ground where it belongs, heaped around a dormant non-human force that has no interest in making it resurface.

Plunder in *Beowulf*

Before turning to two complementary barrows with which the epic concludes – the dragon's hoard and the hero's burial mound – let us look at two instances of plunder and its relationship to storytelling of *Beowulf*. It is impossible and unproductive to record every instance of spoils because of their sheer abundance. Here I am most interested in two artefacts that frustrate attempts of characters to place them in an advantageous context. The first is the enormous torque that the protagonist receives from Wealhtheow at the celebration in Heorot after he defeats Grendel. The 'healsbeaga mæst / þara þe ic on foldan gefrægen hæbbe' [the largest of neck-rings that I have ever heard of on earth] (1195–6) has a legendary status for the poet who goes on to compare it to the Brosings' necklace stolen by Hama. The object immediately inspires 'layering and texturing', a brief foray into the mythical past that deepens the moment of narration. Since they can and often do survive humans for long stretches of time, artefacts like this necklace are well suited for time travel. Though later on the readers will witness Beowulf presenting the torque to Hygelac's queen Hygd (2172–4), the author now reveals its more distant future in one of his characteristic flash-forwards:

> Þone hring hæfde Higelac Geata,
> nefa Swertinges nyhstan siðe,
> siðþan he under segne sinc ealgode,
> wælreaf werede; hyne wyrd fornam,
> syþðan he for wlenco wean ahsode,
> fæhðe to Frysum. He þa frætwe wæg,
> eorclanstanas ofer yða ful,
> rice þeoden; he under rande gecranc.
> Gehwearf þa in Francna fæþm feorh cyninges,
> breostgewædu, ond se beah somod.
> Wyrsan wigfrecan wæl reafeden
> æfter guðsceare; Geata leode
> hreawic heoldon. (1202–14)
> [Then Hygelac the Geat, Swerting's grandson, took the ring with him on an expedition, when he defended his treasure, protected his battle-loot under the banner. Events took him, after he asked for trouble, a conflict with the Frisians out of pride. The mighty ruler carried the treasure, precious stones, over the wave-beaker (i.e., the sea); he perished under his shield. Then the king's life passed into the keeping of the Franks (along with) his breast-armour and also this ring. Worse warrior-men plundered the corpse after the slaughter of war. Geatish people held the place of corpses (i.e., their corpses covered the battlefield).]

Peter Baker reminds us that plundering was utterly common and provides numerous examples from the historical record in his book.[37] Not just gold and gems, but anything of value, including underwear, attracted the enemy's attention and reinvigorated his economy.[38] The poet shows Hygelac defending what he took before becoming himself a part of the taking. The Franks seize his life and body (*feorh* means both) in addition to his belongings. Yet the passage also reveals that the Franks who strip his corpse do not deserve the legendary treasure that Wealhtheow gives Beowulf. They are worse fighters or, in Seamus Heaney's felicitous phrase, 'punier warriors' (line 1212).[39] Enabling the poet to move through temporal layers in *Beowulf*, this spectacular artefact shows the appeal of a precious object that does not discriminate between its owners, the nature of which seems to be on the move. The largest necklace that the narrator has heard of takes part in an intricate system of exchange. It invokes the proper mythological context if needed, upholds the honour of individuals who wear it, and strengthens the bonds between aristocrats across gender and tribal affiliation, Danes and Geats and Franks alike. The torque can also, as in this scene, escape the constrictions of the larger value system, signalling an advantageous moment rather than a particular act of heroism.

Another prominent despoiled object refusing to fit a frame beneficial to human society is a hypothetical sword. Upon his return to Geatland, Beowulf reports to Hygelac the situation at Hrothgar's court. He imagines what will happen when the Danish king's daughter Freawaru marries Ingeld the Heathobard to make peace between the two warring tribes. Beowulf predicts that Freawaru's retainer would enter Ingeld's hall carrying 'gomelra lafe, / heard ond hringmæl Heaða-Beardna gestreon' [ancestral heirlooms, heavy and ring-decorated wealth of Heathobards] from the time when they could still bear arms, that is when they were alive (2036–8). A veteran would then recognise the weapon borne by the Dane and tell a son of the fallen man, former owner of the object: 'Meaht ðu, min wine, mece gecnawan / þone þin fæder to gefeohte bær / [...] þær hyne Dene slogon' [Can you, my friend, recognise the sword that your father carried to combat [...] when the Danes slew him] (2047–8, 2050). In response, the young man would kill Freawaru's thane to avenge his father's death, which would frustrate the attempts to make peace through the marriage of Freawaru and Ingeld.

The danger of plunder acknowledged in Beowulf's story to Hygelac comes from its inability to be subsumed into the new context, from the trace of its former owner still legible upon it. If one object can wreak such havoc, what could a hoard full of them do? The *Beowulf*-poet demonstrates in these scenes his understanding of the threat inherent in precious artefacts that circulate in the world of his heroes. They encourage violence, standing in for perils of pathological memory and even idolatry.[40] Still, the poet cannot let the treasure go. He believes in 'the value of worldly goods – that it is good to have them, sad when they're gone. [He cannot] bring himself to speak of them as evils that one is better off without.'[41] On one hand, the author shows his awareness that absorption in his work, to use Evelyn Reynolds's helpful term, would endanger the readers. On the other hand, he realises that some measure of close engagement is necessary. Due to this complex dynamic, the text of *Beowulf* moves between allowing and denying the audience close association with itself, particularly with the artefacts that are supposed to act as repositories of time to ground the readers.[42]

Hoards in *Beowulf*

The dragon's barrow does not likely correspond to any recoverable Anglo-Saxon structure, but it does bring to mind several types of buildings present in early medieval England. It is a composite space, 'layered and textured', much like the literary work that contains it. Beowulf gets a chance to observe it from the inside after vanquishing the dragon with Wiglaf's aid:

> Ða se æðeling giong,
> þæt he bi wealle   wishycgende
> gesæt on sesse;   seah on enta geweorc,
> hu ða stanbogan   stapulum fæste
> ece eorðreced   innan healde. (2715–19)
> [Then the prince, wise in thought, went to sit on a seat by the wall. He looked at the work of giants, how the stone arches firmly held the eternal earth-hall with pillars from within.]

The phrase 'enta geweorc' [the work of giants] appears elsewhere in *Beowulf* as well as in other vernacular verse to describe larger-than-life craftsmanship, veiled in the mystery of past ages. Scholars often note that stone in Old English poems signifies Otherness, whether threatening or simply enchanting, because the Anglo-Saxons preferred to build with timber so much so that even some of their stone constructions imitate appearance of wood non-functionally (making them *skeuomorphs*).[43] The Old English word for 'to build' is *timbr(i)an*.[44] Earlier, as he enters the lair, Beowulf notes the 'stanbogan' [stone arches] (2545), a key architectural element that cannot escape the character's or the author's attention. The description of the barrow might suggest not only a prehistoric structure, 'a monolithic chambered tomb', but also 'a crypt'.[45] At the same time, its interior with stone arches could have been inspired by 'a Christian mausoleum such as the eighth-century vaulted crypt at Repton, Derbyshire'.[46] Reused columns are iconic representations of ancient Rome in many medieval European settings,[47] so *stapolas* [pillars] can point in that direction. Lori Ann Garner explicitly brings up appropriation of sites sacred to prior cultures and art-historical spoliation in Anglo-Saxon England during her discussion of the dragon's barrow; the structure contains 'layers of occupation'.[48]

Created by the mysterious noble race to which the Last Survivor belonged, then filled with their doomed treasures, it becomes a residence of the reptile for three centuries before being partially incorporated into Beowulf's memorial at the end.

Beowulf's barrow, which attempts to subsume, supersede, and surpass the dragon's lair, is a composite space, as well. This is the only structure in the poem for which the author provides some detail about the labour and the length of time that it required (ten days). The distinction that he seems to make here would result from his desire to separate 'the remote past' of the dragon's barrow and 'a more tangible past' of Beowulf.[49] Along with the buried treasure that previously belonged to the vanquished reptile, the funerary mound consists of wood, that favoured building material of the Anglo-Saxons, and earth.[50] Thus, the monumental ending image of the poem 'tie[s] together several of the poem's architectural themes. Wood is heroic but also vulnerable to fire [...] earth suggests a space for refuge but also death. All are key components in the architectural world of Old English poetry and serve to symbolize the world of *Beowulf* in its totality.'[51] Garner argues that the text finishes with a heterogeneous vision, beautiful in its many parts, but ambivalent. The very power of the ending of *Beowulf* depends on the sense of disturbance inherent in the image of something buried yet present just underneath the surface, of resplendent and destructive energy awaiting reactivation.

Poet as a hoarder

The trope of *Beowulf*-poet as an architect is common in scholarship for a good reason. For instance, not only do the two barrows echo each other, but so do the four funerals of Scyld Sceafing, Hildeburh's kin, the treasure by the Lone Survivor (possibly grave-goods 'sanitised' slightly by the author) and Beowulf.[52] Similar mirroring happens in the three 'halls' of Heorot, Grendelkin's mere, and the dragon's lair.[53] The multilayered, richly textured structure that the poet creates has been imagined variously as a container for a number of early medieval genres, a *summa literarum*,[54] or an artefact in motion, in a constant state of assembly and reassembly, in which 'space and time intersect in an ongoing continuum'.[55] More specifically architectural is the comparison of the poem to a building incorporating *spolia*. Closer to the poetics of *spolia* that I propose elsewhere, R. M. Liuzza makes an analogy between *Beowulf* and 'an Anglo-Saxon church made from the salvaged stones of a Roman temple'.⁵⁶ Haruko Momma writes more generally of the Anglo-Saxon verse that '[w]e could perhaps compare an Old English poem to medieval architecture whose material was taken from diverse locations in place and time, and whose construct has been repeatedly altered by renovations, additions, and demolitions.'⁵⁷ All these parallels imply that the poet has elegantly and successfully put his material together, to which most readers of *Beowulf* can attest. Furthermore, he ends the poem on a triumphant, monumental, memorialising note. What happens after Beowulf's death is, again, a matter of course: wars come in cycles, and the fact that the Geats will experience enormous suffering does not imply that they are doomed to extinction.⁵⁸

Yet we know of the doubleness of vision that pervades the poem, famously termed 'the appositive style' by Fred Robinson.⁵⁹ With the sense of harmonious blending of different elements appears its mirror image – the Grendel to its Beowulf, the mere to its Heorot – hoarding. The narratives about pagans winning gold and fame could be valuable or worthless, depending on the reader's perspective. Liuzza makes yet another analogy: 'like the hapless, nameless thief who plunders the dragon's cave, the poet rifles the hoard of the past to unearth both gleaming treasure and useless trappings'.⁶⁰ Could we, then, in the spirit of layering and texturing, and leaving many questions unanswered, add one more characterisation of the *Beowulf* poet to the list? He has already been seen as a self-assured historian-architect in control of his material and fully confident about the worth of his undertaking, and as a less confident, more doubtful artist with a deep awareness of the ambivalent complexities of his endeavour. Additionally, we can propose a figure who, like those resistant hoarders of today studied by Scott Herring, attempts to maintain an unconventional, perhaps yet-unfathomed connection to his collection of artefacts.

Frost and Steketee argue that hoarding results from an impulse generally shared by people everywhere to preserve and collect objects that hold personal meaning to them.⁶¹ According to some estimates, one-third of American adults are collectors and two-thirds of all households contain at least one collector.⁶² The difference between a collection and a hoard would centre on the presence (or absence) of an organising principle. Even so, pinpointing organising principles can be rather subjective, as we gather from negative responses of earlier scholars to 'digressions' in *Beowulf*. Psychologists nowadays prefer to look for '[d]istress or impairment' as the determining component in distinguishing between 'eccentricity and pathology'.⁶³

In this chapter I am not interested in diagnosing the anonymous poet of *Beowulf*, but rather in exploring the border between collecting and hoarding inherent in the text to produce a stimulating reading of it. While most of humanity may display some hoarding tendencies or 'share some of the hoarding orientation',[64] hoarders have something in common with artists. Frost and Steketee write that '[f]or hoarders, every object in rich in detail. [...] In this way, the physical world of hoarders is different and much more *expansive* than that of the rest of us. [...] [they] are undeniably free of the usual rules that affect how we view and treat our own stuff.'[65] Towards the end of *Beowulf*, the monument to the hero that incorporates his body and the dragon's hoard bespeaks expansion as it towers 'heah ond brad, / weglidendum wide gesyne' [high and broad, visible to seafarers far and wide] (3153–4). Further, Frost and Steketee state that 'an inordinate number of hoarders' self-identify as artists, and that hoarding can be seen as 'a kind of giftedness, a special talent for seeing beauty, utility, and meaning in things'. The psychologists warn, however, that the gift brings with it 'a curse'.[66] The objects buried by the Lone Survivor in the hoard in *Beowulf* are cursed, but what bearing, if any, this curse has on the events at the very end of the poem is unclear.

Bennett, contrary to the argument above, states that hoarders do not put together 'the found-art assemblage' intentionally, consciously, like contemporary visual artists, but join their bodies to the hoard, thus visibly acknowledging its material power. Whilst they share 'a sensibility', hoarders and artists are not the same because utility and aesthetics do not play the foremost role in the thinking of the former.[67] Bennett hopes to gather insights about things in general – how they engage with humans, and vice versa –from listening to hoarders, individuals to whom she attributes a special skill.[68] She brings up a paradox useful for our analysis of *Beowulf*. On one hand, she agrees with Gould, Heidegger, and Adorno when they emphasise 'recalcitrance, elusiveness, and the ability to impede (and thus perhaps to chasten) the will to truth', while, at the same time, she point outs that the three philosophers ignore 'the power that things have to draw us near and provoke our deep attachments to them'.[69] These objects inspire us to bond with them while simultaneously resisting us.

Hoarding in the modern sense appears appropriate to discussion of *Beowulf* on another level, as well. Amassed possessions create a sense of security in addition to a sense of threat: 'The irony that [Irene's, one of the hoarders interviewed] hoard could be comforting and tormenting at the same time was clear to her.'[70] There is a connection to trauma in a number of cases. The events presented in *Beowulf*, especially those in the last part of the poem, following the protagonist's fifty years of prosperous rule, do not lack for trauma, whether on a collective or individual level. The difference is that the Lone Survivor buries his treasure, which may feature dead horses and hawks as funeral goods,[71] rather than immerse himself in it. Perhaps the fact that the hoard rests in the earth, as intact as it could be, provides some solace; the entire material record of the Lone Survivor's race, their bodies and belongings, remain in one place and safe from the depredations of enemies, at least for a period of time. The dragon's past is not sufficiently clear to draw conclusions about it; besides, imaginary reptilian history may not be understandable in human terms, let alone prone to analysis. In the text as a whole, in the shape in which it survives, the poet's hoarding of materials about pagan heroes, their virtues and shortcomings, might function as a metaphorical bulwark against ravages inflicted by humans or passing of time, these undeniably transhistoric phenomena.

Psychologists argue that accumulating objects corresponds to nesting, insulating self from the menacing world by building soft, safe spaces.[72] The architectural world of *Beowulf* does not favour such spaces except for the final image of Beowulf's barrow, a mound made of earth. Many items inside that soft structure consist of hard materials: the war-gear heaped on it has metallic parts and sharp edges. Perhaps the rotting away leads to blending, to heterogeneous elements melding together, and the pagan comfort of funerary goods (as objects that may come of use to the venerable departed in their afterlives) joins dark yet primeval pleasures of the Freudian death drive. Bennett presents the breath-taking evidence that people are, from the point of view of biology, environments composed of numerous, albeit mostly invisible, organisms, nutrients, and chemicals.[73] Hoarders would unconsciously pay homage to this apparently universal situation. Always/already intricate assemblages of various matter as humans, they strive towards even more compositeness.

Today's hoarders typically feel that things provide an incredible connection to the world, often through a narrative that they hold within themselves.[74] The more things they pile up, their logic goes, the more and firmer connections they establish. To put it differently, hoards provide a fantasy of overcoming loss though simultaneous presence of various points in time: the past in which the hoarder obtained the object, the future in which it may become potentially useful or even transform the owner's identity for the better.[75] They do not simply function as an *aide-mémoire*, but also '[allow the hoarder] to re-experience a past event'.[76] The *Beowulf* poet packs so much narrative material in his work employing a similar strategy. Flashbacks and flashforwards, for which the poem is now famous, ensure its survival by opening it up to several temporal dimensions; the paradoxically elusive material culture gives it a grounding. Overcoming the terror of death, one significant comfort afforded to hoarders by their accumulated objects,[77] appears to be behind the ending of the poem. Strangely, the power to bypass death comes from assemblages permeated by death. As Catherine Karkov reminds us concerning the elements of the Staffordshire Hoard, 'They are objects surrounded by violence, meant to do violence, and have been violently treated themselves'.[78] Violence is inherent, perhaps even ever-present in real and imaginary Anglo-Saxon hoards.

A particularly strong sense of loss pervades the second part of *Beowulf*. Quite aside from the layering of the pagan past, so many characters die, including the Last Survivor, the dragon, and Beowulf himself. The readers get a sense that the leaderless Geats have much to lose amidst the lamentation for the protagonist. What remains of Beowulf is the smoke from his cremation pyre, a beautifully ambiguous image. 'Heofon rece swealg' [Heaven swallowed the smoke] (3155). Nevertheless, the poet does not allow us to forget the sheer materiality of the past so easily. Despite the indications of dark days ahead for the Geats, *Beowulf* ends with a vision of a beacon, an assemblage of a corpse and amassed treasure that will – and does (if we take the barrow as a stand in for the text) – survive. The treasure is still there; it lives on. In the act of reading, we are uncovering it and looking at it. '[F]orleton eorla gestreon eorðan healdan, / gold on greote, *þær hit nu gen lifað*, / eldum swa unnyt swa hyt æror wæs' [the earls let the earth hold the treasure, gold in the ground, *where it still lives now*, as useless to people as it had been before (my emphasis)] (3166–8). We end with a paradox. Loss seeps into everything, but there is also too much past that weighs on us, not only metaphorically. We collect things of some or no worth, trying continuously to establish a meaningful relationship with them.

Notes

1 Here is a quick reminder of these events. The winged reptile discovers what happened. He attacks the surrounding area, burning down

Beowulf's splendid hall. Beowulf insists on fighting the monster alone. He attacks the dragon, but, fatally wounded, he needs back-up. No one comes to his aid other than Wiglaf, but they kill the creature together. Beowulf asks Wiglaf to bring some of the treasure to him so that he can gaze upon it. The hero wishes that a barrow be built for him. He says nothing about reburial of the hoard. After the protagonist's death, Geats, led by Wiglaf, have him cremated with some treasure and then buried in a specially created memorial mound visible from the sea. Beowulf's subjects mourn him. The poet suggests that hard times are in store for the Geats now that they are vulnerable to an attack from the neighbouring tribes. The poem, however, ends with a note of praise of the hero, 'manna mildust ond monðwærust,/ leodum liðost ond lofgeornost' [the mildest of men and most humane, the kindest of people and most eager for fame] (3181–2).

2 For a brief introduction, see Karen Eileen Overbey and Maggie M. Williams, 'Hoards, Hoarders, Hordes, and Hoarding', *Postmedieval*, 7 (2016), 339–45. Overbey and Williams describe the Staffordshire Hoard as 'a work-in-progress, a living artifact' (p. 342).

3 Gale R. Owen Crocker, *The Four Funerals in 'Beowulf' and the Structure of the Poem* (Manchester: Manchester University Press, 2000), p. 62.

4 David A. Hinton, *Gold & Gilt, Pots & Pins: Possessions and People in Medieval Britain* (Oxford: Oxford University Press, 2005), pp. 108 (ninth century), 119 (tenth century).

5 Ibid., p. 119.

6 Jennifer Borland and Louise Siddons, 'From Hoarders to the Hoard: Giving Disciplinary Legitimacy to Undisciplined Collecting', *Postmedieval*, 7 (2016), 407–20, at 408–9.

7 Frank, '*Beowulf* and Sutton Hoo'. Leslie Webster underlines that even the scenes that seem substantiated by archaeological findings are 'a literary construction' (p. 193). In short, 'It is a poem, not an archaeological textbook' (p. 184). Leslie Webster, 'Archaeology and *Beowulf*', in Bruce Mitchell and Fred C. Robinson (eds), *Beowulf* (Oxford: Blackwell, 1998), pp. 183–94.

8 Peter S. Baker, *Honour, Exchange and Violence in 'Beowulf'* (Cambridge: D. S. Brewer, 2013), p. 37–8. Catherine M. Hills suggests that the hoards in the poem feature exclusively gold in order to appear distant and extraordinary, different to the more down-to-earth Viking treasure-troves filled with 'more silver than gold'. Catherine M. Hills, '*Beowulf* and Archaeology', in Robert E. Bjork and John D. Niles (eds), *A 'Beowulf' Handbook* (Lincoln: University of Nebraska Press, 1997), pp. 291–310, at 306.

9 Gale R. Owen-Crocker, *The Four Funerals in 'Beowulf'*, p. 99.

10 See Patricia Silber, 'Gold and its Significance in *Beowulf*', *Annuale Mediaevale*, 18 (1977), 5–19, at 16, and Peter Baker's second chapter, 'Loot and the Economy of Honour', esp. pp. 41–2. Speaking about

a real hoard, the one from Staffordshire, Borland and Siddons urge their readers to think about its danger – its compilation 'under duress' and its treasures being 'fragments of weapons with associations of intimidation and bloodshed' ('From Hoarders to the Hoard', p. 410).

11 Questions like these hold interest for any reconstruction of the past, still today. Elif Batuman writes about the discovery of Byzantine artefacts and human and animal remains during the recent digging of the Marmaray tunnel under the Bosphorus in Istanbul, Turkey. Her essay ends with provocative questions useful for my discussion: 'If fifteen houses are built on top of one another, which one is the most important? Whose voices should be heard – those of the living or those of the dead? How can we all fit into this world, and how do we get where we're going?' (Elif Batuman, 'The Big Dig', *New Yorker*, 31 August 2015, https://newyorker.com/magazine/2015/08/31/the-big-dig, accessed 12 September 2015).

12 Andy Orchard, *A Critical Companion to 'Beowulf'* (Cambridge: D. S. Brewer, 2003), p. 264.

13 Owen-Crocker, *The Four Funerals in 'Beowulf'*, p. 238.

14 Roberta Frank, 'The *Beowulf* Poet's Sense of History', in Benson and Wenzel (eds), *The Wisdom of Poetry*, pp. 53–65. Rpt. in Donoghue (ed.), *Beowulf: A Verse Translation*, pp. 167–80, at 169–70.

15 Scott Herring, 'Collyer Curiosa: A Brief History of Hoarding', *Criticism*, 53 (2011), 159–88, at 159–60.

16 Sylvia Lavin, 'Architecture in Extremis', *Log*, 22 (2011), 51–61, at 51, 54.

17 Jane Bennett, 'Powers of the Hoard: Further Notes on Material Agency', in Jeffrey Jerome Cohen (ed.), *Animal, Vegetable, Mineral: Ethics and Objects* (Washington, DC: Oliphaunt Books, 2012), pp. 237–69, at 249–50.

18 Borland and Siddons, 'From Hoarders to the Hoard', p. 409.

19 Mary Kate Hurley, *Translation Effects: Language, Time, and Community in Medieval England* (forthcoming), Chapter 5. I thank the author for letting me read her work in draft form.

20 Frank, 'Three Cups and a Funeral in *Beowulf*', pp. 408–9.

21 Ibid., p. 410.

22 Scott Herring, *The Hoarders: Material Deviance in Modern American Culture* (Chicago: University of Chicago Press, 2014), p. 51. Picasso, it turns out, was an even bigger hoarder than Warhol (see Herring's quotation of the art historian John Richardson on p. 76).

23 Randy O. Frost and Gail Steketee, *Stuff: Compulsive Hoarding and the Meaning of Things* (New York: Houghton Mifflin Harcourt, 2010), p. 24.

24 Bjork et al. (eds), *Klaeber's Beowulf*, p. 256.

25 For the insight about modern hoarders laying bare our unarticulated assumptions about the proper use of 'time, value, and objects', see Brian Thill, *Waste* (New York: Bloomsbury, 2015), p. 110.

26 Herring, 'Material Deviance: Theorizing Queer Objecthood', *Postmodern Culture*, 23 (2013), 1–17, at 3. Available at http://www.pomoculture.org/2013/09/03/material-deviance-theorizing-queer-objecthood/.
27 John D. Niles, *'Beowulf': The Poem and its Tradition* (Cambridge, MA: Harvard University Press, 1983), pp. 229–30. See also John Leyerle, 'The Interlace Structure of *Beowulf*', *University of Toronto Quarterly*, 37 (1967), 1–17. Rpt. in Joseph E. Tuso (ed.), *Beowulf: The Donaldson Translation Backgrounds and Sources. Criticism* (New York: Norton, 1975), pp. 158–70, at 168–9.
28 Paul E. Marshall, '*Goldgyfan* or *Goldwlance*: A Christian Apology for *Beowulf* and Treasure', *Studies in Philology*, 107 (2010), 1–24, at 15.
29 Hurley, *Translation Effects*, Chapter 5.
30 I cite the text of 'Maxims II' from *The Anglo-Saxon Minor Poems*, ASPR 6, ed. Elliott V. Dobbie (New York: Columbia University Press, 1942), pp. 55–7. The preceding maxim concerns a sword's place in the lap (of a warrior) and the following one, a fish's proper site of reproduction, the water; these statements demonstrate how intertwined, at least in one work of literature, the aristocratic world of warfare and gift-giving (culture) and the enviroment (nature) could be in Anglo-Saxon imagination.
31 Scott Herring writes extensively about the twenty-first-century fears about old age pensioners creating improper accumulations of stuff in Chapter 4 ('Old Rubbish') of *The Hoarders*: '… rubbish-loving seniors contribute to ongoing trepidation over the appropriate role of objects in the relatively recent invention of "late life." […] [H]oarding owes a debt to long-standing discourses of the aged recluse and her seemingly unnatural relationship to geriatric object cultures' (p. 118).
32 Mary Kate Hurley uses the Anglo-Saxon maxim I quote above to counteract the claim of the poem that the treasure was not beneficial to the dragon. She further argues that *Beowulf* invokes two incommensurable standards of value, human and non-human. Drawing a parallel to the bookworm in Riddle 47, Hurley emphasises that the reptile's use of the hoard should be understood as 'a natural – perhaps even neutral – occurrence' (*Translation Effects*, Chapter 5).
33 Herring discusses Jill from Milwaukee, featured in *Hoarders*, who parts from a rotting pumpkin by saying 'I enjoyed you while you were here. Thank you. Good-bye.' 'Material Deviance', p. 11.
34 Victor I. Scherb, 'Setting and Cultural Memory in Part II of *Beowulf*', *English Studies*, 79 (1998), 109–19, at 114.
35 Michael Alexander (trans.), *'Beowulf': A Verse Translation: Revised Edition* (New York: Penguin, 2001 [rpt. with corrections 2003]), p. xxxviii.
36 Frank, 'Three Cups and a Funeral in *Beowulf*', p. 414.
37 Baker, *Honour, Exchange and Violence*, pp. 42–53.

38 Underwear in a pre-industrial, pre-outsourcing era required intense, expensive labour, so that corpses were completely stripped (ibid., p. 65).
39 Seamus Heaney (trans.), *Beowulf* (London: Faber and Faber, 1999).
40 Thomas Prendergast, ' "Wanton Recollection": The Idolatrous Pleasures of *Beowulf*', *New Literary History*, 30 (1999), 129–41. (His discussion of Beowulf's prediction regarding Freawaru is on p. 135).
41 Baker, *Honour, Exchange and Violence*, p. 230.
42 Evelyn Reynolds, '*Beowulf*'s Poetics of Absorption: Narrative Syntax and the Illusion of Stability in the Fight with Grendel's Mother', *Essays in Medieval Studies*, 31 (2015), 43–64, at 51 (the audience accessing different temporalities through the objects) and 54 (sense of danger for the readers). Reynolds explains the nature of that peril differently to Prendergast: 'In a world of transience, flawed perception, defeated expectation, and mortality, absorption is dangerous ...' (p. 54).
43 Lori Ann Garner, *Structuring Spaces: Oral Poetics and Architecture in Early Medieval England* (Notre Dame: University of Notre Dame Press, 2011), pp. 35–6. One example of such a building is Earl's Barton tower, Northamptonshire, shown as plate 6 in Sally Crawford, *Daily Life in Anglo-Saxon England* (Westport, CT: Greenwood World Publishing, 2009).
44 Garner, *Structuring Spaces*, p. 42.
45 Owen-Crocker, *The Four Funerals in 'Beowulf'*, p. 62.
46 Ibid., p. 64.
47 See Dale Kinney, 'Roman Architectural Spolia', *Proceedings of the American Philosophical Society*, 145 (2001), 138–61. Romanness of the space, even its inspiration by Roman ruins, may be further indicated by the presence of the golden banner ('segn eallgylden ... beacna beorhtost' [a completely golden flag ... the brightest of signs] (lines 2767, 2777)), possibly a legendary Roman standard or *vexillum*. Thornbury, '*Eald enta geweorc* and the Relics of Empire', p. 90. Such a banner emerges also during Scyld's ship burial (47) and as one of the gifts Hrothgar presents it to the protagonist (1021) after the slaying of Grendel. The splendid object connects the three scenes, usually read as typically Germanic, stamping them with a sign of Romanness.
48 Garner, *Structuring Spaces*, p. 58.
49 Owen-Crocker, *The Four Funerals in 'Beowulf'*, 85.
50 Garner, *Structuring Spaces*, p. 64.
51 Ibid.
52 This is Owen-Crocker's argument throughout her book.
53 Michelet, *Creation, Migration, and Conquest*, pp. 74–114.
54 Joseph Harris, '*Beowulf* in Literary History', *Pacific Coast Philology*, 17 (1982), 16–23.

55 Gillian R. Overing, *'Beowulf*: A Poem in Our Time', in Clare A. Lees (ed.), *The Cambridge History of Early Medieval English Literature* (Cambridge: Cambridge University Press, 2013), pp. 309–31, at 323.
56 Liuzza (trans.), *Beowulf*, p. 31.
57 Momma, 'Old English Poetic Form', p. 279.
58 Baker, *Honour, Exchange and Violence*, pp. 232–9.
59 Fred C. Robinson, *'Beowulf' and the Appositive Style* (Knoxville: University of Tennessee Press, 1985).
60 R. M. Liuzza, *'Beowulf*: Monuments, Memory, History', in Johnson and Treharne (eds.), *Readings in Medieval Texts*, pp. 91–108, at 101.
61 Frost and Steketee, *Stuff*, p. 51.
62 Ibid.
63 Ibid., pp. 56 ('eccentricity and pathology'), 58 ('[d]istress or impairment').
64 Ibid., p. 14.
65 Ibid., p. 15. My emphasis.
66 Ibid., p. 211.
67 Bennett, 'Powers of the Hoard', pp. 260–1.
68 Ibid., p. 241.
69 Ibid., p. 243.
70 Frost and Steketee, *Stuff*, p. 39.
71 Owen-Crocker, *The Four Funerals in 'Beowulf'*, p. 69. A prominent subcategory of hoarding in popular imagination is hoarding of animal corpses, often those of pets. Frost and Steketee dedicate an entire chapter (6) to hoarding of *live* animals.
72 Frost and Steketee, *Stuff*, pp. 50–1.
73 Bennett, 'Powers of the Hoard', pp. 256–7.
74 Frost and Steketee, *Stuff*, p. 45.
75 Ibid., pp. 101–2.
76 Ibid., p. 209.
77 Ibid., p. 55. Compare, also, Bennett's statement that 'Hoarding, in other words, is a coping response to human mortality. […] [The] relatively slow rate of decay [of hoarded objects made of various materials in relation to human flesh] presents the reassuring illusion that at least *something* doesn't die' ('Powers of the Hoard', p. 253).
78 Catherine Karkov, 'Hoards, Hoarders, and Other Broken Things', *Postmedieval*, 7 (2016), 456–68, at 459–60.

Afterword
Resistant material remnants in Old English and beyond

Old English

The trajectory of this book begins with a consideration of several riddles that focus on plunder and accumulation, moves through three very different religious epics (*Exodus*, *Andreas*, *Judith*), and concludes with *Beowulf*, the longest poem among them that, not coincidentally, ends with the paradigmatic image of the hero's corpse incorporated into the reburied hoard. My thread throughout, *spolia* and *spolia*-like objects, consistently brings up questions of interaction between the self and the Other, movement between various temporal layers, and intense changes of scale between the minuscule and the gigantic. Embedding plunder in its various manifestations, these poetic texts are conscious of the larger, Continental learned tradition – a fair number of them being translations – while, at the same time, foregrounding their difference in the vernacular. Old English can continue the play of Latin and even surpass it. Martin Irvine has argued in his *Making of Textual Culture: 'Grammatica' and Literary Theory, 350–1150* that *grammatica*, an intricate system underlying Anglo-Saxon textual production in both Latin and Old English, involves several 'macrogenres' which build up in complexity and nestle like Chinese boxes. These building blocks of early medieval literature include gloss, lexicon, compilation, encyclopedia, and library.[1] '[N]o text', Irvine writes, 'is a simple manifestation of a macrogenre, but, as a form of discourse, may be informed by several of these larger models of organization and intelligibility.'[2] Biblical verse, for instance, functions as an elaborate gloss of the Scriptures, appears in compilations like the Junius 11 and Vercelli manuscripts, and so bound forms a part of a larger library. Each part may reflect elements smaller or larger than itself: a compilation is a microcosm of a library, and a library is a macrocosm of compilations.[3] While Irvine does speak of riddles as texts legible through resemblances of concepts contained inside 'the cultural encyclopedia',[4] the frequency with which the enigmatic mode comes up in my discussions of the religious epics and *Beowulf* above suggests that the riddle could easily qualify as one of his macrogenres.

The vernacular enigmas speak of the world familiar from other surviving poetry but often with a non-heroic slant; they also speak of things unmentioned – perhaps, unmentionable – elsewhere. This intertextual dynamic goes both ways. *Exodus*, according to my argument, presents us with the mysterious images of the African woman, the enclosure or *burh*, the pillar of fire and cloud, as a cluster whose 'solution' may be *spolia*. *Andreas* features characters that talk in riddles and displays embedded enigmas, as Irina Dumitrescu demonstrates in her book.[5] *Judith* brings us close to potentially dangerous materiality, only to zoom out from it just in time, paralleling the dynamic between two Creation riddles from the Exeter Book, the accumulating Riddle 40 and the expansive, rapid-moving Riddle 66. *Beowulf* challenges us to answer what no one knows, what happens to its pagan protagonists after death and how to read the amassed treasures, as doomed or desirable or both. Unlike the religious poems which expand at the end to move away from being caught in the details, *Beowulf* concludes with the hoard put out of sight, yet undeniably present under ground.

Because humans feel the need to grapple with the elusive, artists continue to create art. During that process, to escape from constraints of their own time and space, they leave a gap for the viewer or the reader to step in and engage with the work. This book demonstrates that anonymous Anglo-Saxon poets who lived about a millennium ago are no exception. Critics like Lara Farina and Roberta Frank have remarked on the quality of the Old English work, often called indirectness or obliqueness.[6] It is related to the same urge as modesty or decorum, an unwillingness to state graphically, to reveal everything, which could be conceived as a kind of generosity. Such generosity would not burden the audience, inviting it to participate in the literary act whilst being guided by the textual matter, and comforted by the general redemptive, predictable message of the religious texts, but ultimately encouraged to make their own interpretations.

Beyond

To take us 'beyond', I will finally assert that the generous invitation extends to the readers in our own time, too. What do we gain from reading Old English poetry with an eye to our pressing modern concerns? Do we run the risk of falsifying the past when we harness it to speak to the present? Reading two fourteenth-century texts, Chaucer's *Man of Law's Tale* alongside the anonymous Ethiopian sacred narrative *Kebra Nagast* (*The Book of the Glory of Kings*), Suzanne Conklin Akbari speaks of the potential for 'mutual illumination, of [the works] casting an indirect light upon one another'. She further points out that the commonalities between the *Man of Law's Tale* and *Kebra Nagast* arise from their shared Christian ideological background and spiritual geography.[7] My discussion throughout *Borrowed Objects* does not explicitly juxtapose two literary traditions from different corners of the world, but rather implicitly invokes the present day, while mostly addressing epic and enigmatic poetry from about a millennium ago. We still live in a world shaped by the textual tradition in which the Anglo-Saxons participated. The strategies for incorporation of Others, their erasure, or both, have not changed significantly, however much our technology has developed. Conklin Akbari describes her method as following a thing in motion through different medieval literary traditions; in her case, these things are a vessel representing Noah's Ark and a travel writer's body.[8] I have followed individual instances of *spolia* created within seven Exeter Riddles (numbers 14, 20, 29, 40, 49, 60, and 95), *Exodus*, *Andreas*, *Judith*, and *Beowulf*, suggesting that these poems, in all their diversity, conceived of themselves as 'traveling objects'.

To transform Conklin Akbari's trope of mutual illumination, I have attempted to let intricacies of early medieval English verse illuminate our current theoretical thought about the role of material culture in our lives, and vice versa. I also hoped for some mystery, some productive darkness and salutary discomfort, the realisation that both nowadays and in pre-Conquest England we may not know everything about our world, which is precisely what propulses us towards investigation, discovery, and creation. Of course, we must attend to the differences, which are undeniable: one only needs to look at the language of Old English poetry, even edited, even normalised, even emended. In her book that puts ecocriticism and ecotheology in conversation with the Exeter Riddles, Corinne Dale addresses the 'dangers and pitfalls' of allowing modern approaches to the environment to drown Anglo-Saxon literature, but ultimately argues that remaining fixed on the medieval text in the act of close reading and bringing our analysis always back to it should keep the problem at bay.[9] Like Dale, I return to the Old English again and again in hope of letting it provide its own ways of reading. Having agreed with Dale's points, I still ought to admit that I find anachronism a smaller danger than sharply cutting our scholarly

Afterword: Resistant remnants in Old English and beyond

engagement with Anglo-Saxon literature from our lives today, and consigning these texts to venues only accessible to a privileged few. Not communicating the full sophistication of this ancient poetry, even if – especially if – it clashes with some aspects of the official discourses of its time, would do it a disservice.

Anglo-Saxonists like Catherine Karkov and Nicholas Howe already apply and transform postcolonial theory, a useful and inspiring practice in my case, as well. What illumination – or illumination by productive darkness – do we gain when we think of Old English poetic *spolia* alongside later instances of pointed reuse of material culture from a different geography and (unlike Conklin Akbari's pairing of Chaucer and *Kebra Nagast*) from a different set of religious traditions? Karkov cites Finbarr Flood's research on strategic, multivalent reuse of artefacts by Muslims and Hindus in medieval South Asia.[10] Like me, Flood discusses actual plunder and art-historical *spolia* within the same category,[11] and argues for a more nuanced understanding of spoliated artefacts than mere triumphalism or incongruous eclecticism. As an art historian, he turns his attention to visual works of architecture and sculpture, not to their transformations or creation within poetry. In this book I have attempted to heed Flood's call not to neglect the dynamism of plunder that creates a sense of novelty by circulated things that are never, to use a colloquial expression, 'same old'. Flood powerfully states:

> To focus therefore on the innate qualities of looted objects (their constituent materials, or their formal characteristics) or even their meanings in primary contexts is to ignore the shifting narratives through which new meanings are constructed and transmitted, and the capacity of gifted or looted artifacts to develop novel sets of relationships with new communities of subjects and objects.[12]

It is not only that the *spolia* and *spolia*-like objects that emerge in the Exeter Riddles, biblical verse, and *Beowulf* often move beyond any frame we might wish to put around them. Their value does not lie fully either in their material preciousness or their usefulness for exegetical or heroic interpretation. The Old English poems under consideration, for all their variety, display an awareness of this interaction. They appear to know that these artefacts will help them 'develop novel sets of relationships' with future audiences. An ancient practice employing ancient fragments paradoxically results in a new experience.

Another aspect of Finbarr's research that helps illuminate my work concerns an unofficial story just beneath the surface, in his case told by means of the surviving material record. For all their written insistence on monotheistic shunning of 'idols' and expressed zeal for their destruction, medieval Indian Muslim warrior aristocracy had a richer spectrum of responses to Hindu artefacts, informed by politics, economics, and aesthetics.[13] Similarly, the previous chapters indicate that, however central a role religious orthodoxy played for the monastic setting that produced and circulated all Anglo-Saxon texts, our poems display a wider range of attitudes towards the pagan and Jewish past, not exhausted by Christian supersessionism. The poets and presumably their audiences seem to have found *spolia* interesting because they are able to point to other stories, to relieve them of the burden of the present, to hint at, if not open, newer, broader horizons.

Notes

1. Irvine, Martin, *The Making of Textual Culture: 'Grammatica' and Literary Theory, 350–1100* (Cambridge: Cambridge University Press, 1994), p. 426.
2. Ibid., p. 430.
3. Ibid., p. 429.
4. Ibid., p. 438.
5. Dumitrescu, Irina A., *The Experience of Education in Anglo-Saxon Literature* (Cambridge: Cambridge University Press, 2018), p. 123.
6. Farina speaks of 'restraint' in *Christ 1*, a collection of Anglo-Saxon Advent lyrics that inspires 'repeated readings'. Lara Farina, *Erotic Discourse and Early English Religious Writing* (New York: Palgrave, 2006), p. 23. Frank notes '[t]he indirection of Old English alliteration, its ability to signify more than it says' and urges philologists to make 'subtle, indirect, even ironic overtures' in order to encourage 'a shy past to open up'. Frank, Roberta, 'The Unbearable Lightness of Being a Philologist', *The Journal of English and Germanic Philology*, 96 (1997), 486–513, at 495 (alliteration), 513 (overtures).
7. Suzanne Conklin Akbari, 'Modeling Medieval World Literature', *Middle Eastern Literatures*, 20 (2017), 2–17, at 14.
8. Ibid., p. 15.
9. Dale, Corinne, *The Natural World in the Exeter Book Riddles* (Cambridge: D. S. Brewer, 2017), p. 19.
10. Catherine Karkov, 'Postcolonial', in Jacqueline Stodnick and Renée R. Trilling (eds), *A Handbook of Anglo-Saxon Studies*, pp. 149–63, at 152. Finbarr B. Flood, *Objects of Translation: Material Culture and Medieval 'Hindu-Muslim' Encounter* (Princeton: Princeton University Press, 2009).
11. He also speaks of objects exchanged as gifts between rulers along with tribute which is 'institutionalized plunder' (Flood, *Objects of Translation*, p. 127).
12. Ibid., p. 123.
13. Ibid., p. 125.

Bibliography

Primary sources

Aldhelm, *The Riddles of Aldhelm*, ed. James Hall Pitman (New Haven: Yale University Press, 1925).
Augustine, *De doctrina christiana*, ed. R. P. H. Green (Oxford: Oxford University Press, 1996).
Biblia Sacra [The Vulgate], ed. P. Michael Hetzenauer (Regensburg: F. Pustet, 1929).
Blatt, Franz (ed.), *Die lateinischen Bearbeitungen der Acta Andreæ et Matthiæ apud Anthropophagos* (Giessen: Alfred Töpelmann, 1930).
Brooks, Kenneth R. (ed.), *Andreas and the Fates of the Apostles* (Oxford: Clarendon, 1961).
Dobbie, Elliot V. (ed.), *The Anglo-Saxon Minor Poems*, ASPR 6 (New York: Columbia University Press, 1942).
Fulk, R. D., *The Beowulf Manuscript: Complete Texts and The Fight at Finnsburgh* (Cambridge, MA: Harvard University Press, 2010).
Fulk, R. D., Robert E. Bjork, and John D. Niles (Eds), *Klaeber's Beowulf and the Fight at Finnsburg*, 4th edn (Toronto: Toronto University Press, 2008).
Griffith, Mark (ed.), *Judith* (Exeter: University of Exeter Press, 1997).
Irving, Edward B., Jr (ed.), *The Old English Exodus* (New Haven: Yale University Press, 1953.)
Krapp, George P. (ed.), *The Junius Manuscript*, ASPR 1 (New York: Columbia University Press, 1931).
Krapp, George P. and Elliot V. Dobbie (Eds), *The Exeter Book*, ASPR 3 (New York: Columbia University Press, 1935).
Lucas, Peter J. (ed.), *Exodus*, rev. edn (Exeter: University of Exeter Press, 1994).
Muir, Bernard J. (ed.), *The Exeter Anthology of Old English Poetry* (Exeter: University of Exeter Press, 1994).
North, Richard and Michael D. J. Bintley (Eds), *Andreas: An Edition* (Liverpool: University of Liverpool Press, 2016).
Swanton, Michael (ed.), *The Dream of the Rood* (Exeter: University of Exeter Press, 1996).
Timmer, B. J. (ed.), *Judith* (London: Methuen, 1952).

Lexicographic aids

Bosworth, Joseph and T. Northcote Toller, *An Anglo-Saxon Dictionary* (London: Oxford University Press, 1954).
Dictionary of Old English, http://tapor.library.utoronto.ca/doe/
Dictionary of Old English Web Corpus, http://tapor.library.utoronto.ca/doecorpus/
Roberts, Jane et al., *A Thesaurus of Old English* (New York: Rodopi, 2000).
Zoëga, Geir T., *A Concise Dictionary of Old Icelandic* (Oxford: Clarendon, 1926).

Secondary sources

Alexander, Michael, *A History of Old English Literature* (Peterborough, ON: Broadway Press, 2002).
Alexander, Michael (trans.), *'Beowulf': A Verse Translation: Revised Edition* (New York: Penguin, 2001 [rpt. with corrections 2003]).
Arthur, Ciaran, 'Postural Representations of Holofernes in the Old English *Judith*: The Lord who was Laid Low', *English Studies*, 94 (2013), 872–82.
Astill, Grenville, 'Community, Identity and the Later Anglo-Saxon Town: The Case of Southern England', in Wendy Davies et al. (eds), *People and Space in the Middle Ages 300–1300* (Turnhout: Brepols, 2006), pp. 233–54.
Augustine, *On Christian Teaching*, trans. R. P. H. Green (Oxford: Oxford University Press, 1997).
Babcock, William S., 'Harrowing of Hell', in Everett Ferguson (ed.), *Encyclopedia of Early Christianity*, vol. 1 (New York: Garland, 1997), pp. 509–11.
Bachelard, Gaston, *The Poetics of Space*, trans. Maria Jolas (Boston: Beacon Press, 1969).
Bachelard, Gaston, *Air and Dreams: An Essay on the Imagination of Movement*, trans. Edith R. Farrell and C. Frederick Farrell (Dallas: The Dallas Institute of Humanities and Culture, 1988).
Baker, Peter S., *Honour, Exchange and Violence in 'Beowulf'* (Cambridge: D. S. Brewer, 2013).
Batuman, Elif, 'The Big Dig', *New Yorker* (2015), www.newyorker.com/magazine/2015/08/31/the-big-dig, accessed 12 September 2015.
Beechy, Tiffany, 'A Review of *The Cambridge History of Early Medieval English Literature*', *The Medieval Review*, https://scholarworks.iu.edu/journals/index.php/tmr/article/view/18571/24684, accessed 15 March 2017.
Belanoff, Patricia, '*Judith*: Sacred and Secular Heroine', in Helen Damico and John Leyerle (eds), *Heroic Poetry in the Anglo-Saxon Period: Studies in Honor of Jess B. Bessinger, Jr.* (Kalamazoo: Medieval Institute Publications, 1993), pp. 247–64.
Bennett, Jane, 'Powers of the Hoard: Further Notes on Material Agency', in Jeffrey Jerome Cohen (ed.), *Animal, Vegetable, Mineral: Ethics and Objects* (Washington, DC: Oliphaunt Books, 2012), pp. 237–69.

Biggam, C. P., *Grey in Old English: An Interdisciplinary Semantic Study* (London: Runetree Press, 1998).
Bintley, Michael D. J., 'Demythologising Urban Landscapes in *Andreas*', *Leeds Studies in English*, 40 (2009), 105–18.
Bishop, Chris, 'Ambiguous Eroticism in the Exeter Book', *Journal of the Australian Early Medieval Association*, 2 (2006), 9–22.
Bitterli, Dieter, *Say What I Am Called: The Old English Riddles of the Exeter Book and the Anglo-Latin Riddle Tradition* (Toronto: Toronto University Press, 2009).
Blurton, Heather, *Cannibalism in High Medieval English Literature* (New York: Palgrave, 2007).
Boenig, Robert (trans.), *The Acts of Andrew in the Country of the Cannibals: Translations from the Greek, Latin, and Old English* (New York: Garland, 1991).
Borland, Jennifer and Louise Siddons, 'From Hoarders to the Hoard: Giving Disciplinary Legitimacy to Undisciplined Collecting', *Postmedieval*, 7 (2016), 407–20.
Bradley, S. A. J. (trans.), *Anglo-Saxon Poetry: An Anthology of Old English Poems in Prose Translation* (London: Dent, 1982).
Bredehoft, Thomas, *Early English Metre* (Toronto: University of Toronto Press, 2005).
Brenk, Beat, 'Spolia from Constantine to Charlemagne: Aesthetics versus Ideology', *Dumbarton Oak Papers*, 41 (1987), 103–9.
Bright, James W., 'The Relation of the Cædmonian Exodus to the Liturgy', *Modern Language Notes*, 27 (1912), 97–103.
Brodeur, Arthur G., 'A Study of Diction and Style in Three Anglo-Saxon Narrative Poems', in Allan H. Orrick (ed.), *Nordica et Anglica: Studies in Honor of Stefán Einarsson* (The Hague: Mouton, 1968), pp. 97–114.
Brown, Bill, 'Thing Theory', in Bill Brown (ed.), *Things* (Chicago: Chicago University Press, 2004), pp. 1–16.
Brown, Peter, *The Cult of the Saints: Its Rise and Function in Latin Christianity* (Chicago: Chicago University Press, 1981).
Bynum, Caroline Walker, *Fragmentation and Redemption: Essays on Gender and the Human Body in Medieval Religion* (New York: Zone Books, 1991).
Calder, Daniel G., 'Figurative Language and its Contexts in *Andreas:* A Study in Medieval Expressionism', in Phyllis Rugg Brown et al. (eds), *Modes of Interpretation in Old English Literature: Essays in Honour of Stanley B. Greenfield* (Toronto: University of Toronto Press, 1986), pp. 115–36.
Calder, Daniel G. and Stanley Greenfield, *A New Critical History of Old English Literature* (New York: New York University Press, 1986).
Campbell, Jackson, 'Schematic Technique in *Judith*', *English Literary History*, 38 (1971), 155–72.
Campbell, Mary B., *The Witness and the Other World: Exotic European Travel Writing, 400–1600* (Ithaca: Cornell University Press, 1988).
Chabon, Michael, *Maps and Legends: Reading and Writing Along the Borderlands* (San Francisco: McSweeney's Books, 2008).

Chaganti, Seeta, 'Vestigial Signs: Inscription, Performance, and *The Dream of the Rood*', *PMLA*, 125 (2010), 48–72.
Chickering, Howell, 'Poetic Exuberance in the Old English *Judith*', *Studies in Philology*, 106 (2009), 119–36.
Conklin Akbari, Suzanne, 'Modeling Medieval World Literature', *Middle Eastern Literatures*, 20 (2017), 2–17.
Cox, Barrie, 'The Pattern of Old English *burh* in Early Lindsey', *Anglo-Saxon England*, 23 (1994), 35–58.
Crawford, Sally, *Daily Life in Anglo-Saxon England* (Westport, CT: Greenwood World Publishing, 2009).
Crossley-Holland, Kevin (trans.), *The Exeter Riddles: Revised Edition* (London: Enitharmon Press, 2008).
Csikszentmihalyi, Mihaly and Eugene Rochberg-Halton, *The Meaning of Things: Domestic Symbols and the Self* (Cambridge: Cambridge University Press, 1981).
Curtius, Ernst Robert, *European Literature and the Latin Middle Ages*, trans. Willard R. Trask (Princeton: Princeton University Press, 1953).
Dale, Corinne, *The Natural World in the Exeter Book Riddles* (Cambridge: D. S. Brewer, 2017).
Damico, Helen, *Beowulf and the Grendel-Kin: Politics and Poetry in Eleventh-Century England* (Morgantown: West Virginia University Press, 2015).
Daston, Lorraine, 'Introduction: Speechless', in Lorraine Daston (ed.), *Things that Talk: Object Lessons from Art and Science* (New York: Zone Books, 2004), pp. 9–24.
Davies, Joshua, 'The Literary Languages of Old English: Words, Styles, Voices', in Clare Lees (ed.), *The Cambridge History of Early Medieval English Literature* (Cambridge: Cambridge University Press, 2013), pp. 257–77.
De Lacy, Paul, 'Aspects of Christianisation and Cultural Adaptation in the Old English "Judith"', *Neuphilologische Mitteilungen*, 97 (1996), 393–410.
DiNapoli, Robert, 'In the Kingdom of the Blind, the One-Eyed Man is a Seller of Garlic: Depth-Perception and the Poet's Perspective in the Exeter Book Riddles', *English Studies*, 81 (2000), 422–55.
Dockray-Miller, Mary, 'Female Community in the Old English *Judith*', *Studia Neophilologica*, 70 (1998), 165–72.
Dodwell, C. R., *Anglo-Saxon Art: A New Perspective* (Ithaca: Cornell University Press, 1982).
Dumitrescu, Irina A., *The Experience of Education in Anglo-Saxon Literature* (Cambridge: Cambridge University Press, 2018).
Earl, James W., 'The Typological Structure of *Andreas*', in John D. Niles (ed.), *Old English Literature in Context: Ten Essays* (Cambridge: D. S. Brewer, 1980), pp. 66–89.
Eaton, Tim, *Plundering the Past: Roman Stonework in Medieval Britain* (Stroud, Gloucestershire: Tempus, 2000).

Esch, Arnold, 'Spolien', *Archiv für Kulturgeschichte*, 51 (1969), 1–64.

Estes, Heide, 'Feasting with Holofernes: Digesting Judith in Anglo-Saxon England', *Exemplaria*, 15 (2003), 325–50.

Estes, Heide, *Anglo-Saxon Literary Landscapes: Ecotheory and the An Environmental Imagination* (Amsterdam: Amsterdam University Press, 2017).

Farina, Lara, *Erotic Discourse and Early English Religious Writing* (New York: Palgrave, 2006).

Fee, Christopher, 'Productive Destruction: Torture, Text, and the Body in the Old English *Andreas*', *Essays in Medieval Studies*, 11 (1994), 51–62.

Ferhatović, Denis, '*Burh* & *Beam*, Burning Bright: A Study in the Poetic Imagination of the Old English *Exodus*', *Neophilologus*, 94:3 (2010), 509–22.

Ferhatović, Denis, '*Spolia*-Inflected Poetics of the Old English *Andreas*', *Studies in Philology*, 111 (2013), 199–219.

Ferhatović, Denis, '"Life's Interpreter for the New Millennium": On Three Poetic Translations of the Old English *Exodus*', *Forum for Modern Language Studies*, 50 (2014), 233–44.

Flood, Finbarr B., *Objects of Translation: Material Culture and Medieval 'Hindu-Muslim' Encounter* (Princeton: Princeton University Press, 2009).

Foley, John M., 'The Poet's Self-Interruption in *Andreas*', in M. J. Toswell (ed.), *Prosody and Poetics in the Early Middle Ages: Essays in Honour of C. B. Hieatt* (Toronto: University of Toronto Press, 1995), pp. 42–59.

Forsyth, Ilene H., 'Art with History: The Role of Spolia in the Cumulative Work of Art', in Christopher Moss and Katherine Kiefer (eds), *Byzantine East, Latin West. Art-Historical Studies in Honor of Kurt Weitzmann* (Princeton: Department of Art and Archaeology, Princeton University, 1995), pp. 153–62.

Foys, Martin, 'The Undoing of Exeter Book Riddle 47', in Graham D. Caie and Michael D. C. Drout (eds), *Transitional States: Cultural Change, Tradition, and Memory in Medieval England* (Tempe: Arizona Center for Medieval and Renaissance Studies, forthcoming). Available as a pre-publication draft on https://hcommons.org/deposits/item/hc:10515, accessed 23 June 2018.

Frank, Roberta, 'The *Beowulf* Poet's Sense of History', in Larry D. Benson and Siegfried Wenzel (eds), *The Wisdom of Poetry: Essays in Early English Literature in Honor of Morton W. Bloomfield* (Kalamazoo: Medieval Institute Publications, 1982), pp. 53–65. Reprinted in Daniel Donoghue (ed.), *Beowulf: A Verse Translation*, trans. Seamus Heaney (New York: Norton, 2002), pp. 167–80.

Frank, Roberta, 'What Kind of Poetry is "Exodus"?', in Daniel G. Calder and T. Craig Christy (eds), *Germania: Comparative Studies in the Old Germanic Languages and Literatures* (Cambridge: D. S. Brewer, 1988), pp. 191–205.

Frank, Roberta, '*Beowulf* and Sutton Hoo: The Odd Couple', in Calvin B. Kendall and Peter S. Wells (eds), *Voyage to the Other World: The*

Legacy of Sutton Hoo (Minneapolis: University of Minnesota Press, 1992), pp. 47–64.

Frank, Roberta, 'The Unbearable Lightness of Being a Philologist', *The Journal of English and Germanic Philology*, 96 (1997), 486–513.

Frank, Roberta, 'Three Cups and a Funeral in *Beowulf*', in Katherine O'Brien O'Keeffe and Andy Orchard (eds), *Latin Learning and English Lore: Studies in Anglo-Saxon Literature for Michael Lapidge*, I (Toronto: University of Toronto Press, 2005), pp. 407–20.

Frost, Randy O. and Gail Steketee, *Stuff: Compulsive Hoarding and the Meaning of Things* (New York: Houghton Mifflin Harcourt, 2010).

Fry, Donald, 'The Cliff of Death in Old English Poetry', in John Miley Foley (ed.), *Comparative Research on Oral Traditions: A Memorial for Milman Parry* (Columbus, OH: Slavica, 1987), pp. 213–34.

Garner, Lori Ann, 'The Art of Translation in the Old English *Judith*', *Studia Neophilologica*, 73 (2001), 171–83.

Garner, Lori Ann, *Structuring Space: Oral Poetics and Architecture in Early Medieval England* (Notre Dame: University of Notre Dame Press, 2011).

Geary, Patrick, 'Sacred Commodities: The Circulation of Medieval Relics', in Arjun Appadurai (ed.), *The Social Life of Things: Commodities in Cultural Perspective* (Cambridge: Cambridge University Press, 1986), pp. 169–91.

Godden, Malcolm, 'Biblical Literature: The Old Testament', in Malcolm Godden and Michael Lapidge (eds), *The Cambridge Companion to Old English Literature*, 2nd edn (Cambridge: Cambridge University Press, 2013), pp. 214–34.

Godfrey, Mary F., '*Beowulf* and *Judith*: Thematizing Decapitation in Old English Poetry', *Texas Studies in Literature and Language*, 35 (1993), 1–43.

Green, Brian, 'The Mode and Meaning of the Old English "Exodus"', *English Studies in Africa*, 24 (1981), 73–82.

Gross, Kenneth, *The Dream of the Moving Statue* (Ithaca: Cornell University Press, 1992).

Hall, Thomas N., 'The Cross as Green Tree in the *Vindicta Salvatoris* and the Green Rod of Moses in *Exodus*', *English Studies*, 24 (1991), 297–307.

Hansen, Maria Fabricius, *The Eloquence of Appropriation: Prolegomena to an Understanding of Spolia in Early Christian Rome* (Rome: 'L'Erma' di Bretschneider, 2003).

Harris, Joseph, '*Beowulf* in Literary History', *Pacific Coast Philology*, 17 (1982), 16–23.

Hartman, Megan E., 'A Drawn-Out Beheading: Style, Theme, and Hypermetricity in the Old English *Judith*', *Journal of English and Germanic Philology*, 110 (2011), 421–40.

Heaney, Seamus (trans.), *Beowulf* (London: Faber and Faber, 1999).

Heaney, Seamus and Robert Hass, 'Sounding Lines: The Art of Translating Poetry / Seamus Heaney and Robert Hass in Conversation', February 1999, http://repositories.cdlib.org/cgi/viewcontent.cgi?article=1019&context=townsend, accessed 15 March 2017.

Helder, Willem, 'Etham and the Ethiopians in the Old English *Exodus*', *Annuale Mediaevale*, 16 (1975), 5–24.
Herbison, Ivan, 'Generic Adaptation in *Andreas*', in Jane Roberts and Janet Nelson (eds), *Essays in Anglo-Saxon and Related Themes in Memory of Lynne Grundy* (London: Centre for Late Antique and Medieval Studies, 2000), pp. 181–211.
Herring, Scott, 'Collyer Curiosa: A Brief History of Hoarding', *Criticism*, 53 (2011), 159–88.
Herring, Scott, 'Material Deviance: Theorizing Queer Objecthood', *Postmodern Culture*, 23 (2013), 1–17, http://www.pomoculture.org/2013/09/03/material-deviance-theorizing-queer-objecthood/, accessed 21 September 2015.
Herring, Scott, *The Hoarders: Material Deviance in Modern American Culture* (Chicago: University of Chicago Press, 2014).
Hermann, John, *Allegories of War: Language and Violence in Old English Poetry* (Ann Arbor: University of Michigan Press, 1989).
Hieatt, Constance B., 'The Harrowing of Mermedonia: The Typological Patterns in the Old English "Andreas"', *Neuphilologische Mitteilungen*, 77 (1976), 49–62.
Hill, Thomas D., 'The *virga* of Moses and the Old English *Exodus*', in John D. Niles (ed.), *Old English Literature in Context: Ten Essays* (Cambridge: D. S. Brewer, 1980), pp. 57–65.
Hill, Thomas D., 'Wealhtheow as a Foreign Slave: Some Continental Analogues', *Philological Quarterly*, 69 (1990), 106–12.
Hills, Catherine M., 'Beowulf and Archaeology', in Robert E. Bjork and John D. Niles (eds), *A 'Beowulf' Handbook* (Lincoln: University of Nebraska Press, 1997), pp. 291–310.
Hinton, David A., *Gold & Gilt, Pots & Pins: Possessions and People in Medieval Britain* (Oxford: Oxford University Press, 2005).
Hodder, Ian, *Entangled: An Archaeology of the Relationships between Humans and Things* (Oxford: Willey-Blackwell, 2012).
The Holy Bible, *Translated from the Latin Vulgate [Douay-Rheims]* (Baltimore: John Murphy Company, 1899).
Hostetter, Aaron, 'Disruptive Things in *Beowulf*', *New Medieval Literatures*, 17 (2017), 34–61.
Hostetter, Aaron, *Political Appetites: Food in Medieval English Romance* (Columbus: Ohio State University Press, 2017).
Howe, Nicholas, *Migration and Mythmaking in Anglo-Saxon England* (New Haven: Yale University Press, 1989).
Howe, Nicholas, 'Rome: Capital of Anglo-Saxon England', *Journal of Medieval and Early Modern Studies*, 34 (2004), 147–72.
Howe, Nicholas, *Writing the Map of Anglo-Saxon England: Essays in Cultural Geography* (New Haven: Yale University Press, 2008).
Howie, Cary, *Claustrophilia: The Erotics of Enclosure in Medieval Literature* (New York: Palgrave, 2007).
Hume, Kathryn, 'The Concept of the Hall', *Anglo-Saxon England*, 3 (1974), 63–74.

Huppé, Bernard F., *The Web of Words: Structural Analyses of the Old English Poems Vainglory, The Wonder of Creation, The Dream of the Rood, and Judith* (Albany: State University of New York Press, 1970).

Hurley, Mary Kate, *Translation Effects: Language, Time, and Community in Medieval England* (forthcoming).

Ibrišimović-Šabić, Adijata, *'Kameni spavač' Maka Dizdara i ruska književna avangarda [Mak Dizdar's 'Stone Sleeper' and the Russian Literary Avant-Garde]* (Sarajevo: Slavistički komitet, 2010).

Ingham, Patricia, 'From Kinship to Kingship: Mourning, Gender, and Anglo-Saxon Community', in Jennifer C. Vaugh (ed.), *Grief and Gender: 700–1700* (New York: Palgrave, 2003), pp. 18–31.

Irvine, Martin, *The Making of Textual Culture: 'Grammatica' and Literary Theory, 350–1100* (Cambridge: Cambridge University Press, 1994).

Irving, Edward B., Jr, 'A Reading of *Andreas:* The Poem as Poem', *Anglo-Saxon England*, 12 (1983), 215–37.

Irving, Edward B., Jr, 'Heroic Experience in the Old English Riddles', in Katherine O'Brien O'Keeffe (ed.), *Old English Shorter Poems: Basic Readings* (New York: Garland, 1994), pp. 199–212.

Joy, Eileen A., 'On the Hither Side of Time: Tony Kushner's *Homebody/Kabul* and the Old English *Ruin*', *Medieval Perspectives*, 19 (2005), http://www.sieu.edu/~ejoy/HomebodyRuinArticle.htm, accessed 6 October 2018.

Juster, A. M. (trans.), *Saint Aldhelm's Riddles* (Toronto: University of Toronto Press, 2015).

Kabir, Ananya Jahanara, 'Towards a Contra-Modern Aesthetics: Reading the Old English *Andreas* Against an Image of the Virgin of Guadalupe', in Nils Holger Petersen et al. (eds), *Signs of Change: Transformations of Christian Traditions and Their Representations in the Arts, 1000–2000* (New York: Rodopi, 2004), pp. 31–50.

Karimi, Pamela and Nasser Rabbat, 'The Demise and Afterlife of Artifacts', *Aggregate*, http://we-aggregate.org/piece/the-demise-and-afterlife-of-artifacts, accessed 18 December 2016

Karkov, Catherine, *The Art of Anglo-Saxon England* (Woodbridge: Boydell, 2011).

Karkov, Catherine, 'Postcolonial', in Jacqueline Stodnick and Renée R. Trilling (eds), *A Handbook of Anglo-Saxon Studies* (Oxford: Wiley-Blackwell, 2012), pp. 149–63.

Karkov, Catherine, 'Art and Writing: Voice, Image, Object', in Clare A. Lees (ed.), *The Cambridge History of Early Medieval English Literature* (Cambridge: Cambridge University Press, 2013), pp. 73–98.

Karkov, Catherine, 'Hoards, Hoarders, and Other Broken Things', *Postmedieval*, 7 (2016), 456–68.

Kaske, R. E., '*Sapientia et Fortitudo* in the Old English *Judith*', in Larry D. Benson and Siegfried Wenzel (eds), *The Wisdom of Poetry: Essays in Early English Literature in Honor of Morton W. Bloomfield* (Kalamazoo: Medieval Institute Publications, 1982), pp. 13–30.

Kim, Susan, 'Bloody Signs: Circumcision and Pregnancy in the Old English *Judith*', *Exemplaria*, 11 (1999), 285–307.
Kinney, Dale, 'Roman Architectural Spolia', *Proceedings of the American Philosophical Society*, 145 (2001), 138–61.
Kinney, Dale, 'The Concept of Spolia', in Conrad Rudolph (ed.), *A Companion to Medieval Art* (Oxford: Blackwell, 2006), pp. 233–52.
Klein, Stacy, *Ruling Women: Queenship and Gender in Anglo-Saxon Literature* (Notre Dame: Notre Dame Press, 2006).
Klein, Stacy, 'Gender', in Jacqueline Stodnick and Renée R. Trilling (eds), *A Handbook of Anglo-Saxon Studies* (Oxford: Wiley-Blackwell, 2012), pp. 39–54.
Knappett, Carl, *Thinking Through Material Culture: An Interdisciplinary Perspective* (Philadelphia: University of Pensylvannia Press, 2005).
Koppelman, Kate, 'Fearing My Neighbor: The Intimate Other in *Beowulf* and the Old English *Judith*', *Comitatus*, 35 (2004), 1–21.
Kruger, Steven F., 'Oppositions and their Opposition in the Old English *Exodus*', *Neophilologus*, 78 (1994), 165–70.
Kugel, James L. and Rowan A. Greer, *Early Biblical Interpretation* (Philadelphia: The Westminster Press, 1986).
Lane, George Sherman, 'Words for Clothing in the Principal Indo-European Languages', *Language*, 7 (1931), 3–44.
Lapidge, Michael and James L. Rosier (trans.), *The Poetic Works of Aldhelm* (Cambridge: D. S. Brewer, 1985).
Latour, Bruno, 'The Berlin Key or How to do Words with Things', in Paul M. Graves-Brown (ed.), *Matter, Materiality, and Modern Culture* (New York: Routledge, 2000), pp. 10–21.
Lavezzo, Kathy, *The Accommodated Jew: English Anti-Semitism from Bede to Milton* (Ithaca: Cornell University Press, 2016).
Lavin, Sylvia, 'Architecture in Extremis', *Log*, 22 (2011), 51–61.
Lendinara, Patrizia, 'Aspetti della società germanica negli enigmi del Codice Exoniense', *Antichità germaniche*, 1 (2001), 3–41.
Lerer, Seth, *Literacy and Power in Anglo-Saxon Literature* (Lincoln: University of Nebraska Press, 1991).
Leyerle, John, 'The Interlace Structure of *Beowulf*', *University of Toronto Quarterly*, 37 (1967), 1–17.
Liuzza, R. M. (trans.), *Beowulf* (Peterborough, ON: Broadview, 2000).
Liuzza, R. M., '*Beowulf*: Monuments, Memory, History', in David F. Johnson and Elaine Treharne (eds), *Readings in Medieval Texts: Interpreting Old and Middle English Literature* (Oxford: Oxford University Press, 2005), pp. 91–108.
Liuzza, R. M. (trans.), *Exodus*, in Joseph Black et al. (eds), *The Broadview Anthology of British Literature*, vol. 1 (Peterborough, ON: Broadview, 2006), pp. 101–9, at 101.
Lochrie, Karma, 'Gender, Sexual Violence, and the Politics of War in the Old English *Judith*', in Britton J. Harwood and Gillian R. Overing (eds),

Class and Gender in Early English Literature: Intersections (Bloomington: Indiana University Press, 1994), pp. 1–20.

Lockett, Leslie, *Anglo-Saxon Psychologies in the Vernacular and Latin Traditions* (Toronto: University of Toronto Press, 2011).

Lucas, Peter J., '"Judith" and the Woman Hero', *The Yearbook of English Studies*, 22 (1992), 17–27.

Magennis, Hugh, 'No Sex, Please, We're Anglo-Saxons?', *Leeds Studies in English*, 26 (1995), 1–27.

Magennis, Hugh, *Anglo-Saxon Appetites: Food and Drink and their Consumption in Old English and Related Literature* (Dublin: Four Courts Press, 1999).

Marshall, Paul E., '*Goldgyfan* or *Goldwlance*: A Christian Apology for *Beowulf* and Treasure', *Studies in Philology*, 107 (2010), 1–24.

Martin, Ellen E., 'Allegory and the African Woman in the Old English *Exodus*', *Journal of English and Germanic Philology*, 81 (1982), 1–15.

McFadden, Brian, 'Raiding, Reform, and Reaction: Wondrous Creatures in the Exeter Book Riddles', *Texas Studies in Literature and Language*, 50 (2008), 329–51.

Meaney, Audrey, 'Birds on the Stream of Consciousness: Riddles 7 to 10 of the Exeter Book', *Archaeological Review from Cambridge*, 18 (2002), 120–52.

Menocal, María Rosa, *Shards of Love: Exile and the Origins of the Lyric* (Durham: Duke University Press, 1994).

Michelet, Fabienne L., *Creation, Migration, and Conquest: Imaginary Geography and Sense of Space in Old English Literature* (Oxford: Oxford University Press, 2006).

Mitchell, Bruce and Fred C. Robinson, *A Guide to Old English: Fifth Edition* (Oxford: Blackwell, 1992).

Momma, Haruko, 'Epanalepsis: A Retelling of the Judith Story in the Anglo-Saxon Poetic Language', *Studies in the Literary Imagination*, 36 (2003), 59–73.

Momma, Haruko, 'Old English Poetic Form: Genre, Style, Prosody', in Clare A. Lees (ed.), *The Cambridge History of Early Medieval English Literature* (Cambridge: Cambridge University Press, 2013), pp. 278–308.

Morris, Richard, *Churches in the Landscape* (London: J. M. Dent and Sons, 1989).

Mullally, Erin, 'The Cross-Gendered Gift: Weaponry in the Old English *Judith*', *Exemplaria*, 17 (2005), 255–84.

Murphy, Patrick J., *Unriddling the Exeter Riddles* (University Park: Pennsylvania State University Press, 2011).

Neville, Jennifer, 'The Unexpected Treasure of the "Implement Trope": Hierarchical Relationships in the Old English Riddles', *The Review of English Studies*, 62 (2011), 505–19.

Niles, John D., *'Beowulf': The Poem and its Tradition* (Cambridge, MA: Harvard University Press, 1983).

Niles, John D., *Old English Enigmatic Poems and the Play of the Texts* (Turnhout: Brepols, 2006).
Novacich, Sarah, 'The Old English *Exodus* and the Read Sea', *Exemplaria*, 23 (2011), 50–66.
Olsen, Alexandra, 'Inversion and Political Purpose in the Old English *Judith*', *English Studies*, 63 (1982), 289–93.
Openshaw, K. M., 'The Battle between Christ and Satan in the Tiberius Psalter', *Journal of the Warburg and Courtauld Institutes*, 52 (1989), 14–33.
Orchard, Andy, *Pride and Prodigies: Studies in the Monsters of the 'Beowulf'-Manuscript* (Toronto: University of Toronto Press, 1995).
Orchard, Andy, *A Critical Companion to 'Beowulf'* (Cambridge: D. S. Brewer, 2003).
Overbey, Karen Eileen and Maggie M. Williams, 'Hoards, Hoarders, Hordes, and Hoarding', *Postmedieval*, 7 (2016), 339–45.
Overing, Gillian R., '*Beowulf*: A Poem in Our Time', in Clare A. Lees (ed.), *The Cambridge History of Early Medieval English Literature* (Cambridge: Cambridge University Press, 2013), pp. 309–31.
Owen-Crocker, Gale R., *The Four Funerals in 'Beowulf' and the Structure of the Poem* (Manchester: Manchester University Press, 2000).
The Oxford Dictionary of the Christian Church, ed. F. L. Cross, 3rd edn rev., ed. E. A. Livingstone (Oxford: Oxford University Press, 2005).
Papalexandrou, Amy, 'Memory Tattered and Torn: Spolia in the Heartland of Byzantine Hellenism', in Ruth M. Van Dyke and Susan E. Alcock (eds), *Archaelogies of Memory* (Oxford: Blackwell, 2003), pp. 56–80.
Paz, James, *Nonhuman Voices in Anglo-Saxon Literature and Material Culture* (Manchester: Manchester University Press, 2017).
Portnoy, Phyllis, 'Ring Composition and the Digressions of *Exodus*: The "Legacy" of the "Remnant"', *English Studies*, 4 (2001), 289–307.
Portnoy, Phyllis, '*Laf*-Craft in Five Old English Riddles (K-D 5, 20, 56, 71, 91)', *Neophilologus*, 97 (2013), 555–79.
Powell, Kathryn, 'Meditating on Men and Monsters: A Reconsideration of the Thematic Unity of the *Beowulf* Manuscript', *The Review of English Studies*, 57 (2006), 1–15.
Prendergast, Thomas, '"Wanton Recollection": The Idolatrous Pleasures of *Beowulf*', *New Literary History*, 30 (1999), 129–41.
Price, Helen, 'Human and NonHuman in Anglo-Saxon and British Postwar Poetry: Reshaping Literary Ecology' (unpublished doctoral thesis, University of Leeds, 2013).
Ramey, Peter, 'The Riddle of Beauty: The Aesthetics of *Wrætlic* in Old English Verse', *Modern Philology*, 114 (2017), 457–81.
Reading, Amity, 'Baptism, Conversion, and Selfhood in the Old English *Andreas*', *Studies in Philology*, 112 (2015), 1–23.
Renoir, Alain, '*Judith* and the Limits of Poetry', *English Studies*, 43 (1962), 145–55.

Renoir, Alain, 'The Old English *Ruin*: Contrastive Structure and Affective Impact', in Martin Green (ed.), *The Old English Elegies: New Essays in Criticism and Research* (Rutherford, NJ: Farleigh Dickinson Press, 1983), pp. 148–73.

Reynolds, Evelyn, '*Beowulf*'s Poetics of Absorption: Narrative Syntax and the Illusion of Stability in the Fight with Grendel's Mother', *Essays in Medieval Studies*, 31 (2015), 43–64.

Riedinger, Anita R., 'The Formulaic Relationship Between *Beowulf* and *Andreas*', in Helen Damico and John Leyerle (eds), *Heroic Poetry in the Anglo-Saxon Period: Studies in Honor of Jess B. Bessinger, Jr.* (Kalamazoo: Medieval Institute, 1993), pp. 283–312.

Roberts, Michael, *The Jeweled Style: Poetry and Poetics in Late Antiquity* (Ithaca: Cornell, University Press, 1989).

Robinson, Fred C., 'Notes on the Old English *Exodus*', *Anglia*, 80 (1968), 363–78.

Robinson, Fred C., 'Two Aspects of Variation', in Daniel G. Calder (ed.), *Old English Poetry: Essays on Style* (Berkeley: University of California Press, 1979), pp. 127–45.

Robinson, Fred C., *Beowulf' and the Appositive Style* (Knoxville: University of Tennessee Press, 1985).

Rudolf, Winfried, 'Riddling and Reading: Iconicity and Logographs in Exeter Book Riddles 23 and 45', *Anglia*, 130 (2012), 499–525.

Salvador-Bello, Mercedes, 'The Sexual Riddle Type in Aldhelm's Enigmata, the Exeter Book, and Early Medieval Latin', *Philological Quarterly*, 90 (2012), 357–85.

Salvador-Bello, Mercedes, *Isidorean Perceptions of Order: The Exeter Book Riddles and Medieval Latin Enigmata* (Morgantown: West Virginia University Press, 2015).

Saradi, Helen, 'The Use of Ancient Spolia in Byzantine Monuments: The Archaeological and Literary Evidence', *International Journal of the Classical Tradition*, 3 (1997), 395–423.

Savage, Anne, 'The Old English *Exodus* and the Colonization of the Promised Land', in Wendy Scase et al. (eds), *New Medieval Literatures 4* (Oxford: Oxford University Press, 2001), pp. 39–60.

Scheil, Andrew P., *The Footsteps of Israel: Understanding Jews in Anglo-Saxon England* (Ann Arbor: University of Michigan Press, 2004).

Scherb, Victor I., 'Setting and Cultural Memory in Part II of *Beowulf*', *English Studies*, 79 (1998), 109–19.

Schor, Naomi, *Reading in Detail: Aesthetics and the Feminine* (New York: Methuen, 1987).

Schücking, Levin L., *Untersuchungen zur Bedeutungslehre der angelsächsischen Dichtersprache* (Heidelberg: Carl Winters Universitätsbuchhandlung, 1915).

Sebo, Erin, 'Hopkins and Early English Riddling: Solving *The Windhover*?', *Colloquy: Text, Theory, Critique*, 21 (2011), 25–37.

Sebo, Erin, 'The Creation Riddle and Anglo-Saxon Cosmology', in Gale R. Owen-Crocker and Brian W. Schneider (eds), *The Anglo-Saxons: The World through their Eyes* (Manchester: British Archaeological Reports, 2014), pp. 149–56.

Shippey, T. A., *Old English Verse* (London: Hutchinson University Library, 1972).

Shook, Laurence K., 'Riddles Relating to the Anglo-Saxon Scriptorium', in J. Reginald O'Donnell (ed.), *Essays in Honour of Anton Charles Pegis* (Toronto: Toronto University Press, 1974), pp. 215–36.

Sidebottom, Phil, 'Viking Age Stone Monuments and Social Identity in Derbyshire', in Dawn M. Hadley and Julian D. Richards (eds), *Cultures in Contact: Scandinavian Settlement in England in the Ninth and Tenth Centuries* (Turnhout: Brepols, 2000), pp. 213–35.

Silber, Patricia, 'Gold and its Significance in *Beowulf*', *Annuale Mediaevale*, 18 (1977), 5–19.

Sobin, Gustaf, *Ladder of Shadows: Reflecting on Medieval Vestige in Provence and Languedoc* (Berkeley: University of California Press, 2009).

Soper, Harriet, 'Reading the Exeter Book Riddles as Life-Writing', *The Review of English Studies*, 68 (2017), 841–65.

Stanley, E. G., 'Wonder-Smiths and Others: *Smið* Compounds in Old English Poetry – With an Excursus on *Hleahtor*', *Neophilologus*, 101 (2016), 1–28.

Szarmach, Paul E., 'The *Dream of the Rood* as Ekphrasis', in Alastair Minnis and Jane Roberts (eds), *Text, Image, Interpretation: Studies in Anglo-Saxon Literature and its Insular Context in Honour of Éamonn Ó Carragáin* (Turnhout: Brepols, 2007), pp. 267–88.

Szittya, Penn R., 'The Living Stone and the Patriarchs: Typological Imagery in *Andreas*, Lines 706–810', *Journal of English and Germanic Philology*, 72 (1973), 167–74.

Tamburr, Karl, *The Harrowing of Hell in Medieval England* (Woodbridge: Boydell & Brewer, 2007).

Tatarkiewicz, Władysław, *History of Aesthetics, II, Medieval Aesthetics*, trans. R. M. Montgomery (Warsaw: Polish Scientific Publishers, 1970).

Thill, Brian, *Waste* (New York: Bloomsbury, 2015).

Thornbury, Emily V., '*Eald enta geweorc* and the Relics of Empire: Revisiting the Dragon's Lair in *Beowulf*', *Quaestio*, 1 (2000), 82–92.

Tiffany, Daniel, 'Lyric Substance: On Riddles, Materialism, and Poetic Obscurity', *Critical Inquiry*, 28 (2001), 72–98.

Tigges, Wim, 'Snakes and Ladders: Ambiguity and Coherence in the Exeter Riddles and Maxims', in Hank Aertsen and Rolf H. Bremmer, Jr (eds), *Companion to Old English Poetry* (Amsterdam: Vrije Universiteit Press, 1994), pp. 95–118.

Tilghman, Benjamin C., 'On the Enigmatic Nature of Things in Anglo-Saxon Art', *Different Visions: A Journal of New Perspectives on Medieval Art*, 4 (2014), 1–43.

Tolkien, J. R. R., 'Sigelwara land', *Medium Ævum*, 1:3 (1934), 183–96 and 3.2 (1934), 95–111.

Tolkien, J. R. R., *'Beowulf:* The Monsters and the Critics', reprinted partially in Daniel Donoghue (ed.), *Beowulf: A Verse Translation*, trans. Seamus Heaney (New York: Norton, 2002), pp. 103–29.

Treharne, Elaine (ed. and trans.), *Old and Middle English: An Anthology* (Oxford: Blackwell, 2000).

Turkle, Sherry, 'What Makes an Object Evocative?', in Sherry Turkle (ed.), *Evocative Objects: Things We Think With* (Cambridge: Massachusetts Institute of Technology Press, 2007), pp. 307–26.

Vickrey, Joseph F., '"Exodus" and the Tenth Plague', *Archiv für das Studium der neueren Sprachen und Literaturen*, 210 (1973), 41–52.

Vickrey, Joseph F., '"Exodus" and the Robe of Joseph', *Studies in Philology*, 86 (1989), 1–17.

Waterhouse, Ruth, 'Self-Reflexivity and "Wraetlic word" in *Bleak House* and *Andreas*', *The Journal of Narrative Technique*, 18 (1988), 211–25.

Webster, Leslie, 'Archeology and *Beowulf*', in Bruce Mitchell and Fred C. Robinson (eds), *Beowulf* (Oxford: Blackwell, 1998), pp. 183–94.

Wilcox, Jonathan, '"Tell me what I am": The Old English Riddles', in David F. Johnson and Elaine Treharne (eds), *Readings in Medieval Texts: Interpreting Old and Middle English Literature* (Oxford: Oxford University Press, 2005), pp. 46–59.

Wilcox, Miranda, 'Creating the Cloud-Tent-Ship Conceit in *Exodus*', *Anglo-Saxon England*, 40 (2011), 103–50.

Williamson, Craig (ed.), *The Old English Riddles of the Exeter Book* (Chapel Hill: University of North Carolina Press, 1977).

Wilson, James H., *Christian Theology and Old English Poetry* (The Hague: Mouton, 1974).

Wojahn, David (trans.), 'Riddle 40', in Greg Delanty and Michael Matto (eds), *The Word Exchange: Anglo-Saxon Poems in Translation* (New York: Norton, 2011).

Zacher, Samantha, *Rewriting the Old Testament in Anglo-Saxon Verse: Becoming the Chosen People* (New York: Bloomsbury, 2013).

Zumthor, Paul, *La Mesure du Monde: Représentation de l'Espace au Moyen Age* (Paris: Seuil, 1993).

Zweck, Jordan, 'Silence in the Exeter Book Riddles', *Exemplaria*, 28 (2016), 319–36.

Index

Note: An n. following a page number refers to the endnote number.

Ælfric 30n.71, 101
  on the story of Judith 135
alcohol 37, 105, 119–26, 131
  see also Cups, drinking
Alcuin 16, 84n.50
Aldhelm 31n.89
  'De Creatura' 36, 49–51
  on the story of Judith 135
Alfred, the King 20
Alfred Jewel, the 20
alliteration 43, 101, 129, 168n.6
Andreas 86–114, 116, 128
art, Anglo-Saxon concept of 5–7
  Words for 6–7
Augustine 5, 17–18, 65, 83n.33
  Being overzealously applied to Anglo-Saxon literature 30n.71
  On Christian Teaching 17–18
  Soliloquies, Old English translation of 20

Bachelard, Gaston 3, 78
Bennett, Jane 10, 146, 156–7
Beowulf 2, 4–5, 7, 10, 20, 33, 37, 38, 43, 44, 45, 47, 50, 51, 64–5, 69, 73, 87–8, 99, 103, 108, 114n.63, 117–20, 127, 130, 143–63
binaries 19, 34–5, 45, 48, 52, 144
Burh (also spelt *burg*, pl. *byrig*, 'city, enclosure') 1–3, 54,
67–76, 90, 96–102, 104, 107, 115, 121, 123, 128, 129, 130, 131, 133–4, 141n.65
Bynum, Caroline Walker 27n.38
Byzantium 16, 21, 29n.63, 160n.11

cannibals 86–7, 98–9, 104, 112n.41, 117–18
castration 126, 138–9n.32
Chaganti, Seeta 13–14, 28n.48
Charlemagne 16, 29n.63
Chaucer
  The Man of Law's Tale 166, 167
  Swyve 55n.4
circumcision 116, 126
Constantine 15, 28n.45, 81n.8, 138n.24
cræft ('art'; 'skill'; 'trick') 6, 76
cups, drinking 9, 11, 121–2, 127, 147–9
Cynewulf 86, 113n.53, 114n.68
  Elene 28n.45, 81n.8, 86, 138n.24

decapitation 37, 116, 118, 123, 125–8, 131, 132, 133, 134
Dizdar, Mehmedalija Mak 14
duality/doubleness/*double entendre* 35, 42, 44, 57n.26, 58n.46, 63, 77, 94–5, 103, 109, 129, 155

Dream of the Rood, The 11–14, 19, 37, 56n.21, 86, 109

ecocritical concerns 9, 33, 48–53, 57n.29, 71–5, 93, 99–100, 157, 161n.30, 166
ekphrasis 12, 14
entanglement (Ian Hodder) 8
Eros
　'in the broadest sense' 8
Ethiopia 62, 65–6, 71, 72–5, 79, 166
Exodus, The 34, 44, 61–85, 93, 115, 120, 128, 130, 132, 134, 136
Exeter Book riddes 33–60
　Riddle 14 ('horn') 36–9
　Riddle 15 ('vixen' or 'badger') 43
　Riddle 20 ('sword') 39–42
　Riddle 25 ('onion/phallus') 35, 41, 140n.49
　Riddle 27 ('mead') 50
　Riddle 29 ('the sun and the moon') 42–5
　Riddle 32 ('rake') 56–7n.21
　Riddle 40 ('Creation') 48–51
　Riddle 44 ('key/phallus') 41
　Riddle 47 ('bookworm') 45–6, 161n.32
　　Its flowing into Riddle 48 ('chalice') 58n.46
　Riddle 49 ('bookcase/oven') 45–8
　Riddle 57 ('swallows') 46–7
　Riddle 66 ('Creation') 51–3
　Riddle 95 ('book') 53–4

fan fiction 95–6
Frank, Roberta 13, 43, 55n.9, 80, 147, 150, 165
Freud, Sigmund
　joys of the death drive 157
　Freudian readings of *Judith* 120, 126
　see also castration

gender 40–2, 43–5, 63–7, 79, 82n.11, 115–42, 152

hair, human 49, 96–8, 126–7
hands 24, 45, 52–3, 63, 69–70, 74, 76, 81, 90–1, 104, 119, 125–6, 128, 132
Harrowing of Hell, the 18–19, 44, 93–4, 103
Heaney, Seamus 20, 151
hergung ('harrowing') 19
hoarding 36, 40, 45–51, 53, 67, 69, 70, 71, 75, 76, 117, 135, 143–50, 153–58
Hoarders, The (TV show) 146, 147
Holmes, Sherlock 95
homoeroticism
　in Riddle 20 57n.30
Howe, Nicholas 16, 62, 118, 167
humour 34, 112n.31, 133
Husband's Message, The 33, 34
huðe ('plunder') 43
hwilum ('sometimes, at times') 36–8, 40, 46, 54
hypermetric lines 123–6, 134

India, medieval 117, 167–8
Isidore of Seville 20, 31n.89, 54n.1, 73

Jauss, Hans Robert
　theory of reception 7
Judaism and the Jews 62, 81n.8, 94, 105, 111n.24, 116, 119, 168
Judith 37, 50, 73, 108, 115–42

Karkov, Catherine E. 5–6, 158, 167
Kebra Nagast (The Book of the Glory of Kings) 166, 167
kennings 53–4, 58n.42

laf ('remnant', 'leavings') 19, 41, 63–7, 152
Liuzza, R. M. 20, 61, 154–5

Index

'macrogenres' (Martin Irvine) 24, 164–5
Mary, Virgin 28n.46, 79
Maxims II 149
memorialisation 70, 144, 145, 149, 152, 155
Modesty topos 100

obscene expressions in Old English
 clues to in the Riddles 55n.4
Old Norse/Icelandic 58n.42

Phallus 41, 79, 140n.49
Picasso, Pablo 148
 as a hoarder 160n.22
pillars 15–17, 61, 63, 76–80, 86, 89, 94, 102–6, 111n.20, 125, 153
postcoloniality 21, 167
Poikilia/varietas 20–1
 As a postcolonial element 21
poetics, Old English 4, 7, 35, 68, 89, 102, 105, 106, 109, 113n.46, 154

relics 10–14, 19, 24–5, 27n.39, 32n.102, 37
Robinson, Fred C. 2, 65, 85n.55, 155
Rome 15–17, 153
Ruin, The 1–3, 8, 11, 13, 33
runes 73, 86, 109, 127

Szarmach, Paul 5, 12
Seafarer, The 33, 107
Skeuomorph 153

Spolia 15–25 and *passim*
Staffordshire Hoard, the 144, 158, 159n.2, 160n.10
St. Wystan's Crypt, Repton (Derbyshire) 113n.52, 153
Sutton Hoo 144–5

Tolkien, J. R. R. 20, 73
translation 4, 20, 31n.89, 36, 49–53, 62, 87, 115–17, 119, 127–8
Turkle, Sherry 7–8
typology 5, 18, 31n.75, 62, 71, 79–80, 92–5

underwear
 as plunder 151

vernacular 2, 5, 13, 19, 20, 28n.46, 31n.89, 33–4, 49–53, 55n.9, 164
viking invasions 23, 42, 54, 68, 118, 139–40n.44, 159n.8

Wanderer, The 33, 50, 69, 107
Warhol, Andy 148
Welsh, the 33, 46–7, 62, 82n.17
Wonders of the East 73, 117–18
wrætlic, concept and translations of 7, 19, 79, 90. 92
wundenlocc ('braided'; 'curly-haired') 125–6, 140n.49
wyrm ('insect, worm, dragon') 51, 59n.63, 128, 149

Zumthor, Paul 129

EU authorised representative for GPSR:
Easy Access System Europe, Mustamäe tee 50,
10621 Tallinn, Estonia
gpsr.requests@easproject.com

www.ingramcontent.com/pod-product-compliance
Lightning Source LLC
Chambersburg PA
CBHW070357240426
43671CB00013BA/2544